ECONOMIC DEVELOPMENTS AND REFORMS

IN COOPERATION PARTNER COUNTRIES :

*the interrelationship between regional economic
cooperation, security and stability*

L'EVOLUTION ET LES REFORMES ECONOMIQUES

DANS LES PAYS PARTENAIRES DE LA COOPERATION :

*correlation entre la coopération économique régionale,
la sécurité et la stabilité*

Patrick Hardouin • Reiner Weichhardt • Peter Sutcliffe (eds.)

ECONOMIC DEVELOPMENTS AND REFORMS

IN COOPERATION PARTNER COUNTRIES :

*the interrelationship between regional economic
cooperation, security and stability*

Colloquium • 2-4 May 2001 • Bucharest, Romania

L'EVOLUTION ET LES REFORMES ECONOMIQUES

DANS LES PAYS PARTENAIRES DE LA COOPERATION :

*correlation entre la coopération économique régionale,
la sécurité et la stabilité*

Colloque • 2-4 mai 2001 • Bucharest, Roumanie

NATO : ECONOMICS DIRECTORATE AND OFFICE OF
INFORMATION AND PRESS

OTAN : DIRECTION DES AFFAIRES ECONOMIQUES ET BUREAU
DE L'INFORMATION ET DE LA PRESSE

3

HC
244
E24
2001

Copyright © 2001 NATO

All rights reserved. No part of this publication may be reproduced, stored in a retrieval system or transmitted in any form or by any means : electronic, electrostatic, magnetic tape, mechanical, photocopying, recording or otherwise, without permission in writing from the copyright holders.

First edition 2001
ISBN : 92-845-0158-X

This is the latest in a series bringing together papers presented at the NATO colloquia organised by the NATO Economics Directorate and Office of Information and Press on economic issues in the former USSR and Central and East European countries. For further information please write to the Director, Office of Information and Press, 1110 Brussels, Belgium.

The articles contained in this volume represent the views of the authors and do not necessarily reflect the official opinion or policy of member governments or NATO.

Contents

GROUP I: SOUTH-EASTERN EUROPE

GROUP II:
SOUTH CAUCASUS AND CENTRAL ASIA

PLENARY SESSION - CONCLUSION

PREFACE

Reiner Weichhardt

Deputy Director, NATO Economics Directorate

The 2001 NATO Economics Colloquium - a main economic event of the 2001 Action Plan of the Euro-Atlantic Partnership Council (EAPC) - took place in Bucharest from 2-4 May 2001. The conference, chaired by NATO's Director of Economic Affairs, Mr. Patrick Hardouin, dealt with the interrelationship between regional economic cooperation, security and stability. The regions identified as being of particular security concern were South Eastern Europe and South Caucasus/Central Asia, where economic factors play an important rôle.

Around 120 participants from 30 EAPC countries and several international organisations took part. In the introductory session, high level speeches were given by Ambassador Klaus-Peter Klaiber, NATO Assistant Secretary General for Political Affairs; Mr. Mircea Dan Geoana, Romanian Minister of Foreign Affairs; Mr. Ioan Mircea Pascu, Romanian Minister of Defence; and Mr. Jos van Gennip, Chairman of the Economics and Security Committee of the NATO Parliamentary Assembly. During the subsequent plenary session, some of the wider issues related to regional cooperation were raised. The meeting was then divided into two discussion groups dealing with South Eastern Europe and the South Caucasus/Central Asia. The final plenary session was devoted to reports from the discussion groups, assessments and prospects. The concluding speech was given by Mr. Bodo Hombach, Special Coordinator of the Stability Pact for South Eastern Europe.

The exchanges were very lively and stimulating. A wide scale of pertinent questions were addressed, such as:

• the necessity of regional economic cooperation despite low trade connections;

• the risk of regional economic cooperation being hampered by political tensions and conflicts;

• the potential of bilateral versus multilateral regional cooperation;

• the potential and constraints of existing regional cooperation schemes;

• regional economic cooperation as a step towards wider Euro-Atlantic integration;

• the link between economic and environmental regional security;

• energy development and regional cooperation;

• the rôle of international institutions in promoting regional cooperation;

• the extant and future threats to regional security and stability.

A more detailed overview of the presentations and discussions can be found in the Chairman's summary.

This book contains all the papers submitted at the Colloquium, some of them in shortened versions. In main, they represent the state of information at the time of the meeting. Clearly, important events occured after the date of the conference. Firstly, the signature of the Framework Agreement in the former Yugoslav Republic of Macedonia*, signed by political leaders on 13 August 2001, offered a way out of the conflict which had deeply affected the economic situation of the region. Secondly, the events of 11 September 2001, leading to a global fight against terrorism, have had a seminal effect upon geopolitics throughout the regions covered by this book. But to ask authors to revise their papers in the light of recent events would have delayed the publication of this book for an unacceptable period of time. No doubt, both developments have highlighted the close link between economy and security, a core topic of the conference.

Brussels, February 2002

* Turkey recognises the Republic of Macedonia with its constitutional name.

A BRIEF SUMMARY OF PRESENTATIONS AND DEBATE BY THE ECONOMICS DIRECTORATE

"Defence without economic security is illusionary."[1]

Still a Divided Continent

To say that security and economics are now inter-linked is practically a tautology. Beyond the obvious direct linkages relating to armed forces affordability and security of energy supplies, lies the essential provision of human security - against hunger, want, poverty and disease - that states must provide for their populations. If they fail so to do, people will justifiably look to challenge, perhaps violently, the status quo in the belief that they have nothing further to lose. The Cold War brought security and stability of a sort to most of Europe, but in the eastern half of the continent this was the stability of the graveyard. Lacking diversity, initiative and dynamism, societies atrophied and states eventually failed to provide appropriate levels of human security for their citizens, not perhaps in absolute terms but certainly relative to the more dynamic and prosperous societies of the West.

The Iron Curtain barrier is no more, but the prosperity differentials remain. Whether this divide is sustainable in the longer term is open to doubt. Failure to close the gap would first and foremost be a moral failure on the part of the West and a systemic failure for liberal democracy. More specifically, it would likely open up a whole host of related problems with regard to migration, criminality and civil unrest, not to mention the loss of trading potential that much richer and more stable states in South East Europe, the South Caucasus and Central Asia would bring. Certainly, leading politicians and officials of all the states in these regions represented at the Colloquium - and Western experts thereof - were more or less unanimous that the existing magnitude of prosperity differentials would become a source of deep resentment and distrust if not addressed.

Already, some of these regions are to a certain extent seen in the West as unimportant, except as nuisance value and, in the case of the Caspian Sea basin, as a potentially significant supplier of non-OPEC oil. In economic terms, combined they make up considerably less than one half of one percent of global GDP[2] so the threat of "marginalisation" is real. States are also weak internally and local disputes going back generations and in some cases Centuries remain unresolved. Decades of communist authoritarian rule managed to keep the lid on these disputes and ancient grievances, which are now boiling over everywhere; in the former Yugoslavia, in the key Ferghana valley region of Central Asia, and all over the Caucasus. Colloquium participants agreed that a large-scale regional war was unlikely, but that existing local conflicts would likely fester for a long time.

On the subject of wars, one speaker posed the paradoxical question as to whether poverty was the cause of war, revolution and civil unrest or vice versa. Both are obviously true in a mutually reinforcing circle of destruction, but the premise that rich nations do not start wars or that their populations do not violently challenge the status-quo is to some extent disproved by the case of Yugoslavia that was, just over a decade ago, significantly more prosperous than most of its neighbours. Nevertheless, it is necessary to differentiate between the level of welfare and its trend. For example, people in the Soviet Union did not become demonstrably less well off during the Brezhnev era of stagnation; they simply became aware of their growing relative poverty vis a vis the West. The Soviet Union was not therefore a victim of major economic disruption, but more of a growing discontent that rotted the system from within. In this respect, the gap in levels or trends of development and welfare among neighbouring countries or ethnic groups constitutes a major risk for stability and peace. The fight against poverty is also a fight for security.

Better Governance Required

The good news is that a few states previously on the wrong side of the European divide - those in close geographical proximity to the West - have made substantial advances over the past decade and have effectively provided "route maps" for their neighbours to the east and south. For these Central European states, membership of NATO and the EU are either extant or imminent and this fact alone acts as a spur to others. Several speakers from NATO partner countries confirmed that the promise of accession to the EU and NATO has stimulated efforts to reform and harmonise laws with international norms. Others found inspiration from the Baltic example, where three small states overcame old differences and found common cause in economic progress. But we were reminded that peace and stability are not yet evident in the Caucasus and in Central Asia and are not yet self-sustaining in South East Europe where poverty remains widespread and Balkan conflicts continue to fester. If the international community is to prevent the creation of another curtain or division a few hundred miles further east than the old Cold War divide, engagement and cooperation in mutual security and economic issues will be paramount.

In this respect, the logic of the post-war Marshall Plan might remain relevant but with the proviso that although money transfers might be a necessary condition for the narrowing of the gap, cash alone is far short of being a sufficient condition. The task facing those states aspiring to close the gap and to belong to the economic and security institutions of the West was described by one participant as no less than "nation building". In South East Europe, the term nation "re-building" might be more apt, but the key tasks are the same. Institution building, introducing democratic practice and the separation of powers at all levels of society, and, crucially, in ensuring the impartial rule of law. Only then could FDI be successfully absorbed and, more importantly, domestic capital formation begin.

A key problem common to all new and re-emerging states is the relative youth and inexperience of civil and governmental institutions, which leads to poor and opaque governance at federal, regional and local levels. This is characterised by the insider control of an elite few, endemic corruption and the direct opposite of what Mancur Olsen termed "market-augmenting government".[3] This means creating and sustaining governance that is powerful enough to create and protect private property rights and to enforce contracts, yet constrained so as to not, by its own actions, deprive individuals of these same rights. More specifically, creating better governance equals transparency, accountability, predictability, visibility, responsibility, public participation and access to information. In short, the quality of governance determines the quality of democracy. Both induce better economic performance and the benefits in terms of human security that flow therefrom. Of course, the overall standard of governance in all Western countries can at times fall someway short of this ideal paradigm, but good practice can nevertheless be demonstrated and imparted to NATO partner countries if they are open to debate and prepared to learn. To some extent, this is what Colloquia such as this are all about.

At the micro-level, one Colloquium speaker defined "the building blocks of the market system" as book-keeping, auditing, marketing, accounting, improving productivity and contract law. All this is second nature to business in the West, but remain alien concepts to many factory managers in the regions under review. Help at the micro level with skills of this sort can make and in some cases have made a big difference, but there are also examples where larger scale and more general assistance has been wasted through corruption, mismanagement or bureaucratic incompetence. But behind this veneer of official malaise lies an untapped seam of human potential. All that is needed to release this potential are the right incentives and a receptive environment. People are very flexible and ingenious everywhere. They can work either to benefit society or to destroy it with equal vigour. Only when better governance makes it worth their while to do the former rather than the latter will real economic security and stability ensue.

Common Problems - Common Solutions

In all the regions covered by this Colloquium, the problems faced by individual states tended to be common to all of them, these being relative poverty, high rates of unemployment, low investment, indebtedness, ethnic and religious conflicts, and minimal levels of inter-regional trade. In Central Asia can be added water shortages and militant Islamic fundamentalism. Since problems are thus regional in nature, it was strongly felt that regional rather than national solutions were required and, moreover, that regional cooperation should ideally be initiated from within and not imposed from without. Indeed, maybe it would be wrong to assume that any regional cooperation would be a good thing and produce results. One should ask whether these regions are really optimal for something as advanced as a currency union, for which a high degree of monetary and fiscal expertise, not to mention cross-border discipline and trust are required. Most economies in these regions are simply too small and poor, factors that would make some aspects of integration pointless.

But even modest efforts to promote regional cooperation - and there have been many - have generally failed to live up to the high expectations generated by their formation. Regional blocs have been awarded minimal budgets by their member states and have had even less influence. One participant referred to the "spaghetti bowl" of overlapping memberships and drew attention to the persisting conflicts and poverty that these multifarious organisations have signalled failed to address. One problem here could be that genuine regional cooperation requires a sharing or pooling of sovereignty, something that may be difficult for states that have only just gained it to accept. On a more practical level, transport and communication links are still very much nation based.

Regional Awareness and Cooperation

Another identified problem along the above lines is that individual countries in these regions rarely consider themselves as part of a region and do not see the need for closer cooperation. In Central Asia and parts of the Caucasus, rulers often are autocrats who prefer control over coordination and compromise. They cultivate bi-lateral ties and shun multi-lateral initiatives because the former are more easily managed. Despite the existence of blocs modelled on the EU, such as CEFTA (Central European Free Trade Association), the CAEU (Central Asian Economic Union), or BSEC (Black Sea Economic Cooperation), the reality is that the former is seen by its members as an anti-chamber for the EU and NATO. It is not taken seriously because it is not seen as the real thing. As for the other two, member states are moving in a diametrically opposite direction from the ever closer economic union of the EU. Fifteen years ago, both Central Asia and the Caucasus were similar to the EU if we look at factors such as open borders, free trade and a common currency. But today, internal borders bear a physical resemblance to the Iron Curtain itself. The regrettable result has been a very low level of inter-regional trade; in the south Caucasus amounting to a tiny 3% of total trade and not much better at around 10% in Central Asia. But even in Soviet times trade links were stronger with Moscow than with each other.

Small countries have small domestic markets and need to trade and integrate their economies with neighbours more than large countries need to do. In short, they need to adjust to the rules of globalisation and be competitive to be prosperous. The prime Western example of this fact would be the Netherlands. But throughout the regions under review, competitiveness is based upon the price of a few commodities over which they have no control. Cotton, oil and gold are global trade goods not regional ones. Trade in consumer and consumption goods ought to be much higher, but remains minimal because domestic industries in these sectors, if they exist at all, remain small, underdeveloped and subject to unnecessary regulation. In Central Asia, these problems are compounded by the non-convertible status of the Uzbek som, which effectively cuts off the largest market and second largest economy in Central Asia from all its neighbours. It is as if Canada and Mexico were barred from trading with the US. A further problem throughout these regions is persistently high unemployment which merely encourages regimes to find nationalist and protectionist solutions to their economic problems.

And then there is Russia, sadly not represented at this Colloquium. The question was raised as to how far will Russia allow regional cooperation in the southern Caucasus and Central Asia to go? Not very far if the GUUAM grouping (Georgia, Ukraine, Uzbekistan, Azerbaijan and Moldova) is anything to go by. All these states have improved bi-lateral relations with Russia over the past year to the extent that GUUAM is effectively dead. Russia appears as if it wants both to control the near abroad and have a strategic partnership with the EU. Forecasting Russian intentions in this area is a dangerous game. One participant suggested that Russia was going through a slow "learning process" that might result in a more consistent and realistic foreign policy in years to come.

Cooperation is Key

So, as we were starkly reminded by one speaker, in the main strategic areas requiring regional cooperation, these being trade and security, there has been only "abject failure". Another suggested what might be done, urging everyone to insist and insist again. All international agencies and aid donors working in these regions should insist on regional cooperation and concentrate solely on projects that connect states together, not individually to the outside world as at present. The EU has spent Euro1bn in grants, mainly to South East Europe, but has never played a significant political role. Maybe now is the time for that to change, with the EU defining a common policy for these regions which should convince leaders that all the big problems they face are regional not national. Indeed, the Stability Pact for South East Europe highlights the importance of regional economic cooperation, in that no project is taken on board unless at least two countries participate.

Furthermore, multi-national firms working in these regions prefer larger markets and should also insist that national barriers to trade and investment disappear. In this way, it might eventually be possible to demonstrate a dividend of regional cooperation and thereby encourage more of it. In the Caspian Sea region, joint energy investments could be a useful starting point and would improve stability, because it is in all the littoral nations' economic interest to fully develop and market resources.

Final Thoughts

The link between regional cooperation and international security is strong. Under the globalisation process, there is no benefit to be gained from the construction of new economic fortresses, indeed, it would be dangerous to try. The great advantages that accrue from regional cooperation are market enlargement, an enhanced ability to face international competition, the provision of a secure environment for FDI, and the promotion of higher levels of both foreign and local investment. Thus, the great benefit of regional cooperation for international security is to build a real mutual solidarity based on strong micro-economic links.

Still there has been progress. Opportunities to meet and talk (as with this Colloquium) never existed before. We were reminded of the Marshall Plan ideal of a "Europe full and free". Now the unfinished business of moving the western European space eastwards is at hand. All the regions under discussion have recently re-entered history and Colloquium participants felt that it was the duty of all to try and ensure that they do not disappear again. Clearly, the numerous conflicts that persist throughout these regions will need to be settled before any more detailed problem resolution can begin. International capital and support for liberalising change will be important, but slowly building internal strength both at the national and regional levels will be key. Success must start at home.

1.   Quote by a Colloquium speaker during the Introductory Session.

2.   Based on World Bank data for 1999. See World Development Report 2000/2001; pp 274,275 & 316.

3.   'Power and Prosperity - Outgrowing Communist and Capitalist Dictatorships' by Mancur Olsen. Basic Books; 2000.

RESUME SUCCINCT DES EXPOSES ET DES DEBATS, PAR LA DIRECTION ECONOMIQUE

"Sans sécurité économique, la défense est une illusion"[1]

L'Europe, un continent encore divisé

Dire que la sécurité et l'économie sont désormais interdépendantes est presque une évidence. Au-delà des liens directs qui existent manifestement entre l'abordabilité des forces armées et la sécurité des approvisionnements en énergie, il y a la notion essentielle de la sécurité humaine - face à la faim, la précarité, la pauvreté et la maladie - que les Etats doivent à leurs populations. Si les Etats ne s'acquittent pas de cette obligation, les populations tenteront à juste titre de rompre avec le statu quo, parfois de manière violente, estimant qu'elles n'ont plus rien à perdre. La Guerre froide a amené une certaine forme de sécurité et de stabilité dans la plus grande partie de l'Europe, mais, dans la moitié orientale du continent, règne la paix des cimetières. Faute de diversité, d'initiative et de dynamisme, les sociétés se sont atrophiées et les Etats ont finalement été incapables d'offrir à leurs citoyens des niveaux appropriés de sécurité humaine, si ce n'est dans l'absolu, du moins certainement par rapport aux sociétés plus dynamiques et plus prospères de l'Europe occidentale.

Le rideau de fer appartient au passé, mais les écarts de prospérité demeurent. Reste à savoir si cette fracture est supportable à plus long terme. L'incapacité de combler ce fossé serait avant tout un échec moral de la part de l'Ouest, mais ce serait aussi l'échec du système de démocratie libérale. Plus précisément, cela aurait pour effet d'engendrer toute une série de problèmes connexes en relation avec les flux migratoires, la criminalité et les troubles civils, sans parler de la perte du potentiel commercial que pourraient apporter une plus grande richesse et une plus grande stabilité des Etats de l'Europe du Sud-Est, du Sud-Caucase et d'Asie centrale. En tous cas, les principaux hommes politiques et responsables de tous les Etats de ces régions représentés au colloque - ainsi que les experts occidentaux - sont plus ou moins tombés d'accord pour affirmer que l'amplitude actuelle des écarts de prospérité ferait naître un profond ressentiment et une grande méfiance si rien n'était fait pour y remédier.

Déjà, certaines de ces régions sont considérées à l'Ouest comme quantités négligeables, n'était-ce leur éventuelle capacité de nuisance et, dans le cas des pays riverains de la mer Caspienne, comme des fournisseurs de pétrole non-OPEP d'importance moyenne. Sur le plan économique, toutes ces régions mises ensemble représentent nettement moins d'un demi pourcent du PIB mondial[2] et la menace de "marginalisation" est donc bien réelle. Certains Etats se trouvent également dans une situation de faiblesse sur le plan intérieur et des conflits locaux remontant à plusieurs générations, voire parfois à plusieurs siècles, demeurent sans solution. Plusieurs décennies de joug communiste étaient parvenues à étouffer les conflits et les vieilles querelles, qui reprennent maintenant de plus belle un peu partout, dans l'ex-Yougoslavie, dans la zone névralgique de la vallée de la Ferghana en Asie centrale et dans tout le Caucase. Les participants au colloque ont reconnu qu'une guerre régionale à grande échelle était improbable, mais que les conflits locaux actuels pouvaient couver pendant longtemps encore.

A propos de la guerre, un orateur a posé la question paradoxale de savoir si la pauvreté était la cause ou le résultat de la guerre. A l'évidence, les deux assertions se vérifient dans un cycle de destruction où pauvreté et guerre se renforcent mutuellement, mais le postulat selon lequel les pays riches ne déclenchent pas de guerres est démenti dans une certaine mesure par le cas de la Yougoslavie, qui était, il y a tout juste dix ans, beaucoup plus prospère que la plupart de ses voisins. Il faut toutefois faire une distinction entre le niveau de développement social et son évolution. De plus, les disparités entre pays voisins ou groupes ethniques quant aux niveaux ou aux tendances de développement et de bien-être social représentent une grave menace pour la stabilité et la paix. La lutte contre la pauvreté est aussi un combat pour la sécurité.

Nécessité d'une meilleure gouvernance

Un point positif est à signaler : quelques Etats, qui se trouvaient précédemment du mauvais côté de la ligne de partage - les plus proches de l'Ouest, géographiquement parlant - ont fait de grands progrès au cours des dix dernières années et ont en fait "montré le chemin" à leurs voisins de l'est et du sud. Pour ces Etats d'Europe centrale, l'appartenance à l'OTAN et l'UE est déjà effective ou imminente et ce seul fait agit comme un stimulant pour d'autres pays. Plusieurs orateurs de pays partenaires de l'OTAN ont confirmé que la promesse d'une adhésion à l'UE et à l'OTAN avait stimulé les efforts de réforme et d'harmonisation des législations avec les normes internationales. D'autres pays ont été inspirés par l'exemple balte, où trois petits Etats ont surmonté d'anciens clivages et trouvé dans le progrès économique une cause commune. Il a toutefois été rappelé que la paix et la stabilité ne sont pas encore une évidence dans le Caucase et en Asie centrale et qu'elles ne sont pas encore bien établies dans le sud-est de l'Europe, où la pauvreté demeure généralisée et où le conflit des Balkans continue de couver. L'engagement et la coopération dans le domaine de la sécurité mutuelle et de l'économie seront essentiels si la communauté internationale veut empêcher que ne se crée une autre ligne de partage quelques centaines de kilomètres plus à l'est de l'ancien rideau de fer abaissé au moment de la Guerre froide.

A cet égard, la logique du plan Marshall de l'après-guerre pourrait être encore valable aujourd'hui, à une réserve près : même si les transferts financiers sont éventuellement une condition nécessaire pour aplanir les différences, les seuls transferts monétaires sont loin d'être une condition suffisante. Pour l'un des orateurs, la tâche incombant aux Etats désireux d'aplanir les différences et de faire partie des institutions occidentales dans le domaine économique et dans celui de la sécurité serait même propice à l'"édification de la nation". Dans l'Europe du Sud-Est, le terme de "réédification de la nation" serait plus approprié, mais les tâches essentielles sont les mêmes : création d'institutions, introduction de pratiques démocratiques et séparation des pouvoirs à tous les niveaux de la société et, par-dessus tout, application impartiale du principe de légalité. Ces tâches accomplies, les investissements étrangers directs (IED) pourraient alors - et alors seulement - être absorbés de manière satisfaisante et, fait plus important, la formation intérieure de capital pourrait débuter.

Tous les Etats émergents ou renaissants sont confrontés à un problème majeur : la jeunesse et l'inexpérience relatives des institutions civiles et gouvernementales, qui se traduisent par une gouvernance médiocre et opaque aux niveaux fédéral, régional et local. Celle-ci se caractérise par le contrôle interne exercé par une petite élite, par une corruption endémique et par tout le contraire de ce que Mancur Olsen qualifie de "gouvernement favorisant le marché".[3] Cette notion suppose l'établissement et l'exercice d'une gouvernance qui soit suffisamment forte pour créer et protéger les droits de propriété individuelle et faire appliquer des contrats, mais qui soit dans le même temps limitée de manière à éviter que des individus puissent, par son action, être privés de ces mêmes droits. Plus précisément, instaurer une meilleure gouvernance revient à assurer transparence, obligation de rendre des comptes, prévisibilité, visibilité, responsabilité, participation du public et accès à l'information. En résumé, la qualité de la gouvernance détermine la qualité de la démocratie. L'une et l'autre induisent une meilleure performance de l'économie, avec tous les avantages qui en découlent pour la sécurité des personnes. Bien entendu, il arrive que la qualité globale de la gouvernance pratiquée dans tous les pays occidentaux ne corresponde pas toujours à ce paradigme idéal, mais il est toutefois possible de démontrer et d'imposer des règles de bonne gestion aux pays partenaires de l'OTAN si ceux-ci y sont préparés. D'une certaine manière, c'est ce dont il est question dans un colloque tel que celui-ci.

Au niveau microéconomique, un orateur a défini "les éléments constituant le système du marché" comme étant la comptabilité, la vérification des comptes, le marketing, l'amélioration de la productivité et le droit des contrats. Toutes ces notions sont inhérentes aux relations commerciales dans les pays occidentaux, mais elles demeurent étrangères à de nombreux chefs d'entreprises dans les régions considérées. Au niveau microéconomique, une aide consistant à fournir ce type de compétences peut avoir une influence décisive - cela s'est d'ailleurs déjà vérifié - mais il est également arrivé qu'une aide plus globale et à plus grande échelle ait été gaspillée du fait de la corruption, de la mauvaise gestion ou de l'incompétence de bureaucrates. Pourtant, derrière ce malaise officiel apparent, subsiste un gisement inexploité de ressources humaines. Des mesures incitatives appropriées et un environnement propice suffiraient à libérer ce potentiel. Partout dans le monde, les individus ont une grande capacité d'adaptation et d'initiative. Ils peuvent œuvrer avec la même ardeur pour le bien de la société ou pour sa perte. Seule une meilleure gouvernance amenant les individus à préférer la première solution permettra d'instaurer une sécurité et une stabilité économiques réelles.

Mêmes problèmes, mêmes solutions

Dans toutes les régions étudiées à l'occasion du colloque, les problèmes auxquels sont confrontés les différents Etats tendent à être les mêmes : pauvreté relative, taux élevé de chômage, faible niveau des investissements, endettement, conflits religieux et ethniques, niveaux minimums d'échanges commerciaux interrégionaux. En Asie centrale peuvent s'y ajouter la pénurie d'eau et le fondamentalisme islamique militant. Les problèmes étant de nature régionale, il est apparu clairement que des solutions régionales - et non nationales - devaient être trouvées et que, de plus, la coopération régionale devrait dans la mesure du possible être amorcée de l'intérieur et non imposée de l'extérieur. En fait, on croit peut-être à tort que toute coopération régionale est bonne et produit des résultats. Il faudrait se demander si ces régions sont réellement un terrain optimal pour une expérience aussi avancée qu'une union monétaire, qui requiert un niveau élevé de compétences monétaires et budgétaires, sans parler de la discipline et de la confiance qui doivent prévaloir par-delà les frontières. La plupart des économies de ces régions sont simplement trop limitées et trop pauvres, de sorte que certains aspects de leur intégration seraient sans objet.

Toutefois, même les efforts modestes déployés pour promouvoir la coopération régionale - ils ont été nombreux - n'ont généralement pas permis de répondre aux fortes attentes qu'avait suscité leur lancement. Des blocs régionaux n'ont reçu que des budgets minimes de la part de leurs Etats membres et ont ainsi perdu de leur influence. Un participant a fait allusion à l'écheveau des appartenances multiples et a attiré l'attention sur la persistance des conflits et de la pauvreté, auxquels ces diverses organisations n'ont manifestement pas apporté de solution. Le problème qui pourrait se poser à ce niveau est qu'une véritable coopération régionale exige que la souveraineté soit partagée ou exercée en commun, ce qui peut être difficile à accepter pour des Etats venant tout juste de l'acquérir. D'un point de vue plus pratique, les transports et les moyens de communication relèvent encore largement des pays.

Sentiment régional et coopération

Un autre problème peut être dégagé de ce qui précède : les différents pays de ces régions ont rarement un sentiment d'appartenance régionale et ne voient pas la nécessité d'une coopération plus étroite. En Asie centrale et dans certaines parties du Caucase, les dirigeants sont souvent des autocrates qui préfèrent la domination à la coordination et au compromis. Ces dirigeants cultivent les liens bilatéraux, plus faciles à gérer, et fuient les initiatives multilatérales. Il existe bien des blocs calqués sur le modèle de l'UE, dont le CEFTA (Accord de libre-échange centre européen), la CAEU (Union écono- mique d'Asie centrale) ou la BSEC (Coopération économique de la mer Noire), mais, en réalité, le CEFTA est considéré par ses membres comme l'antichambre de l'UE et de l'OTAN et n'est pas pris au sérieux parce qu'il n'est pas perçu comme le véritable objectif. Quant aux Etats membres des deux autres blocs, ils évoluent dans une direction diamétralement opposée à celle prise par l'Union économique européenne, dont la cohésion ne cesse de se renforcer. Il y a quinze ans, l'Asie centrale comme le Caucase ressemblaient à l'UE si l'on considère l'ouverture des frontières, la liberté du commerce et la monnaie commune. Ajourd'hui, les frontières intérieures ont des allures de rideau de fer. Cette évolution s'est malheureusement traduite par un très faible niveau de commerce interrégional, qui, dans le Sud-Caucase, représentait très modestement 3% du volume total des échanges et seulement 10% environ en Asie centrale. Cela étant, même à l'époque soviétique, les relations commerciales étaient plus fortes avec Moscou qu'entre les différents pays de ces régions.

Les petits pays ont des marchés intérieurs limités et, plus que les grands pays, ils doivent faire du commerce et intégrer leurs économies avec celles de leurs voisins. En d'autres termes, ils ont l'obligation de s'adapter aux règles de la mondialisation et d'être compétitifs pour être prospères. A l'Ouest, ce sont les Pays-Bas qui illustrent le mieux cet état de fait. Toutefois, dans les régions considérées, la compétitivité est basée sur le prix de quelques produits de base sur lesquels les régions n'ont aucun contrôle. Le coton, le pétrole et l'or sont des biens qui s'échangent au niveau mondial et non au niveau régional. Les échanges de biens de consommation devraient être beaucoup plus importants, mais ils demeurent limités parce que, dans ces secteurs, les industries nationales, pour autant qu'elles existent, sont encore de petite taille, sous-développées et soumises à une réglementation inutile. En Asie centrale, ces problèmes sont aggravés par la non-convertibilité du som ouzbek, qui isole en fait de ses voisins la plus grande économie de la région et le principal marché d'Asie centrale. C'est comme si le Canada et le Mexique se voyaient empêchés de commercer avec les Etats-Unis. Un autre problème continue de se poser dans l'ensemble de ces régions : le fort taux de chômage, qui encourage tout simplement les régimes à trouver des remèdes nationalistes et protectionnistes à leurs difficultés économiques.

Il faut enfin parler de la Russie, qui n'était malheureusement pas représentée au colloque. La question a été posée de savoir dans quelle mesure la Russie autorisera le développement d'une coopération régionale dans le Sud-Caucase et en Asie centrale. Si l'on considère le groupe GUUAM (Géorgie, Ukraine, Ouzbékistan, Azerbaïdjan et Moldova) comme l'exemple d'une telle coopération, la réponse doit être "dans une mesure très limitée". Tous les Etats de ce groupe ont amélioré leurs relations bilatérales avec la Russie l'année dernière, pour la raison que le groupe GUAAM n'est plus. La Russie semble vouloir à la fois contrôler l'"étranger proche" et établir un partenariat stratégique avec l'UE. Il est hasardeux de prédire les intentions de la Russie dans ce domaine. Un participant a suggéré que la Russie était engagée dans un lent "processus d'apprentissage" qui pourrait aboutir, dans les années à venir, à une politique étrangère plus cohérente et plus réaliste.

La coopération est essentielle

Ainsi, comme l'a rappelé sans détours un orateur, les principaux domaines stratégiques appelant une coopération régionale, à savoir le commerce et la sécurité, n'ont connu que des échecs cuisants. Un participant a proposé une approche possible, invitant instamment chacun à insister sans relâche. Toutes les agences internationales et les organismes d'aide travaillant dans ces régions devraient insister sur la coopération régionale et faire porter exclusivement leurs efforts sur des projets mettant en relation plusieurs Etats entre eux, et non un Etat avec le monde extérieur, comme c'est le cas à présent. L'UE a dépensé 1 milliard d'euros en subventions, principalement destinées à l'Europe du Sud-Est, mais elle n'a jamais joué de véritable rôle politique. Peut-être est-il temps maintenant que cela change et que l'UE définisse une politique commune pour ces régions dont le but serait de convaincre les dirigeants que tous les problèmes majeurs auxquels ils sont confrontés sont régionaux et non nationaux. D'ailleurs, le Pacte de stabilité pour l'Europe du Sud-Est souligne l'importance de la coopération économique régionale et stipule qu'aucun projet n'est accepté si au moins deux pays n'y participent pas.

Quant aux entreprises multinationales actives dans ces régions, qui préfèrent des marchés plus importants, elles devraient elles aussi insister pour que soient levées les entraves au commerce et à l'investissement imposées au niveau national. Il serait ainsi enfin possible de démontrer l'un des avantages de la coopération régionale et donc d'encourager son développement. Dans la région de la mer Caspienne, des investissements conjoints dans le secteur de l'énergie pourraient être un bon point de départ et un facteur de stabilité, car tous les pays ont un intérêt économique dans le plein développement et la commercialisation de leurs ressources.

Observations finales

La coopération régionale et la sécurité internationale sont étroitement liées. Dans le processus de mondialisation, nul n'a intérêt à édifier de nouvelles forteresses économiques et il serait même hasardeux de s'y risquer. Les avantages substantiels offerts par la copération régionale sont l'élargissement des marchés, l'amélioration de la compétitivité au niveau international, le développement d'un environnement sûr pour les IED, ainsi que l'élévation du niveau des investissements, tant étrangers que nationaux. Ainsi, le grand intérêt que présente la coopération régionale pour la sécurité internationale est d'instaurer une réelle solidarité mutuelle basée sur des liens microéconomiques forts.

Quoi qu'il en soit, des progrès ont été accomplis. Jamais auparavant de telles possibilités de rencontre et d'échange (comme ce fut le cas lors du colloque) n'ont existé. L'idéal d'une "Europe libre et entière" contenu dans le plan Marshall nous a été rappelé. Aujourd'hui, la tâche inachevée consistant à étendre vers l'est l'espace de l'Europe occidentale est à notre portée. Toutes les régions étudiées lors du colloque ont fait leur retour dans l'histoire et les participants ont estimé qu'il était du devoir de tous de veiller à ce qu'elles n'en sortent pas une nouvelle fois. Bien entendu, les nombreux conflits sévissant encore dans ces régions devront être réglés avant que l'on puisse commencer à résoudre des problèmes plus spécifiques. L'apport de capitaux internationaux et le soutien apporté à la libéralisation des échanges auront une importance certaine, mais, peu à peu, l'établissement d'un pouvoir interne, au niveau national comme au niveau régional, jouera un rôle essentiel. C'est par là que passe le chemin de la réussite.

1. Citation d'un orateur lors de la séance d'ouverture du colloque.

2. D'après les chiffres de la Banque mondiale pour 1999. Voir World Development Report 2000/2001- pp. 274, 275 & 316

3. "Power and Prosperity – Outgrowing Communist and Capitalist Dictatorships" by Mancur Olsen. Basic Books 2000.

PLENARY SESSION

WELCOMING REMARKS AT THE 2001 NATO ECONOMICS COLLOQUIUM, 3 MAY 2001, BUCHAREST, ROMANIA

Ambassador Klaus-Peter Klaiber

NATO Assistant Secretary General for Political Affairs

Distinguished Ministers, Members of Parliament, Dear Guests,

I want to start by welcoming all the participants in this year's NATO Economics Colloquium. Let me also, on behalf of NATO, extend sincere thanks to the Government of Romania for hosting this meeting in Bucharest. Thanks are also due to the NATO Parliamentary Assembly for its own active involvement in this year's colloquium.

The theme for this colloquium - he relationship between economics and security - is a fascinating one and one which, not just from NATO's point of view, has become more compelling since the end of the Cold War.

During the Cold War, economics and security were linked in a rather straightforward way: strong economies provided the cash to fund strong militaries, which in turn provided the physical security within which our countries were able to undertake economic activity. In the post-Cold War period, our focus has shifted. Right across Central and Eastern Europe, economic development has become very much a security challenge in and of itself. And the reason is clear. Economic difficulties, or even collapse, cause political instability. And instability leads to the kind of security challenges we all face in the post-Cold War period - ethnic and religious hatred, crime and corruption, terrorism and weapons trafficking.

None of these challenges can be addressed in isolation. No single country can hope to tackle them alone. NATO, for its part, has long understood that these challenges required a pro-active approach, reaching out to non-member countries, and working together with other institutions capable of complementing its efforts.

That is why, ten years ago, the Alliance launched a policy of partnership and cooperation with its former adversaries in Central and Eastern Europe. This policy has been a tremendous success. More and more countries have opted to participate, and cooperation has steadily widened and deepened. And now, in 2001, NATO is the dynamo at the centre of an inclusive and dynamic framework of security relationships that stretches all across the European continent, and still continues to develop further.

The Alliance's policy of partnership and cooperation has always had a significant economic component, starting with the North Atlantic Cooperation Council at the beginning of the 1990s, and continuing with the Partnership for Peace and the Euro-Atlantic Partnership Council later on during the decade. NATO's special relationships with Russia and with Ukraine also have a distinct economic dimension.

The reason for this is clear. Although NATO is not an economic organisation as such, the Alliance and its member countries possess considerable expertise in several areas where economic and security considerations intertwine - expertise which Allies have been keen to share with Partner countries, and from which Partner countries have been keen to benefit. Hence, over the years, in all of NATO's partnership relations, considerable attention has been devoted to such issues as defence resource management, the restructuring of defence industries, and the reintegration into civil society of decommissioned military personnel.

It is fair to say that these efforts are paying off. Despite real and complex challenges, governments throughout Central and Eastern Europe have managed to implement bold but crucial economic reforms. NATO has done its best to support these efforts - and the Alliance is determined to stay the course.

This colloquium is another important step forward. Together, we will take a particular look at regional economic cooperation, which is a key element of any successful economic reform programme, as well as a vital contribution to regional stability and security. Hence, this colloquium will assess the current state of existing regional economic cooperation initiatives, prospects for further bilateral and multilateral schemes, individual sectors where cooperation appears particularly promising, ways in which regional economic cooperation can foster integration more widely, and the role of the international community in promoting such processes.

The colloquium will also devote particular attention to two regions: South-East Europe, and the South Caucasus and Central Asia. I think this special focus is entirely justified, since these two regions are of significant concern - for economic as well as broader political reasons.

The Alliance, and the international community more generally, has been actively engaged in South East Europe for a number of years. The positive results of this involvement are unmistakable. Peace has been restored, communities are being rebuilt, and refugees are returning home. It is evident, at the same time, that peace and stability are not yet self-sustaining. And as long as that is the case, the international community will need to remain engaged, or its efforts will have been in vain.

In addition to its direct military engagement in Bosnia and Kosovo, the Alliance is fostering positive change in the region in other ways as well. Several South East European countries benefit from cooperation and consultation with NATO through the Partnership for Peace and the Euro-Atlantic Partnership Council. The last country to join these fora was Croatia, about a year ago, when a democratic, Western-oriented government had replaced the authoritarian regime of President Tudjman. Not surprisingly, the newly democratic Federal Republic of Yugoslavia has recently also expressed interest in joining PfP and the EAPC. Another important incentive for positive change is the prospect of actual admission into NATO, which is a key foreign policy objective of several countries in the region, and a possibility which the Alliance is very deliberately keeping open to all interested European countries.

Together with NATO, a range of other international organisations, and of course many individual nations, are assisting the countries of South East Europe as well. They are doing so in a variety of ways, complementing each other in the common effort to bring the countries of the region back into the European mainstream, where they belong. In addition to NATO's efforts, those of the European Union in the realm of reconstruction and economic assistance are of particular importance. Security and economics go together - they reinforce each other. That was the logic that underpinned the Marshall Plan and NATO back in the late 1940s. The same logic now applies to South East Europe.

Like the countries of South East Europe, those in the Caucasus and Central Asia have also moved closer towards the Alliance in recent years, notably by participating actively in PfP and the EAPC. Practical cooperation has developed in a whole range of areas, stretching from scientific cooperation, through civil emergency planning, to defence reform. In the context of the EAPC, regional ad hoc working groups have held highly interesting political consultations on security concerns specific to the Caucasus and Central Asia. And there is still considerable potential for more fruitful partnership in other areas of mutual interest as well.

One of those areas of mutual concern is clearly the ongoing effort to bring lasting peace and stability to the Caucasus. Of course, NATO does not claim a lead role in facilitating the peace processes in this region. That responsibility falls first and foremost to the parties of the region, who must find a way to agree on a peaceful way forward. And of course, the OSCE and the United Nations are vital brokers in this region as well, as is the Minsk Group. But, through PfP and the EAPC, NATO stands ready to support all these efforts, because the Alliance believes that this entire region deserves peace and stability - and the economic investment and prosperity that goes with it. Indeed, it goes almost without saying that the region will never enjoy the economic prosperity it deserves until the security situation is stabilised.

Let me conclude. NATO is not an economic organisation, and has neither the mandate nor the resources to fund specific economic assistance programmes. However, the Alliance has always understood that there is a close inter-relationship between security and economics.

In the post-Cold War period, our concerns have focused on the potentially destabilising effect of economic weaknesses in the countries to our east. Hence, ever since its inception, the Alliance's policy of partnership and cooperation has had a significant economic component.

Over the years, initiatives such as the Partnership for Peace and the Euro-Atlantic Partnership Council have been enormously successful. Today, they allow all of NATO's 27 Partner countries - including those in South East Europe, the Caucasus and Central Asia - to draw concrete benefits from the Alliance's broad experience and expertise in a wide range of areas, including in security-related economic issues.

The Alliance is determined to continue to pursue this course of action. To continue to offer its Partners the opportunity to work with and benefit from NATO, according to their own security interests and practical abilities. And yes, to further deepen and widen this cooperation even more in the future.

The decision taken several years ago to open the NATO Economics Colloquium to participation by Partners has been a most propitious one. It has allowed Partners to benefit from and contribute to NATO's work in the economic area, it has enriched the level of debate, and has thus also been of benefit to NATO country participants.

I am convinced that the decision to accept the generous offer of one of our Partner countries to host the Colloquium will also prove a wise one. You have a very interesting programme ahead of you, in a great setting and a wonderful city. I thank the Romanian authorities once again for their generous hospitality, and wish you all a most interesting and enjoyable meeting.

REGIONAL ECONOMIC CO-OPERATION AND INTEGRATION INTO WIDER EURO-ATLANTIC STRUCTURES - THE MUTUALLY REINFORCING LINK

Ambassador Lazar Comanescu

Head of the Mission of Romania to NATO and WEU

Economic Development and Cooperation - Sine Qua-Non of Security and Stability

At the previous NATO Economics Colloquium where I also had the honour to be a lead speaker, I started with a quotation saying that "it has long been a staple in international relations that economics and security conflict with each other".[1] With the hope you will not conclude that all I can do is make quotations, I will venture a couple more.

First, from Article 2 of the Washington Treaty of 1949:

"The Parties will contribute toward the further development of peaceful and friendly international relations by strengthening their free institutions, by bringing about a better understanding of the principles upon which these institutions are founded, and by promoting conditions of stability and wellbeing. They will seek to eliminate conflict in their international economic policies and will encourage economic collaboration between any or all of them."[2]

This article speaks for itself, and represents alongside the famous Article 5 what NATO has been all about. And Article 2 is particularly relevant for our debate in this 2001 NATO Economics Colloquium, because it speaks about encouraging economic collaboration among the Allies. That is, NATO stimulates economic co-operation as economic co-operation strengthens NATO.

Second, by the NATO Secretary General on 15 March 2001 at the British Chamber of Commerce in Belgium:

"Nowhere else has the link between economics and security been more explicit than in the twin project of the Marshall Plan and NATO.

Indeed, as US President Truman later put it, the Marshall Plan and NATO were 'two halves of the same walnut'. And when you look at how far we have come, this twin project has brought spectacular dividends".[3]

This is also a very good definition for the project that the Euro-Atlantic community is now facing in Central and Eastern Europe - on one hand, to encourage political and economic integration, whilst on the other to strengthen and project security and stability.

Today, the threats to Euro-Atlantic security and to the Balkans in particular are of a different nature than in the former so-called "bipolar world". They involve new types of "complications". Globalisation - alongside its multiple positive effects - gives rise to new challenges: smuggling, organised crime, terrorism, illegal migration, economic instability, failure in reforms, and threats to the environment. Such are the current consequences of the heavy burden of transition.[4]

The concept of security itself has thus been undergoing a transformation process with economic, political, social and environmental aspects becoming more and more evident. The old perception or maybe the old cliché that one has to choose - more or less visibly - between economy and security on the assumption that it is almost impossible to effectively address both simultaneously does not now apply.

Many have thought and still think that with regard to security, what should matter most would be national sovereignty and security from external attack. All other concerns, including pursuit of economic well being, were considered to be of lesser importance. But these clearly are artificial priorities, even if one would use a narrow definition of security.

First, they ignore the material and economic underpinnings of military power and national security. Second, they take for granted that states are independent both from the international economy and from the domestic environment when mobilising economic resources in support of security objectives. Or, to achieve national security objectives in an interdependent world with an interdependent or global economy, any state of whatever size must have access to a wide array of resources (often called "strategic goods"). Hence an important economic dilemma: should countries attempt to produce as many of these strategic requirements as possible domestically, by striving for autarky, or should they trade for them on the international market? Autarky of course is inconceivable today. It entails both economic costs, since it promotes economic inefficiency, and strategic costs, since it requires countries to produce defence goods that it may not be well suited to produce. The resource acquisition dilemma is, in fact, part of a broader political economy dilemma with profound security implications: whether to organise the national economy in accordance with the principles of economic nationalism or those of economic integration.

The reliance of states on both domestic support and international sources of supply in order to meet their security complicates military strategies, but, at the same time and much more importantly, it affords opportunities to achieve strategic goals through economic means rather than military force.

Translating the Economic Experience of Western Europe to CEE

Everyone has to admit that a divide between a secure and economically prosperous West and a less secure, less prosperous East is not sustainable. So, the challenge ahead is quite clear: there is a clear need to create economic prosperity and political stability in the whole Euro-Atlantic area.

One of the major ideas is to apply, adapted to the present circumstances, the formula that worked so well in Europe's Western half, which was to build stability through Euro-Atlantic structures, thereby helping to foster economic prosperity. And then promoting economic prosperity to lock in stability. This is the very definition of a mutually reinforcing process. Good for stability, therefore good for investment, therefore good for prosperity.[5] That said and bearing in mind the links between economics, security and stability, it has become more and more obvious over the past years that countries belonging to CEE could not imagine their own future other than within the European and Euro-Atlantic structures. It is equally obvious - or at least it should be - that developing and strengthening regional economic co-operation is one of the first major steps towards integration. For this, action-oriented regional projects are required with clear designs.

Some reluctance was registered in this respect immediately after 1989, mainly because of COMECON's previous experiences. Later on and slowly, the need for and the potential of regional links began to be exploited. One indisputable proof was the emergence of market players that are competitive in both domestic and international business environments. Private firms largely oriented towards profit maximisation displayed a strong tendency to address regional co-operation by means of redistributive operations borne by growth in real output and the efficient use of production factors.

Everyone has to recognise that regional (economic) co-operation is indeed very helpful in ongoing preparations for integration. It is beneficial for each of the participants and it is an important factor in promoting economic development. It also contributes to strengthening confidence and, as a consequence, to broadening stability and security.

Without sound and sustainable economic development, no real and lasting solution can be found to problems such as those in SEE. The relationship with international financial institutions is very important in order to ensure foreign financing and access to capital markets. But, in the end, the key factor remains the capacity of every country to attract private capital. Prescriptions cannot be "offered" but "success stories" have occurred.

Solutions involving "robust" processes of restructuring and privatisation, export promotion, expansion of key economic sectors (processing industry, construction, trade), and the development of a future IT-based economy could lead to substantial economic growth and the integration into wider Euro-Atlantic structures. All of these did not come from nowhere but as results of "lessons learned" during the past decade. Drawing upon that experience, Romania's included, one could at the very least identify the following lessons:[6]

• Constructive relations with neighbours. The foundation of new regional policies can be built through bilateral treaties, but also by encouraging and initiating various arrangements of sub-regional co-operation. These have to begin by looking towards the future and not to the past;

• Not being part of the problem is important. Trying to be part of the solution is essential. Whether it is spurring initiatives of regional co-operation, building solidarity and support for NATO-led operations (like SFOR and KFOR) or assuming the OSCE Chairmanship, Romania, like other countries in the region, is showing that it is committed to provide greater stability and security to the international environment;

• Developing team spirit. Solving problems with one's neighbours is not enough. Their diversity could startle anyone with the curiosity to look into the network of (sub-) regional co-operation arrangements in Central and SEE. The Central European Free Trade Agreement, the Central European Initiative, the Black Sea Economic Co-operation Organisation, the South-East European Co-operation Process, the South East European Defence Ministerial, the NATO/SEEI - just to name a few - have done a lot in terms of building confidence and laying the groundwork for more comprehensive forms of integration. Off course, Romania, like most of the countries involved, does not see all these arrangements as substitutes for NATO or EU, but as instruments for speeding preparations for membership.

• Learning - and sharing - the rules of the democratic game and of market economic behaviour, these being the rule of law, respect for human rights and fundamental freedoms, building a strong civil society, freedom of the press, and participation of national minorities in the decision making process;

• Getting the economy right. In this context, the Stability Pact for South-East Europe continues to show how important it is to build synergy among all partners involved in building security, stability and prosperity in the whole Euro-Atlantic area.

Let us try to see where we are, both from the perspective of these lessons and from the various schemes of co-operation which I have already mentioned. What needs to be done to upgrade and substantiate further regional economic co-operation as an instrument to promote stability, security and integration?

• CEFTA

The CEFTA is harmonised with WTO principles. WTO membership in itself dictates the reduction of customs protection and the limitation of subsides. But CEFTA also combines its multilateral general part with bilateral agreements on the liberalisation of trade among members. The results speak for themselves: trade among CEFTA members increased significantly. CEFTA has also proved to be a good "training ground" for EU membership.

• Cross-Border Projects

Past experiences in this field, be they bilateral projects or Euro-regions related ones, are more than encouraging and have started to bear fruit. It emerged that developing infrastructure programs in support and/or part of economic development and regional integration could create the road to stability and prosperity. That applies to South Eastern Europe as well and the Stability Pact is a key factor for the success of such endeavours.

Indeed, without adequate infrastructure services (transport, energy, telecoms and water) linking countries together, trade cannot flourish; and without adequate communication facilities, citizens of different countries cannot be in reliable contact with each other, which also constrains possibilities for trade. It is important to stress, however, that while infrastructure is essential it is not sufficient. Investments without the reforms necessary to strengthen institutions and promote development of the private sector will not be sustainable and will not generate their full potential benefits in terms of durable economic growth and prosperity for the region.

No doubt, infrastructure has important regional dimensions. First, significant efficiency gains could be made by pursuing infrastructure development regionally rather than on a national level. Second, since the benefits from regional projects are realised beyond national borders, fair mechanisms for both financing and burden sharing of these regional projects could be established, again at a regional level.

• BSECO

The Black Sea region has always been at the crossroads of East-West, North-South routes. But beyond that, countries forming BSECO comprise an area of nearly 20 million square km, a market of over 330 million people (where, in some sectors, supply still remains behind demand) and an annual foreign trade capacity of over US$300bn. It also encompasses a mixture of long histories, rich cultures and diverse life styles.

Cooperation within the Black Sea region would certainly bring a "fresh breeze" in international relations. Having these prospects in mind, Heads of State or Government of 11 countries in the region decided to form BSECO on the following terms: "confrontation is out, co-operation is in" and "isolation is out, engagement is in".[7] The aim of BSECO is - and will continue to be - the establishment of BSEC-wide security, stability and prosperity. Its major mechanism - regional economic co-operation. One additional and particularly important aspect, especially from the perspective of NATO enlargement, is that BSECO's membership consists of countries which are already members of the Alliance, countries which aspire to that position and, finally, countries that for one reason or another do not envisage seeking or are unlikely to ever get NATO membership. Developing important economic projects within BSECO would nevertheless contribute to strengthening confidence among those countries and thus to a diminishing of perceptions within some of them that enhancing NATO is directed against somebody.

That applies also to co-operation in the Baltic and Barents Seas. Hence the idea that I fully subscribe to of a working relationship among these "sea-based" regional schemes of co-operation.

One thing is certain: alongside individual internal preparation efforts and transformations, cooperation through (regional) projects of common interest should be an engine driving the CEE - and especially SEE - towards the West. Without bankable projects, regional and sub-regional initiatives will however continue to remain mainly politically oriented structures.

Prospects for Regional (Economic) Co-operation in the Framework of Integration Demarches

There is no doubt that one of the main challenges, especially for SEE countries in the coming years, lie in creating a reliable institutional and policy environment which attracts investment flows and encourages both the growth of a new private sector and the restructuring of the old. Such an environment would also improve the functioning of markets, foster entrepreneurial and market skills, and, last but not least, strengthen the confidence of the population in the reform process(es).

41

Of course, the primary responsibility for shaping the response to the transition challenges lies with the countries themselves. Internal adjustments (reforms, functional market economy, and fight against corruption) should be made as significant and indispensable steps towards a healthy (economic) climate. The political support for reform, which is crucial to its success, must be constructed internally. However, the international community could make a major contribution, working in partnership with countries in transition. These countries have opened their markets and are reorienting their trade. The international community could work towards promoting the growth and further opening of markets into the world economy. This is not easy but it can be done. One essential ingredient is the (political) will.

To reach concrete results in this respect means, inter alia[8]:

• Co-ordination and correlation among various (sub-) regional initiatives;

• Developing sound co-operative projects (e.g. re/building bridges over the Danube);

• Substantial involvement of foreign investors, both public and private (with possible margins of preferences for companies/joint-ventures from the region).

Some prerequisites for bringing lasting stability and sustainable development in the CEE region could be addressed as follows:

• EU and NATO Enlargement

Successful EU enlargement is economically and politically a win-win situation for all parties concerned. It is clear that the question is no longer "if" but rather "when" and "how" the EU will enlarge. Given the immense political progress that most candidate countries have demonstrated, the grounds for optimism remain sound. One should look to the way in which trade between each of the CEE countries and the EU area has evolved to see this. Indeed, the EU has already become for all of them by far the main trade and economic partner.

As for NATO, it became absolutely clear that prospects for enlargement are an important stimulating factor for investment and economic development. The case of the three youngest members of the Alliance is convincing proof in this respect. Moreover, prospects for NATO membership clearly stimulate co-operative attitudes. One example in this respect is NATO's SEEI project, the development of which has so far been quite promising. The drafting of the SEECAP (Southeast Europe Common Assessment Paper on Regional Security Challenges and Opportunities) has almost been completed. As it stands, the current draft sets out the common perceptions on the strategic environment, the political, military, economic, environmental, civil emergency and social challenges to security and stability in Southeast Europe. The document has been designed as a beginning and not as an end in itself, looking ahead in terms of concrete follow up to address the challenges identified.

Another example is that to prepare for NATO membership, all aspirant countries need sound and deep reforms in the defence sector and this has important economic implications. Such transformations cannot be made other than through close co-operation with partners from NATO member states. It is particularly important that they also stimulate co-operation and exchange of experience among the aspirants themselves, thus contributing to the development of a new (i.e. allied type) defence culture. The MAP process is a case in point.

Everyone is aware that there is no magic formula when it comes to promoting long-term security and stability. This goes also for regional co-operation, which is a catalyst, but not a panacea. Regional leadership and ownership should have to go hand in hand with international engagement and commitment. Certain complex issues will have to be addressed, on both a short- and mid-term basis, with the international community's strong support. EU and NATO are majors in the field. So goes for prospects of membership in them.

• Interregional Trade

There is little doubt that intra-regional trade can expand and be a stimulus for growth, even though the economic structures of some of the countries are quite similar, leaving less room for obvious increased trade opportunities based on structural complementaries. The size of the economies and markets of South Eastern Europe suggest that the stimulus would be far smaller than the stimulus provided by closer integration with the EU and should not be seen as an alternative to EU integration; but progress in intra-regional integration is needed both for its direct economic benefits and the contribution it makes to the wider political integration of these countries. At the same time, increased intra-regional trade should not imply the re-establishment of some of the economic links that existed under the former COMECON, which would be neither desirable nor feasible.

That is why, in the case of SEE, Romania considers that speeding up the implementation of the economic dimension of the Stability Pact is crucial. Indeed, success in promoting the other two dimensions - namely security/stability and human rights/democracy - will greatly depend upon the Table II evolutions.

Effective integration demarches require a critical mass of projects. Volume, as well as quality of projects, are important. That is why all initiatives, regional ones included, have to adopt a strategic approach to portfolio management. This means that both the stock of existing projects and the flow of new commitments have to be managed to pursue economic and social goals whilst balancing risks and costs. Specific tools are required to underpin this approach. These include, inter alia, ex ante and ex post assessments of economic and social impact, effective risk-based allocation of resources and a more detailed framework for managing and monitoring costs and profitability. There is also a great need for transparency and predictability as incentives for investment and economic growth. In this respect, priorities could be itemised as follows[9] :

• Setting up a sound financial sector, which commands the confidence of the population, facilitates transactions, and intermediates effectively and efficiently between savers and (foreign) investors. Special attention has to be paid to building financial services that serve the needs of the real economy, including those of small and medium-sized enterprises;

• Business start-ups and the growth of SMEs are vital to transition particularly through the nurturing of entrepreneurship, new jobs and social stability. An institutional (international) commitment to SMEs could use instruments like credit lines, microlending, equity and venture funds, and technical assistance;

• Sound, market-based and customer-oriented infrastructure is a key component of progress. Infrastructure operations could pursue a full range of financing structures (including private, sovereign and public/private partnerships);

• The scale and nature of the industrial legacy of the command economy pose a major challenge. One has to seek to support the restructuring of potentially viable (large) enterprises by carefully selecting projects that have a strong "demonstration effect". Experience has shown the importance of strategic investors.

• Equity investment could have a powerful impact in providing risk capital and promoting sound business practices and corporate governance.

• Sound and reliable institutional and policy environments are essential for generating the investment flows needed to move transition forward. A sound investment climate is based on a supportive and effective regulatory framework, business integrity and sound corporate governance, limits to bureaucratic interference, a firm stance against corrupt practices, fair and predictable taxation, and transparent accounting.

Co-operation between neighbours is essential in setting priorities and allocating resources. It generates self-confidence and a spirit of co-ownership. "Cross-border problems demand cross-border responses to ensure that security and prosperity are accessible to all." (10) Massive trade and development cannot be stimulated as long as political and security risks endure. That is why there might be two major points to plead for. The first one is that European and Euro-Atlantic institutions should enlarge as soon as possible. The second one comes from a national prospective: Romania to be included - as soon as possible - in these processes.

1. "Economic Developments and Reforms in Cooperation Partner Countries: The Link between Economics, Security and Stability", NATO Economics Colloquium, Brussels, 3-5 November 1999;

2. The North-Atlantic Treaty, Washington D.C., April 4, 1949;

3. "Security and Prosperity: Two Halves of the Same Walnut", Speech by the Rt. Hon. Lord Robertson of Port Ellen, PC, Secretary General of NATO, to the British Chamber of Commerce in Belgium, Brussels, 15 March 2001;

4. "The Alliance's Strategic Concept", Washington D.C., 23-24 April, 1999;

5. "Security and Prosperity: Two Halves of the Same Walnut", Speech by the Rt. Hon. Lord Robertson of Port Ellen, PC, Secretary General of NATO, to the British Chamber of Commerce in Belgium, Brussels, 15 March 2001;

6. Government of Romania, Government Program 2000-2004, "Relaunching National Economy";

7. "Priorities of Romania's Chairmanship-in-Office of the Black Sea Economic Co-operation Organisation" (1 May -1 November 2000);

8. "Economic Developments and Reforms in Cooperation Partner Countries: The Link between Economics, Security and Stability", NATO Economics Colloquium, Brussels, 3-5 November 1999;

9. Government of Romania, Government Program 2000-2004, "Relaunching National Economy";

10. Address by Romanian Foreign Minister, H.E. Mircea Dan Geoana, OSCE Chairman-in-Office, to the OSCE Seminar on "Transparency and Good Governance in Economic Matters; Institutions, Governance and Economic Performance" (Bucharest, 27-28 March 2001).

BLACK SEA ECONOMIC COOPERATION: VISION AND OPPORTUNITIES

Ambassador Nurver Nures

Former First Deputy Secretary General,
Black Sea Economic Cooperation (BSEC), Istanbul

BSEC Emerging in a World of Flux

Upheavals in the flow of history are also periods of critical risks and major opportunities. The demise of the Soviet Union in December 1991 was a turning point of this magnitude. It gave rise to a number of new actors as independent states, extending from Central Asia to Central Europe, and give rise naturally to a process of new "nation building" across the Eurasian landmass. Two words easy to say, but in fact a formidable mission to realise.

This event drastically changed political relations in global terms; confrontation in essence yielded to dialogue, isolation to cooperation and interdependence. Global vision, regional strategies, and national policies gained recognition as the transition to a market economy began. These dramatic developments continue to proceed against a moving global theatre where change is the rule, constant renewal is its corollary and knowledge-based, information-driven computer science and technology the powerhouse behind.

A range of these factors along with the political search by the former Soviet Republics for identity and security in a new league of free and independent states - and the appeal of possible benefits regional cooperation may offer - are the dynamics which laid the ground for regional cooperation. Hence eleven states, i.e. Albania, Armenia, Azerbaijan, Bulgaria, Georgia, Greece, Moldova, Romania, Russia, Turkey and Ukraine, initially led by Ankara, established the Black Sea Economic Cooperation (BSEC) on 25 June 1992 which has been, with the enactment (May 1998) of a Charter, transformed into a full-fledged regional economic organisation with a legal identity and recognition on the international stage.

The Charter is a political testament to the abiding political commitment of its member states to the BSEC and its aims. It also specifies the priority areas of cooperation, such as trade and economic development, transport and communication, energy, banking and finance, agriculture and agro-industry, science and technology.

BSEC Set-Up

BSEC operates on five different platforms:

• *Intergovernmental:* The Council of Foreign Ministers is the ultimate authority which charts the course of the BSEC process and is equipped with decision making power. A Committee of Senior Officials acts on behalf of the Ministers, functioning as a board where all BSEC matters are discussed and presented to the Council for final approval. The Permanent International Secretariat (PERMS), founded in Istanbul (March 1994), provides secretarial services under a Secretary General, and is essentially an intergovernmental body exercising its work and responsibility within the same parameter. Subsidiary organs operating generally in the format of Committees are active in specific economic sectors. The Chairmanship and venue of Council Meetings rotate among member states bi-annually, in alphabetic order. The host of the Council Meeting assumes sessional Chairmanship as the chief coordinator within BSEC for the following term. The Secretary General is subject to appointment by the member states every four years and is responsible for the Secretariat's daily management. In the engagement of professional staff to the secretariat, equitable distribution based on geographic location is the principle. Up to now, the executive staff and the three Secretaries General have been of diplomatic origin.

• *Interparliamentarian:* The Parliamentary Assembly (PABSEC) is composed of parliamentary groups from the eleven national parliaments and provides BSEC with constant support, especially in legislative matters. PABSEC and PERMIS operate in regular interaction.

• *Interbusiness:* Private sector driven, established in 1992. The BSEC Business Council is the responsible body. This is equipped with a Secretariat in Istanbul, operates under a Secretary General and run by a Board of Directors. It functions as a forum for BSEC businessmen. It is expected to develop into an enduring centre of interaction by way of wide ranging business-oriented activities, including incubating joint ventures.

• *Interfinance:* BSEC Trade and Development Bank (BSTDB) is the financial pillar of the organisation. It was founded in March 1998 and started operation in July 1999, located in Thessaloniki. It operates on commercial principles and follows private banking norms. Its initial capital is composed of quotas assigned to the member states in accordance with a special scale and is expected to reach an authorised capital level of SDR1bn (c. US$1.35bn) upon fulfilment of quota purchases. The Bank's niche is the promotion of regional cooperation as an integral component of economic development. It has a dual function; to finance bankable projects in the BSEC region and to cultivate channels of investment flows by developing active relations with international banking and financial circles.

• *Interacademic:* It brings together scientists, scholars, researchers, academicians and representatives from other institutions with a view to translating the rich end diverse scientific, technological and intellectual resources of the region into projects that promote development and well-being. In relation with such exchanges, the International Centre for Black Sea Studies (ICBSS) located in Athens has its own status and operates independently under the umbrella of BSEC. The lack of any policy-oriented, pragmatic research or study relevant to the region was the reason behind its foundation.

What Does BSEC Signify?

Pivotal to three continents, Europe-Asia-Africa, and encompassing a large portion of the Eurasian landmass, the BSEC covers an area of nearly 20 million sq.km. It spreads across nine time-zones, includes eight seas (some inland) where important sea lanes cross, has a market of 330 million people and annual foreign trade exceeding US$300bn, and possesses large crude oil and natural gas reserves second only to the Gulf. Moreover, the BSEC region is home to a rich and diverse population ranging from top scientists, academicians, well-educated professionals, experienced technicians to both skilled and unskilled labour. The region has a broad-based industrial capacity, extensive fertile agricultural land and abundant forests. It has a large and diverse food processing potential, wealth in basic commodities and intermediary goods and a rich tourism-base waiting to be discovered and exploited.

With these appealing assets, can the Black Sea region uplift itself and assume its deserved place and role in the larger European

Foremost is that any international organisation can only be as strong and effective as the moral, political and material support accorded to it by its partners. The Secretariat acting on behalf of the organisation is not an exception to this rule. There is moral and political support, but material support is very much in short supply. Scarce funds cause strain on the Secretariat; there are no funds for detailed technical investigations such as feasibility studies; and a lack of technical experts make project development - which member states urgently need - extremely difficult. The Secretariat can at best coordinate multilateral work and strives to harmonise positions, but it can neither give guidance nor lead. It can follow up resolutions and initiatives, but can neither monitor nor force implementation. Thus a new look to the PERMIS is unavoidable.

In order to make the Secretariat operate more effectively and improve work toward project production, member states are faced with two main options:

• PERMIS remains intact, its operation continuing as before. New understanding among the member states would need to be reached, in that they must take it as imperative to implement resolutions made and within a specific time reference. This should be accompanied by an effective monitoring mechanism, regularly reporting on the progress of implementation. These improvements would be completed if measures were put in place to redress failure in implementation by any member state. All this would constitute a major advance over present practice.

• Transform the present setup into a project-oriented Secretariat, equipped with competent technical experts while keeping a nucleus of inter-governmental representatives, such as diplomats. Technical experts from the private sector are to be preferred for reasons of professionalism and unbiased performance. Funds should be made available to PERMIS in order to finance project development. This option would allow the Secretariat added scope for initiative, but added authorisation is also needed. Under the umbrella of PERMIS, meetings could be arranged composed of permanent technical experts with full authority, to be assigned by the national governments. The experts would remain in the payroll of the latter. The experts must have easy access to decision makers in their home state and be made responsible until the project is complete.

Regarding both of these options, another very critical point deserves special attention. The extensive orientation involving numerous sectors under review needs to be replaced by intensive concentration limiting areas and topics to those cross-sectoral and cross-border fields where achievements will be that much greater. As I see it, herebelow are the locomotive sectors, which would create a lasting impact on the BSEC process, accompanied by comments on the progress made so far:

Regional trade has failed to live up to expectations

Economic transition has disturbed region-wide trade patterns and volumes. This will continue for sometime. Russia is still the focal point in the flow of regional trade although its share is falling, as states shift their trade direction to third countries, mainly in Western Europe. So far, intra-regional trade has remained below expectations. BSEC encourages membership of the WTO and integration into the global trading system. Sustained development of intra-regional trade would be a step in this direction. However, the removal of barriers to trade, including non-tariff barriers, has yet to appear on the agenda of the BSEC. The decision on the establishment of a free trade area, given a background of meagre trade levels among the members, is destined to remain a distant objective. The easing of border controls is indispensable for the growth of trade, but this has not advanced so far beyond the stage of discussion. Moreover, the relaxation of visa regulations has failed to occur in general, although a few BSEC members have eased their restrictions a little, Turkey in particular.

Transportation and communications are in urgent need of renewal

Although these constitute the strategic component of economic integration, the required improvements to these systems are beyond the capacity of national budgets and new investments have been minor. The system will have to go through a heavy construction and investment phase sooner rather than later. Nevertheless, BSEC has initiated regular, structured contacts between itself and the EU in the field of transport. The Black Sea basin is recognised within the EU system of Pan-European Transit Corridors, which have been further extended to cover Central Asia in the framework of the Transport Corridor Europe-Caucasus-Asia (TRACECA). A map produced by the BSEC covering rail and road links, ports and shipping routes in the region up to 2005 aims to create harmonised links when new projects are launched by national governments. The BSEC has been instrumental is promoting regional concepts for this critical sector. Out of the seven principal communication projects in hand, three have been completed and are already in operation.

The Black Sea - a promising bread basket

The Black Sea itself has a major potential in intra-regional and international trade. So far, actual trade has failed to realise this potential, mainly due to problems at the ports around the Black Sea. In its hinterland, some 150 million people make a living, many relying on trade and related business. That is, the Black Sea is not only a stage for trade but also a bread basket for the many. The efforts of BSEC, supported by the European Commission, have failed to improve so far the state of affairs at the ports.

Problems centre on two sets of issues. Firstly, modernising ports with advanced machinery and equipment is unavoidable but understandably difficult at this stage of transition, because of a shortage of capital. Secondly, investment alone is not enough. Organisational and administrative measures to facilitate the movement of vessels, the flow of goods and a change in bureaucratic mentality are also needed. Briefly, cooperation among the ports would yield manifold benefits, by easing trade and improving the well being of the millions living in the Black Sea basin.

BSEC region - an emerging big actor in global energy diplomacy

Oil has been the single item which influenced most the flow of diplomatic history in the last hundred years. Oil and natural gas resources in the Caspian basin, given ever increasing new discoveries, have already cast this area into the centre of global competition.

Oil and natural gas can also be assessed in terms of regional peace, security and stability. It should be remembered here how the Coal and Steel Union between Germany and France marked the end of WW2 animosities and the beginning towards peace and security. The rapidly emerging intra-regional energy market and demand from third countries is giving rise to a network of pipelines and terminals for the transport of oil and natural gas within the region and to markets abroad. This involves a critical interdependence between energy-rich and energy-poor countries and is bound to cement relations, strengthen mutual trust, encourage and diversify intra-regional trade, create new jobs, promote the flow of investments and technology and accelerate growth. Clearly, oil and natural gas are energising agents that will further consolidate the region and usher it more effectively into the international trading system. Movements towards this need to be encouraged and supported. It is notable that this strategic issue is considered as "hot" at the bilateral level and is not taken as a point of discussion in the BSEC process.

Nevertheless, intergovernmental work by all the members on the interconnection of electric power grids has reached the stage of a feasibility study, but has been awaiting financing for the last two years. This project should not be missed.

BSTDB crucial in project financing

This bank has been built by the participation of the member states on the principle of self-help at a time of very serious capital shortage. It therefore deserves special credit. Since inauguration in July 1999, it has received over 204 project proposals. The interest in it is obvious. The amount of credits approved so far exceed US$140m of which US$51m are earmarked for trade financing and the rest for project finance. Trade financing operates through national financial institutions to draw them into this field. In these activities, the Bank aims to promote economic development, the transition to market economics and integration within the region.

Relations with the World Bank, IBRD, IFC, and EBRD are under progress and co-financing operations took place in this frame. At the present initial stage, BSTDB operations appear encouraging. Fulfilment of the purchase of the quotas by the member states would expand the volume and scope of financing and impact upon financial markets where BSTDB hopes to assume a growing presence. This would also impress the international rating agencies, so important for the image of the Bank.

SMEs need a business-friendly environment

More than 95 % of enterprises in Greece and Turkey are small and medium-size business units. A similar pattern is also emerging in the Black Sea region as transition moves forward. Well aware of their weight in economies in general, PERMIS together with the active support of the Conrad Adenauer Foundation have arranged an SME Program comprising some ten workshops since 1998 addressing pressing issues confronting SMEs. They helped to make the authorities aware of the crucial role SMEs have in development, transition, employment, distribution of earnings and wellbeing. Beyond this, however, progress in member states towards building the necessary legal infrastructure and the institutional framework supportive to SMEs has been limited. Implementation has moved slowly.

Tourism - fosters peace and aids wellbeing

Tourism is coming alive in the Black Sea region. In the new environment of the region, inward-looking societies under duress became outward-oriented, stimulating for the first time in the Black Sea area the movement of many people across national frontiers. This can only be defined as dramatic, as indigenous people discover one-another for the first time in an environment of peace and security. It has proved to be a rewarding and exhilarating experience. It constitutes a priceless, long-term investment in peace and stability. A striking example in this respect is that the past animosity between Russians and Turks is now largely forgotten.

The region also witnessed the fact that tourism leads to personal relations, that it opens up new avenues of cooperation, fosters cultural exchange, stimulates trade, encourages investment, and generates many service-sector jobs. This is only a beginning for tourism in the Black Sea region, which has very much more to offer in this field. The many related business opportunities need to be discovered and cultivated. Greece and Turkey both have experience of the tourism industry and could impart their knowledge to the other member states, which could benefit from their accumulated experience and know-how. However, those other members need to take the initiative and come forward with a meaningful program indicating priority requirements.

Conclusions

• In a state of global flux, the downfall of the Soviet Union set the stage where we see a new political and economic reality emerging - the revival of EURASIA. The transition from an historical, volatile and adversarial relationship to one of cooperation is a long-term and painful journey, which cannot be accomplished overnight. Deep down, this is probably the main reason for the slow progress of the BSEC.

• It would be no surprise, therefore, if transformation still continues to occupy minds and strategies in the mid 21st Century. In this great task, there are many risks great and small. All must be prepared to face such developments, and in this respect, NATO's remote but sustained watch will be indispensable.

• The Eurasian people have for the first time in decades if not centuries seized the opportunity to shape and make their future and fortune. In the present transition and nation-building stage, beyond self-help, they look to the West, in particular the EU. If they are not let down, transition will gain pace and peace and security will acquire further strength. The free world owes this support. In this respect, Russia's reconciliation with the new order is of special importance for a smooth transformation.

• BSEC is the only international forum in the region where member states participate on their own free will without any outside interference. It is a standing platform which also provides scope for discussion of political issues on a bilateral level, outside of BSEC meetings.

• Russia is the largest economy followed by Turkey within BSEC. They also rank one and two in a larger area extending from East Asia to Central Europe, from the Balkans to the Middle East, which covers 24 million km.sq. with a market of 550 million people. Consequently, both have unique positions within BSEC. Without Russia, the organisation loses its political significance, trade flows and related business. Russia's increasing engagement in BSEC is invaluable economically as well politically. Without Turkey, an important emerging market as producer and consumer would be missed and, in its absence, overpowering political forces would curtail freedom of action, determine the course of events and thereby seriously weaken the interest of other members in collective cooperation.

• The EU is the principal mover determining Europe's future architecture on a firm base of peace and prosperity. The BSEC is a recent starter and is mandated to transform the Black Sea area into a region of peace and progress. The ongoing evolution in this process is but part and parcel of the changes taking place in the European

A majority of countries in the region are participating in a number of projects and programs related to the energy and transport sectors. There are also many pipeline projects in which our states are involved. Georgia supports a multiplicity of these projects and related transit routes. But these routes should meet the challenges towards the securing of independence and sovereignty of the states, facilitate their democratic reforms and market oriented transformations, as well as create a stable energy security environment.

Concerning relations at the global level, allow me to propose that the goals of countries in transition are best served by such strong and forward-moving international organisations like UN, OSCE, WTO, NATO, and the EU. This argument can be explained by the following: assistance rendered by these organisations, the United States, European countries and partners from Asia is an essential element for the promotion of security and stability in our region.

A few words about the UN role in promoting security and sustainable economic development. There are two separate directions. What we need is a new model of interaction and inter-coordination between these two crucial issues. Keeping in mind the universal character of the UN, it could substantially contribute to the elaboration and implementation of such a model of stability and prosperity on this basis.

Within the context of inter-regional relations, collaboration between the economic structures of Europe and Asia is supposed to be very progressive. Undoubtedly, by close interaction with such structures as UN/ECE, UN/ESCAP, ECO and others, the countries in transition have a good chance to be really involved in global economic processes, enlarge their financial opportunities and, especially important, to set up a sustainable environment of cooperation. It is obvious that Eurasian economic cooperation is not only a need of small countries in transition but also a need of the developed countries. The countries in transition need investment, while the developed ones are interested in new markets and the utilisation of local natural wealth. The developed countries are also interested in the "export" of democracy and market economics to the Newly Independent States, which in turn will strengthen stability and the spirit of partnership in our region.

These observations lead to the following conclusion in accordance with Georgia's participation in the integration process at all levels: **Georgia considers its fully-fledged integration into sub-regional,**

regional and inter-regional organisations and initiatives both as a core necessity to meet today's challenges and, above all, to secure the future economic growth of the country.

ENSURING PEACE AND STABILITY IN THE ECE REGION THROUGH COOPERATION: THE ROLE OF THE UNITED NATIONS ECONOMIC COMMISSION FOR EUROPE

Danuta Hübner

United Nations Under Secretary General and Executive Secretary, United Nations Economic Commission for Europe, Geneva [1]

Peace and stability do not come without a systematic effort aimed at preserving them. Regretfully, people tend to forget how destructive violent conflicts and wars are; how easy and quickly the entire livelihood of a nation can be destroyed, and how long it takes and how difficult it is to restore it. The temptation to solve a societal conflict by coercive methods is always there, so, it is crucial to continuously work on mitigating risks of conflict that could otherwise lead to the outbreak of violence.

One of the most important risk factors is the lack of economic growth, and a significant group of the UN/ECE member states has been suffering from prolonged economic stagnation and decline. Given the economic situation and development trends in the ECE region, the Economic Commission for Europe has been focussing on promoting cooperation between member states at the regional and sub-regional levels in order to expand opportunities for growth. The Commission provides support for cooperation in such economic areas as transport, trade, energy, human settlement, environment, entrepreneurship, industry restructuring, and small- and medium-sized enterprise development. This support in such cases like SECI, SPECA and South Caucasus aims at expanding newly emerged economies by the creation of a sub-regional market. This can be achieved by promoting a reduction of non-economic barriers, the harmonisation of standards and regulations, and the improvement or build-up of national capacities in an attempt to compensate for insufficient market space and limited income-generating opportunities. In some other cases, for example the CEI, the UN/ECE has been assisting member states in their efforts to develop an enabling environment for entrepreneurial and investment activities, and, therefore, to ensure that fragile economic recovery and growth are sustained.

The patterns of economic growth and development in the ECE region, however, have been showing a tendency to diverge. Furthermore, in some sub-regions and countries, this trend has been accompanied by negative structural changes and a regressive adjustment of human resources. Thus, for example, the share of the agricultural sector in total employment has been decreasing in Hungary, Czech Republic, Poland, Slovenia and Slovakia, but increasing in Romania, Bulgaria and some other South European countries. The share of agriculture in total value added has fallen, however, in all the above countries with the exception of Bulgaria. The share of industry in total employment has diminished in all listed countries except South Europe, so did its share in total value added with the exception of Czech Republic. While the service sector has become the major provider of employment in the countries under consideration, its share in total value added has declined in Bulgaria and the Czech Republic.

Results of a recent analysis of structural change in the countries of Central and Eastern Europe revealed that whereas some countries show clear signs of catching up with the more advanced EU countries, others such as Romania and Bulgaria seem trapped in the specialisation profile typical for less developed countries, while losing their earlier comparative advantages.

Structural changes and the overall economic situation in the countries of the CIS are even more alarming with most countries having moved backward in terms of industrial development and real GDP. The erosion of real gross fixed capital formation has been most dramatic in Armenia, Ukraine, the Russian Federation and Georgia, respectively, by 88%, 84%, 83% and 81% between 1989 and 1999. Real industrial output fell most in Georgia and Azerbaijan, correspondingly by 84% and 72%. Real GDP has remained far below the pre-transition level in most countries with the lowest levels in Moldova, Georgia and Ukraine (respectively 32%, 34% and 39% of the 1989 level).

It is obvious that such a divergence in development may lead to a cumulative effect over time with some countries joining the ranks of the most advanced member states of the ECE region and some becoming marginalised and returning to the pre-industrial stage. Such a possibility constitutes a potential threat to stability and security in the ECE region and requires a collective effort to avoid a new divide. This is especially important in the light of recent social trends, existing cultural and institutional frameworks, demographic trends and the historic legacy of ethnic conflicts in the countries at risk.

The social costs of transition in most countries of the CIS have been extremely unequally distributed among social and ethnic groups, and between poor and rich. In fact, a redistribution of national wealth of such a magnitude and over such a short time-span does not have an historic analogue. With impoverishment, income polarisation and growing social inequalities along ethnic, social and other boundaries, the risk of large-scale conflict has been aggravated. Furthermore, apart from open confrontations and wars such as the civil war in Tajikistan or the Karabakh conflict, so-called "hotbeds" in the region (especially in Central Asia and South Caucasus) with a mixed ethnicity and a relatively high frequency of ethnic group violence have been agitated by the consequences of environment degradation, adding water and land issues to the grievances of the local communities. Mutual territorial claims and disputes among the countries of the above regions constitute another dimension to the crisis situation.

Finally, the problems faced by the countries that emerged from the remnants of Yugoslavia are, in many respects, similar to those of the CIS, including both inherited structural problems and the consequences of civil war.

The UN/ECE strategy under these circumstances is, first and foremost:

• to focus its limited resources and activities on disadvantaged and vulnerable countries;

• to provide assistance in trade and border-crossing facilitation;

• to assist in developing an enabling environment for entrepreneurial activities and SMEs;

• to assist in mitigating energy and industrial crisis by promoting efficient energy and production practices;

• to assist in improving human settlements;

• to assist in building national capacities for improving the environment and preventing further environmental degradation;

• to provide a neutral forum for parties in confrontation;

• to mitigate tension between countries by involving them in joint projects addressing trans-boundaries;

• to alleviate poverty through promoting entrepreneurial activities among the poor and disadvantaged groups;

• to promote innovative forms of partnership to remove development bottlenecks;

• to bring the member states together to discuss and address emerging developmental problems.

The UN/ECE regards itself as a collective instrument of its member states. Depending on their political will, this instrument may become an effective tool in finding a solution to the problems faced by the countries of the region. It may be left intact, but the problems will not go away. It should be remembered that the ECE region, over the last 10 years, has moved up to the second place among the world regions, following Asia, in terms of the total number of refugees and internally displaced people, which currently stands at more than 7 million. The overall situation remains tense, as the development problems of some of the countries of the region receive increasing attention and financial support from major donors, while some others continue to be largely neglected, or given attention only in those instances that could have a direct effect on the advanced countries, such as migration, trafficking in people, weapons and drugs, or corruption. The primary causes of these phenomena, however, are economic, and require an economic remedy.

1. Written contribution

GROUP I : SOUTH-EASTERN EUROPE

INSIGHTS INTO BALKAN ECONOMIC INTERDEPENDENCIES

Krassen Stanchev

Executive Director, Institute for Market Economies, Sofia

Introduction

The Balkans has a broad but poorly defined development agenda. Factors that support and are likely to support the search for development and prosperity in the near future are the following:

• In most countries the transition to market economy and democracy has become irreversible;

• Leaders express commitments to follow the path of sustainable growth and prosperity combined with a vision of (re-) building their nations. In a response to this the international community launches a number of supporting initiatives;

• They all justify the need for an explicit local "ownership" and the inclusion of Balkan social capital in global competition.

There are factors, however, that are likely to counteract the seeds and efforts of development. For example, political wishes still need to be translated into practicalities and policy measures. It is already a conventional wisdom that long-lasting Balkan controversies stem from the unfinished formation of nation-states in the region (a process, which in other parts of Europe occurred between the 17th and 19th Centuries) and that this process contributes to intra-regional economic disparities. Kosovo is undergoing such nation-state formation. FR Yugoslavia is "defending" its national pride and territory. Montenegro is embarking on the nation-state path. Macedonia faces the challenge of defending its status quo.

Many constitutions in the region prevent flexibility on ethnic issues in their concept of statehood, envisage a constituent nation[1], ban autonomy[2], restrict foreigners from owning land, or prohibit political representation of ethnic and religious minorities.[3] To this list one should add constitutional provision for inefficient government machinery, protected monopolies and the ambiguous manner of imposing duties on citizenry through minor government acts.

In the 20th century most countries have used some form of "soft" ethnic cleansing; e.g., the last pre-Yugoslavian case was the expulsion of Bulgarian ethnic Turks in May-June 1989 to neighbouring Turkey (after they were deprived of their property rights). Similar events or negotiated "exchanges" of population, not very different from cleansing and deprivation, have been reoccurring in the last 120 years or so. Memories are alive while there is no critical mass of orientation towards the future.

While economic and political links between Balkan countries and the international community improved in the second half of 1999 and 2000, in 2001 the attempt of the UN and NATO to contain conflict within the borders of Kosovo failed and the aggression "leaked" from this UN protected territory into neighboring Macedonia, a country that originally had no formal involvement with the conflict in the province. In the light of prospects for economic cooperation and prosperity, it does not matter whether the territory is perceived as merely a "logistics site" for the politically dissatisfied Albanian minority in Macedonia or whether it is considered as a home base for "terrorist raids" of armed troops.[4] The fact of the matter is that the undecided status of Kosovo and the failure to organise (legitimate) representative democracy is reproducing the model of chetnik (i.e. guerilla) tactics of late 19th and early 20th Century national movements in the Balkans. These tactics revitalise political rhetoric and interethnic attitudes of the past, jeopardize fragile trust that business and trade opportunities would eventually make a difference, and scare away private sector and foreign investment in the region. Last but not least, the failures of democratic policies ensures the dominance of semi-legal and semi-informal economic interests in vast sub-regional territories, diminishing the chances of peace and order.

Problems

The idea of this paper is to provide some insights as to what extent transition Balkan economies represent indigenous roots of integration. International initiatives such as the Stability Pact assume that economic freedom, prosperity and rooted democracy would bring normality back to the region and would integrate it. There is a tacit believe that if economies are more interdependent, governments and people are less likely to resort to violence, since companies and citizens have much to loose. At the same time, both the Stability Pact and the EU Stabilisation and Association Agreement failed to prevent the March to May 2001 crisis in Macedonia.

Global economic divisions are different from those the world lived in even a decade ago. Reform leaders coped with the legacies of COMECON and re-oriented their capital and trade flows. These economies seek a niche in the global economy. The political process of building a nation state in a mid to late 19th Century manner, when homocentric European alliances were presumed as a territorial expansion of economic influence, is rather odd. Then, territorial identity was perceived as a precondition of prosperity, to be used as a governments' bargaining chip to seek rents from one alliance or another. Balkan nations, then, had fallen victim to these notions, fighting several wars with one another. Now, prosperity depends on competitiveness and innovation, on whether a national economy falls into the group of technology producing or technology consuming economies. If in the 19th Century it was somehow politically justifiable to fight for territorial influence in the Balkans, at the end of the 20th Century it was not. The region does not provide natural resources on which other economies depend, so there is no need to protect investment and trade routes.

Balkan countries faced different challenges. Slovenia from day one has 60% trade with the EU. Bulgarian COMECON trade in the 1970s and 1980s averaged around 60%, in Czechoslovakia it was over 50%, in Romania less than 30%, Hungary 40% and in Poland 50%.[5] The non-transition Balkan states, Greece and Turkey, are also different, one being a part of the EU single market, and the other in a free trade agreement with EU and a virtually free trade relationship with the Middle East (and Israeli) markets. The issue is whether and how it is possible to convert this diversity into mutual benefit. The Balkans do not constitute an economic notion, rather a political one.

Policy Objectives

Declared objectives of Balkan economic recovery fall into the area of socio-political engineering of a "neighbour-success" development pattern, which intends to compensate to a certain extent for the declining share of the region and individual countries in the global economy, and be a vehicle for enlarging individual countries' markets, and constitute a path to better competitiveness.

Table 1: Per Capita GDP as a %age of the West - 1870-1989

	1870	1913	1938	1973	1989
Western Europe	44	44	44	45	40
Overseas West	32	30	35	38	32

Source: Ivan T. Berend, From Plan to Market, From Regime Change to Sustained Growth in Central and Eastern Europe, Economic Survey of Europe, UNECE, 2000, No 2/3, p. 49, a quotation of A. Madison, Monitoring the World Economy 1820-1992, OECD, Paris, 1995, p. 212.

GDP per capita comparisons suggest that between 1870 and 1989, neither market nor central planning could generate prosperity at best available standards. CEE countries did not change their relative position vis-à-vis Western Europe and the West in general. The situation of the Balkan countries is likely to be worse than in CEE.

Trade Conditions

Like elsewhere, a critical mass of publicly supported orientation towards prosperity requires that there is a political consensus for structural change and exports to sophisticated markets. This consensus is expected to contribute to higher flexibility and lesser dependence on export receipts from physical access to major trade partners when conflict and/or non-tariff barriers interrupt traditional trade routes. In other words, regional integration alone is no substitute for general reform and restructuring efforts.

In terms of trade to GDP, there is a significant difference between Bulgaria, Bosnia and Herzegovina (B&H), and Macedonia with the highest ratios of trade to GDP, the medium ratios of Croatia and Romania, and the smaller international exchanges of Albania, and FR Yugoslavia (FRY). In Albania, reasons for this are the small size of industries, low productivity levels and wide spread economic informality. In the FRY, the ratio reflects distortions due to embargoes, sanctions and military conflicts.

Table 2: Trade Openness - 1998 (%)

	Exports+Imports as % of GDP
Albania	34
B&H	83
Bulgaria	91
Croatia	61
Yugoslavia	40
Macedonia	91
Romania	58

Source: World Bank[6]

The greater openness of Bulgaria and Macedonia is evidence of having got some fundamentals right, such as establishing trade contacts and cooperation links with a potential to cluster internationally.

The EU is the biggest trading partner for all SEE economies. On the other hand, in 1998, transition Balkans together had merely 1.6% of EU imports and 4.4% of exports. It is thus clearly no major market for the EU. Excluding Bulgaria and Romania, it is less than 1% of EU imports. The alternative Balkan market has its own peculiarities. **Tables 3** and **4** below show the distribution of main trade partners in 1998.

Table 3: Balkan Ranks of Trade Partners (Imports, % in 1998)

PARTNERS/ RANKS	AL	B&H	BG	CR	FRY	MK	RO	Balkans
Balkans (incl. Slovenia)	6.9	43.4	3.4	12.1	17.4	28.9	1.5	11.5
EU	79	41.5	44.6	58.1	72.6	52.8	56	56.1
I	38.7 (Ita)	14.7 (Ger)	13.9 (Ger)	20.5 (Ger)	25.2 (Ger)	14.4 (Ger)	17.5 (Ita)	
II	24.4 (Cre)	11.8 (Ita)	7.9 (Ita)	19 (Ita)	22.7 (Ita)	13.8 (Ita)	17.4 (Ger)	
III	7.9 (Ger)	4.9 (Aus)	6.4 (Gre)	5.1 (Fra)	8.8 (Aus)	8.9 (Aus)	6.9 (Fra)	
Industrial world	81.9	44.8	53.4	71.1	78.9	57.7	65.4	65.1

Source: IMF Direction of Trade, own calculations.

For Bulgaria, proximity matters in trade with Greece, a third partner since 1994 and EU member. Bosnia and Herzegovina, FR Yugoslavia and Macedonia have around one-fifth or more of their trade with a neighbouring country from the Balkans.

Table 4: Balkan Ranks of Trade Partners (Exports, % in 1998)

PARTNERS/ RANKS	AL	BiH	BG	CR	FRY	MK	RO	Balkans
Balkans (incl. Slovenia)	3	39.3	7.7	25.3	25.9	22.8	3.3	11.5
EU	88.8	50.9	47.9	45.8	71.7	51.8	62.8	58
I	58.9 (Ita)	22.3 (Ita)	13.1 (Ita)	18.4 (Ita)	28 (Ita)	22.4 (Ger)	22.3 (Ita)	
II	12.8 (Gre)	18.8 (Ger)	10.9 (Ger)	17.3 (Ger)	25.5 (Ger)	11.4 (Ita)	19.5 (Ger)	
III	8.3 (Ger)	4.5 (Aus)	9.2 (Gre)	2.3 (Fra)	5.3 (Fra)	3.7 (Bel)	5.9 (Fra)	
Industrial world	94	54	56.7	53.4	71.7	65.9	70.7	65.6

Source: IMF Direction of Trade, own calculations

With exports, the situation is basically the same. But it is obvious that Croatia exports rather extensively to neighbouring countries. Again Bosnia & Herzegovina, FR Yugoslavia and Macedonia have relatively high neighbour shares in their exports. Data for other years do not suggest a different picture.[7] At the same time it is obvious that these three countries experienced internal civic conflict and violence. A possible explanation for this coincidence of larger regional trade exposure and internal conflict is that the greater the trade, the greater the temptation to resort to physical (direct) control over trade roots and territories in order to extort taxes.

In general, however, Balkan countries trade over 60% with EU and the industrialised West, but not with one another. This fact might be justified by following reasons:

• Regional integration of a low-income economy with low-income countries usually makes an economy poorer;

• Demand is weak and relatively unsophisticated, and competitive companies chose more complex markets;

• The countries in the region have relatively similar product and quality structures;

• Instability of the regional markets in monetary and political terms;

• Inefficient contract enforcement and dispute resolution; tariff and non-tariff barriers; companies also avoid risks related to civic conflicts and insurgencies.

Economic Sizes and Balkan Cooperation

Economies and company structures are not well positioned to prevent external constraints to regional and indigenous development. Most economies are led by private sectors and services, which are rarely competitive. Foreign direct investment is negligible in absolute and in per-capita terms. The level of foreign ownership in Spain is 42%, in Poland 12%, and in Romania 6%.[8] Economic interdependence (besides Croatia in Bosnia-Herzegovina) is no factor. Mutual penetration of bank sectors is zero, with the exception of some Turkish and Greek banks. Foreign ownership in banking sectors used to be a rare phenomenon until recently. The presence of foreign (international) banks ranks from more than 80% of the respective sectors of Bulgaria and Bosnia & Herzegovina to zero in FR Yugoslavia and Kosovo. A common practice used to be transferring payments to a neighbouring country via international correspondent banks or using cash, and, in FR Yugoslavia, to have an account in part of the ex-republic from where to carry in cash. Domestic, not to mention regional (or of regional significance) commodity exchanges, do not exist or function badly. Links between capital markets are at the level of irregular correspondence. Cross-border clusters are the exception, even between countries never torn by recent wars and conflicts (e.g. Bulgaria and Romania).[9]

The dependency on international initiatives, constellations and agreements and the inability to cope with past legacies in Balkan countries is jeopardized by the fact that these are low income economies. Bulgaria's GDP per capita is just one-fifth of the EU lower rank economies. The average SEE GDP per capita at market exchange rate in 1998 was US$1,793. Lowest GDP per capita is Albania (US$1,110) and the highest Croatia (US$4,635). The total SEE GDP was US$94.92 billion, only 0.32% of the value of 1998 world output. If we exclude Romania (which is roughly 40% of the total SEE), remaining SEE GDP for 1998 is US$58.12 billion, i.e. 0.2% of the world output. Thus (excluding Romania) total SEE GDP was roughly one-twelfth of the combined 1998 public procurement budget of the EU member states.

A company demographics of low-income economies might be considerd as typically consisting of three groups of companies:

• **Subsistence** firms, in which there is little distinction between household and company finance, and which have high "social" value added but little or no value for the economy as a whole;

• **Survival** companies, which are incorporated, niche filling, relatively immobile, dependent on "single" suppliers or markets;

• **Competitive** companies, which are driven by productivity and quality of operations and are mobile, adjustable to the demand of a sophisticated market.

From these three groups, it is likely that the first prevails in number while the share of the third group is negligible. In this demographics, sole proprietorship firms are more likely to belong to the first category. In Bulgaria, one of the relatively well established Balkan economies, the picture is the following. 85% of the registered enterprises are sole proprietorships; 150,000 (i.e. roughly one-third) might be considered active (i.e. pay taxes or report more profits than losses). The share of competitive companies of all registered is just 5-7%, although these produced 35% of gross value added in 1999.

It is difficult to underestimate the political impact of this situation. Subsistence companies could be a subject of welfare policies and usually in high-income economies of the EU they are. Votes are where the majority is and there is pressure to support survival and subsistence companies at the expense of competitive ones. In Bulgaria and the Balkans they advocate welfare-like policies, requesting subsidies and protectionism and their demands often serve as substitute for the economic rationale of domestic and international policies.

Political Pre-conditions of Economic Cooperation

Since there is no indigenous critical mass - at the level of the firm - for cooperation and thinking about the future, attention again must be directed to more or less pure political conditions. There are two main political pre-conditions to convert the region into the recovery and development path. The first is to avoid the legacy risks. Such risks may occur when new realities reproduce the heritage of the 1990s or when post-Kosovo initiatives, opportunities, policies and instruments are rejected by local or Western democracies, and fail to behave in an economically rational manner.

The second condition is to avoid deeper divisions of legitimate execution of power in the Balkans. It is likely that geographic location, meaning the proximity and availability of traditional (pre-1999) trade routes and markets, will have a predominant importance in the short and medium term. Companies from and economies in the Balkan countries will naturally seek diversity and alternatives to pre-WW1 links and routes. The philosophy of both governments and chetniks here has often been that nations (not companies) compete; seeking rents from others is a norm. As Arben Xhaferi said recently in an interview for IWPR: "I explain [the outbreak of violence in Macedonia] as ethnic competition: to whom does the state belong?"

Domestic and intra-regional conditions that would eliminate sticky political and economic divisions in SEE are as follows:

• To avoid consistent failures of Balkan countries, leaders must agree on long-lasting peace agreements and constitutional orders;

• To reduce discrepancies in economic rules of the game within the region[10] and between different speeds of market and democratic reforms, including those related to EU-accession;

• To re-address aspirations to build nation-states at the expense of others, combined with a lack of respect for human and minority rights.

There is no shortage of international initiatives as well as of desire to be a member of those initiatives and structures, as Table 5 below demonstrates.

States	Key trade related organizations				Key agreements			South-East Europe Initiatives				
UN/ECE	WTO	WCO	OECD	ICC	European Union (TR)	European Union (PECO)	EFTA	BSEC	CEI	SECI	SE Stabty. Pact	SE Trade Initve.
Albania	(WTO)	WCO			GSP		(UTA)	BSEC	CEI	SECI	SESP	SETI
B&H					ATP		(UTA)		CEI	SECI	SESP	SETI
Bulgaria	WTO	WCO		ICC	EAA& invit.	PECO	FTA	BSEC	CEI	SECI	SESP	SETI
Macedonia	(WTO)	WCO		(ICC)	TCA	SAA	(UTA)		CEI	SECI	SESP	SETI
Croatia	(WTO)	WCO		ICC	ATP	SAA	(UTA)		CEI	SECI	SESP	SETI
Romania	WTO	WCO		ICC	EAA& invit.	PECO	FTA	BSEC	CEI	SECI	SESP	SETI
Yugoslavia				INCC NC		(SAA)	(UTA)				SESP	(SETI)

Notes: Brackets mean either a procedure to join (ratify) or status of an observer and/or unclearly defined membership.

In addition to the listed initiatives and institutions, Bulgaria and Romania are also members of the Central European Free Trade Agreement (CEFTA). It seems, however, that these initiatives and domestic and regional policies proceed as if on two parallel, rarely interchangeable levels. Kosovo does not have and cannot have a place in the above table due to its undecided status. The membership of Macedonia in almost all relevant initiatives and institutions and the Stabilisation and Association Agreement with the EU seems not to contribute to the stability of the country.

In all SEE countries, domestic policies have been delaying reforms. Wars and conflicts aggravated and still prolong high country risks and worsen the ill effects of the lack of institution building. Therefore, regional initiatives and policies must not be perceived as a substitute for core market and democratisation reforms.

1. E.g., the Croatian Constitution says: "Croatia, the nation-state of the Croatian people and the state of other nationalities and minorities which are its citizens"; the Macedonian Constitution contains a similar statement: "Macedonia, the national state of the Macedonian people, which guarantees the complete civic equality and permanent cohabitation of the Macedonian people with the Albanians, Turks, Roma, and other nationalities living there." The Bulgarian Constitution states that "the official language is Bulgarian" (Article 3), while 10% of the citizenry has the Turkish as mother tongue.

2. E.g., Article 21 of the Bulgarian Constitution.

3. E.g., in the Constitution of Bulgaria one may find the statement; "the traditional religion [in the country] is the Orthodox Christian congregation" (Article 13.2), and that political parties established on "ethnic, racial or religious lines" are not allowed (Article 11.4). While such parties exist de facto it is almost impossible to implement this provision de jure.

4. The former explanation has been recently used by Veton Surroi, the publisher of the main Kosovo newspaper, Koha Ditore (see "Renewed Ethnic Reform Would Defuse Macedonian Conflict", International Herald Tribune, March 27, 2001, p.10); the latter interpretation was suggested by the prime minister of Macedonia, Ljupco Georgievski, in a public statement on March 19, 2001 and has been used by Yugoslav officials to describe insurgencies in the Presevo region earlier this year; while US, EU and NATO officials used the enigmatic and less decisive definitions of "extremism" and "armed extremists".

5. Rumen Dobrinski, Transition Failures: Anatomy of the Bulgarian Crisis, Vienna, WIIW, 1997, p.7.

6. Trade Integration for SEE in the Context of the Stability Pact, World Bank, 2000, p. 55.

7. The constellations have changed with regard to Bulgaria: in 2000 its Balkan trade tripled, due to petroleum exports to FR Yugoslavia and the free trade agreement with Macedonia, which in 2000 equaled Russia in Bulgarian exports.

8. Source: Heriot-Watt University, UK, quoted by: Francis Harris, "Join at your Peril," Business Central Europe, March, 1999, 12.

9. Petya Mandova, Krassen Stanchev, To Cluster or Not: Cross Danube Firm Level Co-operation, (http://www.ime-bg.org).

10. See: Krassen Stanchev, "Market Reforms in the Balkans: Barriers and Challenges," Balkan Transitions, edited by Ivailo Dichev, (Sofia, ACCESS, 1997).

11. ECE - Economic Commission for Europe, Geneva; WTO - World Trade Organization, Geneva; WCO - World Customs Organization, Brussels; OECD - Organization for Economic Cooperation and Development, Paris; ICC - International Chamber of Commerce, Paris (important for setting rules of conduct and international dispute resolution); EU - European Union, Brussels; EFTA - European Free Trade Association, Brussels; BSEC - Black Sea Economic Cooperation; CEI - Central European Initiative; SECI - Southeast European Cooperative Initiative; SESP - Southeast Europe Stability Pact; SETI - Southeast Europe Trade Initiative (SETI is an advocacy group, securing businesses' support for values and projects of SECI and SESP); SAA - Stabilisation and Association Agreement; EAA - European Association Agreement; TR - Trade Relations; PECO - Pan European Cumulation of Origin; FTA - Free Trade Agreement; CU - Customs Union ; ATP - Autonomous Trade Preferences; GSP - Generalized System of Preferences; TCA - Trade and Cooperation Agreement; UTA - Unilateral Trade Agreement (an EU model to liberalise tariffs for the western Balkans).

SOUTHEAST EUROPEAN ECONOMIC PROSPECTS IN VIEW OF RECENT POLITICAL DEVELOPMENTS

Vladimir Gligorov

Professor, The Vienna Institute for International Economic Studies and OECD

Introduction

After the momentous political changes in Croatia and Serbia and generally positive political developments in the region last year, economic prospects for Southeast Europe (SEE) looked better than at any time in the last ten years or so.[1] Indeed, 2000 was the first in a long time that saw positive growth in all SEE states. Though there were reasons to believe that this positive economic performance may not be easy to sustain because of significant and persistent macroeconomic disequilibria and uneven microeconomic transition, still it looked as if the region has finally chosen to walk the path of transition and development. These hopes have been somewhat shattered by the renewed security concerns centred, this time, on Macedonia. Though the impact of the current crisis in Macedonia is not easy to assess, it is clear that it will not be without costs, both political and economic. In addition, there is the potential for other crisis points to emerge or re-emerge, especially depending on the way the crisis in Macedonia develops and is resolved. Thus, the economic prospects still depend to a very large extent on the way political and security issues are resolved. In this paper, the possible course of economic developments in the short and medium run will be assessed in view of the political and security flash points and their potential, if any, to lead to a more general instability in SEE.

Overview of Current Economic Developments in SEE

Most assessments of current economic developments in particular SEE countries are encouraging.[2] They emphasise:

- continued price stability, except in Yugoslavia and Romania;

- positive growth rates in 2000, everywhere, in some cases after

85

years of stagnation or low growth (e.g., Macedonia) and in other cases after shorter or prolonged recessions (e.g., Croatia and Romania);

• accelerated structural reforms in Bulgaria, Macedonia, Croatia and even Bosnia and Herzegovina and Albania;

• more positive prospects for foreign investments due to greater domestic interest in attracting them and to improved risk assessments on the part of foreign investors;

• improved intra-regional and inter-regional co-operation (with Central Europe, the EU and the rest of the world);

• and, in general, the sustainability of these positive trends at least in the short and medium run.[3]

One could add that the initial developments in Yugoslavia, after the momentous political change in the autumn of 2000, have been assessed as promising,[4] and that the difficult negotiations between the IMF and Romania seem to be moving towards some kind of a positive resolution.[5]

Of course, it is hard not to notice the persistence of high unemployment throughout the region, of fiscal fragility and of external imbalances in addition to large black markets, pervasive corruption and significant economic criminality. Still, it is easier to deal with all of these problems when the economies are growing than when they are not. Thus, the two key targets that have been set for the region on the basis of developments in 2000 are sustained stability and growth. Most of the economic programmes of the countries in the region have been geared towards achieving these two goals.

Obviously, the conditions that would be conducive to achieving these goals, apart from the adoption of an appropriate reform strategy and a coherent economic policy, are improved domestic and regional security, political stability and the continuation of regional and wider integration. The changes in Serbia and Croatia last year were seen precisely as contributing to these conditions being fulfilled. In addition to those, the elections in Bosnia and Herzegovina in late 2000 were seen as going mostly in the same direction.[6] The same process of democratisation was seen as taking root or developing further in the rest of the region too. Finally, it was believed that the prospect of EU integration would displace the political attractiveness of local animosities.

These positive developments were seen as supportive of the programme of making this region, or most of the region, self-sustainable especially in cases in which foreign aid has played a vital role over the last decade. The sub-region in the Balkans that depends to a significant extent on foreign private and public aid is quite large. It includes Bosnia and Herzegovina, Kosovo, Montenegro, Macedonia and Albania. Now Serbia has to be added to this list.[7] The other three countries, Croatia, Romania and Bulgaria, do not depend on outright foreign aid all that much, though various other types of help and special consideration, together with financial and technical assistance, are quite important.[8] The shift to self-sustainability was supposed to take place over the next five or so years,[9] but this is probably unrealistic given the heavy political and security agenda that has to be dealt with. Indeed, at the beginning of 2001 the political and security situation looks significantly worse than it looked at the end of the year 2000.

Nationalism Strikes Back

The problem with the positive analysis of trends in 2000 was that it disregarded the strength of nationalism and also the fragility of some of the security and political arrangements. The pro-democratic changes in the region have stirred nationalist reactions that underline the fragility of the whole security and political construction on which SEE stability and development are based. This has exposed the key problem with the internal and the external approach to the region, namely that it has been based on the premise that nationalism should be appeased rather than completely illegitimatised. It has also not been taken fully into account that democracy and nationalism do not go together and that the nationalists will have to react if democracy appears to be taking root.

This reaction has now arrived. It is again shaking the political structures in SEE and will undoubtedly have serious economic consequences for the countries affected. The resurgence of the many faces of SEE nationalism has already been noticed by scholars and commentators[10] so I will concentrate on what is at the moment the most critical issue, that of Macedonia.

The reason that the current Albanian revolt in Macedonia can be defined as nationalistic is twofold. First, the key demand is territorial, i.e., the control of ethnic territories.[11] Second, the Albanians using violence to achieve their political ends are recruited from outside as well as from inside Macedonia. This is a movement that is almost to the dot analogous to the Serbian and the Croat ones. In the latter cases, the cause of the nationalists was also territorial and they assumed the existence of ethnic solidarity from all the Serbs and all the Croats wherever they happened to live.

There are two aspects of Albanian nationalism, however, that distinguishes it from the other two. This nationalism is revolutionary and has been somewhat legitimised internationally. It is revolutionary because it puts out political goals that do not really justify the violent actions that are taken to achieve them. Thus, for instance, equal rights under the constitution are demanded, but that would justify demons-trations or other types of political actions and not armed insurrection. It is also said that the existing Albanian parties that take part in the Macedonian parliament and government are unrepresentative and corrupt, which would suggest that an alternative party rather than a paramilitary organisation should be formed.

The other aspect of this nationalism is that it can claim some international legitimacy (even if it uses violent means to achieve political ends) in view of the support for the insurrection in Kosovo in 1998 and 1999. There is some confusion in the international circles about the nature of this support.[12] The fact that it was justified as humanitarian does not mean that whenever there is any violation of human rights, true or alleged, armed revolt is justified and will be supported. Because, first, gross violations of human rights are needed and, second, the legal and democratic means to remedy those should be completely absent. This was arguably the case in Kosovo, but it is not the case in Macedonia.

This confusion has another consequence that has to be taken into account. The international support for the resistance in Kosovo is not the same as the support for the separation of Kosovo from Yugoslavia. This is in keeping with basic international principles. This does not mean that Kosovo cannot become an independent political entity sometime in the future. What it means is that the support for human rights and for the right to democratic government and indeed even for national self-determination is not necessarily the same as the support for national independence, i.e., for a separate state.[13] Indeed, the very nature of the defence of human rights that took place in Kosovo goes somewhat against the principle of self-determination to the extent that the latter can lead to national independence and to the change of national borders only through peaceful means. Because of that and also because of the subsequent democratisation of Serbia, the international community is unlikely to support the independence of Kosovo if it is not achieved in a peaceful and negotiated way. The same argument applies to Bosnia and Herzegovina and indeed to all the other contested territories in the Balkans.

The change of borders by the use of violence is not something that the international community will feel comfortable with and an agreement on that, for instance in the Security Council, is not to be expected either in the case of Kosovo or in the other cases.

With all that in mind, the Macedonian crisis has to be seen as a very serious one indeed. Though it has calmed down somewhat, it cannot be expected to be completely resolved in a short period of time and certainly not through half-hearted political concessions that will not be seen as satisfying the demands of the nationalists. However, the full justification and acceptance of the demands of the nationalists cannot but lead to a new round of balkanisation throughout the region or in any case of a large part of it.

This is the dilemma that hangs over the political debate in Macedonia. At this moment, it is not clear how it is going to be resolved. With the means used not being matched by the ends sought, there is an ambiguity in the strategies followed by the various political actors in Macedonia that is certain to create problems in the political discussions and negotiations that have already started in Skopje. Those should have come up with a political resolution of the "ethnic competition" in Macedonia by the end of June 2001. This is an obligation that the Macedonian government has undertaken in the context of the political discussions with the representatives of the international community. The negotiations are being held under the constant pressure of the threat of the resurgence of violence if they do not end up with the desired outcome. As the demand of the Albanian representatives is the change of the constitution in a way which is unacceptable to the Macedonians and as the threat by the paramilitaries is that conflicts will continue if the changes are not adopted, the compromise solution is rather difficult to see at this particular point in time.

Economic Consequences

The economic consequences of the Macedonian crisis are not so easy to assess. This is because it is difficult to predict the likely development of the crisis. There are, perhaps, the following possibilities in terms of duration:

- quick resolution;

- somewhat prolonged, low-level conflict;

- gradual deterioration;

- sharp deterioration;

- prolonged sharp conflict (i.e., civil war).

Assuming that it is a localised, low-level, but somewhat prolonged conflict (possibly with gradual deterioration), the consequences can be confined to Macedonia and Kosovo with the neighbouring countries being little affected. The immediate economic consequences for Macedonia can already be assessed. The IMF has already realised that Macedonia will not be able to fulfil the targets set by the recent agreement. In particular, the accelerated structural reforms, involving the downsizing of the public administration and closing down of loss-making enterprises will have to be postponed. Also, exports will suffer, especially those destined for Kosovo. Public obligations will rise because of the costs of military intervention and because of the costs of destruction and migration. Internal trade will suffer too, so the overall economic picture would worsen significantly.

It will become much more difficult to sustain the already tenuous external position and with that the stability of the currency. Macedonia runs a large trade deficit, which could be sustained, at the current exchange rate, only with the help of private and public transfers and increasingly with foreign direct investments. Private transfers will suffer, as will investment. Therefore, a need may arise to adjust the exchange rate. A sharp depreciation[14] should clearly be avoided for the time being at least because it may have serious destabilising effects.

For this to be achieved, it will be crucial to see how official foreign transfers will perform. The initial reaction by the EU has been to set aside some additional money to support some of the programmes that aim to meet some of the Albanian demands, e.g., the opening of the University in Tetovo and greater inclusion of Albanians in public services. Some technical support for the military has been promised. It can be expected that some support for refugees and displaced people will be forthcoming too. However, if the crisis is prolonged and the economic situation deteriorates further, other types of support will be necessary in order to avoid further macroeconomic destabilisation.

In this context, it is very significant that the EU has decided to proceed with the signing of the Stabilisation and Association Agreement (SAA) with Macedonia irrespective of the crisis that has developed since the SAA was negotiated and initialled (late 2000). Indeed, Macedonia is a front runner in this new type of association agreements and it is important for the stability of the country that it does not lose pace in its integration with the EU.

Apart from Macedonia, the most affected region is that of Kosovo. Because of the lack of data, it is difficult to assess the extent of economic inter-dependence between Macedonia and Kosovo. Clearly, the main route to Kosovo is through Macedonia.[15] Connections with Albania are not good and those with Serbia are mostly closed. Looking at the available data on the Kosovo economy,[16] it is evident that this province depends very much on imports and on official transfers. At least half of the Kosovo budget is covered from foreign grants. Also, all imports are paid for from transfers - Kosovo exports are effectively zero. Thus, the Kosovo economy depends significantly on its relations with Macedonia and on the steady inflow of foreign aid.

Obviously, if trade with Macedonia suffers, this will hurt Kosovo. More importantly, if the international community decides that it does not want to continue with its generous support for Kosovo, there will be a significant deterioration in public finances. Finally, violent conflicts in Macedonia will postpone the process of state building in Kosovo, which will have negative effects on investments and on economic development in general. Thus, the costs of the Macedonian crisis for Kosovo could be very significant.

Moreover, the costs of the current crisis will be born disproportionately by the Albanian population in Macedonia. The economic relations between the Albanian part of Skopje, of Tetovo, the whole of Western Macedonia and Kosovo are much more developed than between the Macedonian parts and Kosovo. Thus, both physical destruction and economic loss is going to fall mainly, though not exclusively, on the Albanian population both in Macedonia and in Kosovo. Also, and more importantly, investments in Western Macedonia, i.e., in the region populated by Albanians, will continue to suffer, especially those in industry and in public projects. Thus, economic development, which is the one key factor for political stability in Western Macedonia, will not occur. Indeed, in Western Macedonia, as in Macedonia as a whole, rapid economic development and social modernisation are the key to political and social stability. Wars and ethnic conflicts are of course bad catalysts for that kind of change.

Assuming still that the conflict will be a localised but a prolonged one, there will be some negative consequences for the Bulgarian and the Albanian economies. Those will mostly consist of the increased costs of foreign investments. Direct economic dependencies between Macedonia and both Bulgaria and Albania are not very high and will certainly not increase in the context of the increased security risks. There is some trade, but it is not vital and it will not necessarily suffer. However, the regional risk will increase and that will have consequences for foreign investments both official and private. Some of the important regional projects under the Stability Pact will be negatively affected and some of the private investments with a regional component will also be more difficult to implement.[17]

There will be some negative consequences for the Serbian economy too, because Macedonia is an important trade partner and especially because the conflict in Macedonia is not independent from the similar conflict in Southern Serbia. Clearly, the latter cannot destabilise Serbia, but may drain some of its resources and may have some negative influence on political developments in Serbia (e.g., on the scaling down of the role of the military). It may have adverse effects on the economic development of the southern part of Serbia and of central Serbia in general. This may further complicate the relations between Vojvodina, Belgrade and central Serbia, as Vojvodina stands to gain much more from the political and economic changes in Serbia than either Belgrade or central Serbia do. Indeed, further transfers of public money from Vojvodina to central Serbia, which may be even more necessary given the adverse security developments in Serbia, may create problems for the government in Belgrade.

Political and Economic Contagion

Other countries in the region should not be affected all that much by the current conflict, assuming that it is localised. However, given the nationalist environment in which it is taking place, problems of different types and intensities may be expected to emerge throughout the region and that may have negative economic consequences that cannot be easily assessed or quantified at this early stage. These developments will depend very much on the behaviour of the international community, especially of the EU and the US. If they fail to take a firm stand against the resurgent nationalism throughout the region, quite far-reaching negative consequences can be anticipated.

There are other leftovers from the dissolution of former Yugoslavia and from the Balkan wars in the nineties, in addition to the conflict in Macedonia, some of which are potentially destabilising. The incomplete list includes:

- the Kosovo question;

- the constitutional development of Bosnia and Herzegovina;

- the issue of the independence of Montenegro;

- the constitutional arrangement for Yugoslavia, i.e., Serbia.

The rest of the Balkans seems unaffected by internal problems of the same kind, though this is probably somewhat misleading. However, if the four problems listed above develop in an unfavourable way, the whole region may be more or less destabilised.

These four major problem areas have to be seen together with the current crisis in Macedonia in order to have an understanding of the scope of the problems that the current set up in the SEE creates and contains. Looking at the possible contagion mechanisms from whichever of these four problems to the others, two most general ones can be singled out:

- The first is that of general instability and the attached uncertainty. If one takes the example of Kosovo, it becomes clear that the unsettled political status of Kosovo increases the instability in the whole region through the increase in the uncertainty of what is permanent and what is provisional. The same is true for the possible contagion effect of the eventual decision of Montenegro to declare independence from Yugoslavia. This is also mainly the effect that constitutional debates and decisions in Serbia may have on its immediate neighbours (e.g., Bosnia and Herzegovina and Macedonia);

• The second is that of principles followed and applied. The decisions taken locally have to be accepted by the international community. Unlike inter-state relations, which do not have to go beyond common interests, the legitimacy bestowed on the national decision by the international community has to be based on principles if not on international law. Therefore, the constitutional arrangement that is accepted in one case sets a precedent for all the other cases. This is what is so bothersome to many countries in the region when it comes to the issue of the re-drawing of the borders. Once borders are changed in one case, the principle is being violated and a new one, that of the acceptability of the redrawing of the borders is being promoted. This applies to all the other issues, and not only to that of borders. For instance, if the federalisation of Macedonia is accepted, so may the federalisation of Kosovo, and so on.

Clearly, the current situation is unsustainable. To estimate more exactly the potential risks that these all these security and political problems may give rise to, at least two things have to be known. One is the final regional set-up that may be emerging and the other is the process by which it will be reached (these two may not be independent of each other). It could be argued that if the process is democratic, then the final status may not be settled before the process runs its course. However, the use of non-democratic means cannot be excluded and because of that there may be a need to have an idea of where these developments are going in order to minimise the possible security and other risks that are sure to arise. Clearly, EU integration is the end to which most of the reasonable political actors in the region are inclined. However, for the region to be integrated into the EU, it has to solve all outstanding security and political problems. Therefore, some idea of how the intra-regional set up is going to look like would be useful in strengthening the pro-democratic and pro-European political actors.

The Weak States

The key security, political and economic problem of the SEE is to be found in the weakness of its constituent states[18] that are weak constitutionally, politically and economically.

Clearly, constitutional problems are the most fundamental ones and have been discussed throughout this paper.[19] It is enough here to point out that many countries in the SEE have unclear borders and have internally and externally limited sovereignty.[20] One has only to think of the constitutional constructs like those to be found in Bosnia and Herzegovina and Yugoslavia to see the point. Other countries have constitutional problems too, as already discussed, while the biggest problem is the constitutional status of Kosovo, which is in fact impossible to define.

The key consequence of these constitutional deficiencies is the shaky or non-existent rule of law. Without the rule of law, the provision of security is at best an imperfect one. Again, the extreme example is Kosovo where there is no legislative power at all, as there is little if any other legitimate power, and that fact accounts for the bad security situation both in Kosovo itself and nearby. However, the deficiencies in the rule of law are widespread throughout the region. Those deficiencies have negative consequences for other institutions as well, so the region has to go through the process of institution building together with that of state building.

Politically, these states are in a process of democratisation, at best. Again, they are at different stages in this process, but none of the SEE countries can yet be described as a stable, functioning and sustainable democracy. Still, the situation that the region is facing now is fundamentally different from the one that prevailed immediately after the end of socialism and during the dissolution of former Yugoslavia. There are three differences to consider:

• The general acceptance of democratic means to solve political problems. After the fall of Milosevic, the non-democratic forces are only those who support paramilitaries whether those are Albanian or not. Though the paramilitary forces present a significant threat, they are still facing mainly pro-democratic parties and governments and cannot expect to muster international support even if sometimes they purport to be aiming at political goals that have wide support among the respective population. Thus, nationalists cannot expect to get international support for the use of violent means to achieve political aims, as they in some cases could during the dissolution of former Yugoslavia;

• The partly changed structure of public preferences. While in the past political preferences dominated over economic ones, this ranking has been partly reversed in many countries. This is something one hopes to see even more in Bosnia and Herzegovina and in Kosovo, while the reversal is almost complete in all the other states;

• The role of EU integration. Though the issue of integration still does not dominate the domestic political agenda in SEE, it has certainly increased in importance. With the speed up of the process of association, the issues pertaining to EU integration will become even more prominent. This will give significant leverage to the EU to influence developments both in the region and in particular countries in a positive way. Indeed, the current crisis in Macedonia is an obvious test of that.

Economically, states in SEE are, for the most part, captured. They tend to respond to domestic and international interest groups rather than to their electorates. This is a well-documented fact. Other economic characteristics of SEE are discussed in more detail in the next section on "Economic Prospects".

The weakness of states in SEE cannot be completely overcome by promises of EU integration, because such integration will not take place without these states becoming strong. That means that they respect the rule of law, are sustainable democracies and follow economic policies that respond to the preferences of its citizens. In SEE the strong state is identified with the strongly sovereign and paternalistic state,[21] which is not what I have in mind here. Clearly, the process of EU integration leads to the modification of the traditional concept of sovereignty. But it stresses even more the need for legality, legitimacy and democratic responsiveness.

There are opinions that the states are weak because they are multi-ethnic and that they will strengthen if they are ethnically homogenous. Thus, some commentators push for further ethnic separation and for further disintegration of the ethnically mixed states. This judgement is not really supported by the facts of SEE development. It cannot be said that the states that are ethnically more homogenous are also stronger in term of rule of law. Romania, Bulgaria and Albania have weak states, though they are reasonably ethnically homogenous, at least by Balkan standards. Croatia is not much different, though it is now quite homogenous in ethnic terms. This points to the fact that ethnic homogeneity is not a sufficient condition for existence of a well-functioning state. It is also not a necessary condition either, as there are quite a number of ethnically heterogeneous states outside of the Balkans that are quite successful. By a strong state, I mean one that is based on the rule of law and where there is no reason to expect that ethnic heterogeneity would be a barrier to the determined and consistent implementation of the rule of law.

Ideas about the necessity of ethnic homogeneity in the Balkans are mostly propagated out of ignorance and by relying on comparisons of dubious value. It has been argued that a stable state in Europe, and thus in the Balkans, requires that at least 80% of the population of a state belongs to the dominant ethnic community. Otherwise, ethnic conflicts are to be expected. A rather comprehensive study of ethnic conflicts in the world, however, seems to show that precisely the opposite is true: multi-ethnic states are more stable than those with small minorities.[22] This finding can be supported by the history of ethnic conflicts in the Balkans. In most cases, the worst ethnic cleansing has happened in areas where there is one dominant ethnic group that wants to get rid of one or more minorities. This, if correct, would argue for regional integration, and thus for the increased role of multi-ethnic coexistence, rather than for ethnic disintegration.

Economic Prospects

Given the political and security problems outlined above, what are the economic prospects for SEE? Short-term economic prospects depend on the sources of growth from 2000 remaining extant and upon the non-appearance of external shocks that might emerge. Growth in 2000 was the consequence of a better export performance in most countries of the region.[23] This was due to higher growth in the EU, which cannot be expected to be repeated in 2001. There was some increase in investments into some SEE countries, especially of foreign investments (e.g., in Macedonia). This should continue to be the case because most countries are hard pressed for foreign currency in order to pay for their mounting public debts. Private consumption is still depressed, while public consumption has been recovering in a number of cases. The latter cannot be expected to continue to grow this year, however, except in some cases, e.g., in Serbia. Therefore, overall growth should not be much better in 2001 than it was in 2000. Though some countries may do better and some worse.

Short-term growth prospects may deteriorate through internal and external shocks. Apart from the security and political changes that have already been discussed above, there are those that may arise out of the unfinished process of transition. For instance, in the case of Serbia, a slowdown of growth is projected in 2001 due to the need to stabilise the economy and to start the process of transition in earnest. In the case of Croatia, growth is not expected to accelerate significantly due to the need to reduce public expenditures in order to get the fiscal deficit under control. Growth prospects in Romania could also be affected by the need to tighten fiscal and monetary policies in order to bring inflation down, though that was not originally the intention of the new government, at least not this year.

The need to accelerate the process of transition may lead to medium-term growth prospects that are rather less than spectacular. More importantly, in the medium-term, there are a number of macro-economic imbalances that may instigate sharp adjustments that might in turn lead to the slowdown of growth or to a recession in some cases. In many cases, the exchange rate is misaligned and may have to be adjusted. In others, the fiscal situation is unsustainable and a protracted adjustment may fuel a prolonged low growth rate. Finally, social pressure, as a consequence of the high rate of unemployment, may lead to a slowdown in microeconomic adjustment and that may lead to low productivity growth rates and thus to low GDP growth as well.

It cannot be expected that political and security uncertainties will be resolved in the medium-term in order to provide a positive boost to economic growth. Therefore, the level of uncertainty in the region will remain pretty much the same, though serious crisis, e.g., in Macedonia, cannot be excluded. If that were to happen, the regional economic prospects would only get worse.

Conclusion

SEE is facing a new source of instability. The potential for the conflict in Macedonia to destabilise the whole region is great. However, the most probable development of the crisis is that it will be localised and will be somewhat prolonged. That will have significant negative economic consequences for Macedonia and for Kosovo and non-negligible consequences for Albania, Serbia and Bulgaria. However, the situation has changed in the last couple of years or so, with democratic parties and institutions taking over from more authoritarian and bellicose political actors. Therefore, the challenge that resurgent nationalism poses is to the strength of the rule of law and of democracy. This applies to the other fundamental political and indeed constitutional issues that arise in a number of countries in the region. In this context, sustainable economic improvement is vitally important. This will depend on the way macroeconomic imbalances are handled in the medium run and with transition progress. Also, and most importantly, steady progress with intra-regional and EU integration is crucial.

Appendix: Selected Macroeconomic Indicators in South East European Countries, 1998-2000

	ALB[1]	B&H[1,2]	BUL	CRO	MAC	ROM	YUG[3]
GDP, real change in % p.a.							
1998	8.0	18	3.5	2.5	2.9	-5.4	2.5
1999	7.3	8	2.4	-0.4	2.7	-3.2	-17.7
2000	7.8	10	5.0	3.5	5.1	1.6	7.0
Consumer inflation, change in % p.a.							
1998	20.9	5 / 2	22.3	5.7	0.8	59.1	29.9
1999	0.4	0 / 14	0.3	4.2	-1.1	45.8	44.9
2000	-0.2	0 / 12[4]	9.9	6.2	10.6	45.7	85.6
Unemployment rate, in %, end-2000	18.4[5]	39 / 41[6]	17.9	22.6	32[7]	10.5	26.7
Current account, % of GDP							
1998	-1.5[8]	-28.2	-0.5	-0.7	-8.8	-7.2	-6.4
1999	-4.2[8]	-17.4	-5.3	-7.6	-3.9	-3.8	-3.4
2000	-4.0[8]	.	-5.8	-4.2	-9.7	-3.8	-7.7
General government balance, % of GDP							
1998	-10.4	-7.4	1.0	0.6	-0.6	-4.1	-6.1
1999	-11.5	-5.7	-1.0	-2.0	1.0	-4.0	.
2000	-9.5	-3 / -4	-0.7[9]	-3.9[9]	3.5	-3.6[9]	.
GDP per capita, USD at PPP, in 2000	2893[10]	.	5600	7640	4880	6200	3500[11]

Notes: 1) Unless otherwise indicated, figures for 2000 for Albania and Bosnia and Herzegovina represent IMF estimates. - 2) In case two figures are given, the first one refers to the Federation, the second to Republika Srpska. - 3) From 1999 excluding Kosovo and Metohia. - 4) As of mid-2000, year-on-year. - 5) End-1999. - 6) Mid-2000. - 7) Annual average, according to LFS data. - 8) Including official transfers. - 9) Central government only. - 10) In 1998. - 11) Estimation as of 1999 by Prof. Pavle Petrovic, University of Belgrade.

Source: WIIW Database incorporating national and international statistics.

References

Collier, P. (2000), Economic Causes of Civil Conflict and Their Implications for Policy. The World Bank.

Department of Reconstruction, New Economic Faculty (2001), Partnership in Kosovo: Reconstruction 1999-2000.

EBRD (2001), BIH Country Strategy Paper.

Gligorov, V. (1994), Why Do Countries Break Up? The Case of Yugoslavia. Uppsala: Acta Universitatis Upsaliansis.

Gligorov, V. (2000a), "The Economic Viability of Kosovo". International Spectator.

Gligorov, V., ed., (2000b), Balkan Reconstruction: Economic Aspects. WIIW.

Gligorov, V. (2000c), "Bosnia and Herzegovina: Reconstruction without Development", Journal of Southeast European and Black Sea Studies, Vol. 1, number 1.

Gligorov, V. (2000d), "Notes on the Stability Pact", Journal of Southeast European and Black Sea Studies, Vol. 1, number 1.

Gligorov, V. (2001a), "State in the Balkans", to be published.

Gligorov, V. (2001b), Southeast Europe: Business Prospects. Bank Austria.

Gligorov, V. (2001c), "Kosovo's Economy: An Overview", to be published.

Gligorov, V., N. Sundstrom (1999), "The Costs of the Kosovo Crisis", Country Studies 12.

Gligorov, V., N. Sundstrom (2001), "Change in Serbia", Social Market Foundation Working Paper 3.

IMF Macedonia (2000), Former Yugoslav Republic of Macedonia: Recent Economic Developments.

IMF Macedonia (2000), Former Yugoslav Republic of Macedonia: Staff Report for the 2000 Article IV Consultation.

IMF Romania (2000), Romania: 2000 Article IV Consultation -- Staff Report; Statement by Staff Representative; and Public Information Notice Following Consultation.

IMF Romania (2001), Romania: Selected Issues and Statistical Appendix.

IMF BiH (2001), Bosnia and Herzegovina: Fourth and Fifth Review Under the Stand-By Arrangement and Requests for Extension and Rephasing of the Arrangement--Staff Report and Press Release on the Executive Board Discussion.

IMF Croatia (2001), Republic of Croatia: 2000 Article IV Consultation and Request for a Stand-By Arrangement--Staff Report; Staff Statement; Public Information Notice and Press Release on the Executive Board Discussion; and Statement by the Authorities of Croatia.

IMF Albania (2001), Albania: First Review Under the Third Annual Arrangement Under the Poverty Reduction and Growth Facility and Request for Waiver of Performance Criteria--Staff Report; Staff Statement; News Brief on the Executive Discussion; and Statement by Authorities of Albania.

IMF Yugoslavia (2001), Federal Republic of Yugoslavia: Membership and Request for Emergency Postconflict Assistance--Staff Report, and Press Release on the Executive Board Discussion.

IMF Kosovo (2001), Kosovo: Macroeconomic Issues and Financial Sustainability.

IMF Bulgaria (2001), Bulgaria: Selected Issues and Statistical Appendix.

IMF Bulgaria (2001), Bulgaria: 2000 Article IV Consultation and Fifth Review Under the Extended Arrangement--Staff Report; Staff Statement; Public Information Notice and News Brief on the Executive Board Discussion; and Statement by the Authorities of Bulgaria.

Independent International Commission on Kosovo (2000), The Kosovo Report: Conflict, International Response, Lessons Learned. Oxford University Press.

Podkaminer, L. et al. (2001), The Transition Economies: Externally Conditioned Improvements in 2000, Slowdowns and Adjustments Likely in 2001 and 2002. WIIW Research Reports, No. 275.

Rawls, J. (1999), The Law of Peoples. Harvard University Press.

Suroi, V. (2001), "Renewed Ethnic Reform Would Defuse Macedonian Conflict", International Herald Tribune, March 27.

Tamir, Y. (1993), Liberal Nationalism. Princeton University Press.

UNMIK (2001), Kosovo Budget for 2001, and Public Reconstruction Investment Proposals for 2001-2003.

WIIW, Southeast Europe: Economic Statistics. WIIW.

World Bank (2000), The Road to Stability and Prosperity in Southeast Europe. The World Bank.

World Bank Bulgaria (2001), Bulgaria - Country Economic Memorandum: The Dual Challenge of Transition and Accession.

World Bank Yugoslavia (2000), Federal Republic of Yugoslavia - Recent Economic Developments and Key Policy Challenges.

World Bank Kosovo, Federal Republic of Yugoslavia (Serbia and Montenegro) (Kosovo) (2001), Economic and Social reforms for Peace and Reconciliation.

Xhaferi, A. (2001), "An Optimist in Panic: An Interview with Arben Xhaferi", IWPR Balkan Crisis Reports, number 236.

1. Detailed analysis of these recent developments can be found in Gligorov (2001b). For a description of the main developments in the last ten years or so see World Bank (2000). For a discussion of the main problems that economic reconstruction of SEE faces, see Gligorov (2000b).

2. For the recent development of key economic indicators, see the table in the appendix. For comprehensive data on the economic development in Southeast Europe, see WIIW (2001).

3. This is the assessment to be found in various country reports by the IMF and The World Bank. See, for instance, IMF on Croatia and Albania, and before that on Macedonia. See the World Bank study on Bulgaria and EBRD study on Bosnia and Herzegovina.

4. See IMF and the World Bank on Yugoslavia.

5. According to the statement by the chief negotiator of the IMF.

6. A number of other elections in the region were seen as generally encouraging, though not always up to the more optimistic expectations.

7. The extent of aid dependence is hard to assess precisely. Public aid arrives from different and diffuse sources. Private transfers are even more difficult to trace because they arrive in all kinds of ways, in many cases not through the banking system. Still, just by looking at the information on the EU aid and assistance, it is clear that their contribution is vital.

8. Again, EU aid and assistance of one kind or another plays a crucial role.

9. See World Bank (2000).

10. E.g., for the latter in the op-ed pieces by D. Owen, W. Petritsch, C. Bildt, R. Holbrooke among others.

11. There are some differences between the demands of the Albanian political leaders in Macedonia and those put out by the paramilitaries. The difference is on the issue of federalisation of Macedonia. Some, like the leaders of the DPA (the major Albanian party in Macedonia, which is a member of the coalition government) are against federalisation. The paramilitaries, however, are for federalisation and eventual secession. On the whole issue see Xhaferi (2001) who defines the current conflict as "ethnic competition". He also says that the demands of the political and the military leaders of the Albanians in Macedonia are the same, which introduces an ambiguity in view of the difference pointed to above.

12. "War is a catalyst for change", writes Veton Suroi (2001) expressing succinctly this confusion about the legitimacy of violence.

13. On this, for instance, see Tamir (1993) and Rawls (1999).

14. Macedonian denar has slipped from 31 to 33 denars for one German mark.

15. Throughout the crisis there were demands from the international administration in Kosovo to keep the border with Macedonia open because its closure is having negative effects on the Kosovo economy.

16. For whatever data there is, see IMF on Kosovo. For some discussion of the economic development of Kosovo see Gligorov (2001c).

17. More on that in Gligorov (2000d).

18. More on that in Gligorov (2001b).

19. For some background discussion of constitutional problems of former Yugoslavia, see Gligorov (1994).

20. Sovereignty may be limited by contractual arrangements, as in the case of membership in a confederation or a union. It can also be limited by imposition or by circumstances, the latter being the case with the countries in the SEE with significant international involvement.

21. More on that in Gligorov (2001a).

22. Collier (2000).

23. Details on that see in Podkaminer et al. (2001).

REGIONAL COOPERATION AND INTEGRATION IN THE BALKANS - A HISTORICAL CHALLENGE FOR A DIFFERENT FUTURE

Genc Ruli

Professor, Institute for Contemporary Studies, Tirana

Regional cooperation in South-Eastern Europe (SEE) has never been so important as today. A multitude of motives, economic and non-economic, now exist to intensify regional cooperation, which in turn would help to induce growth, to strengthen security and political stability and to promote development and modernisation in SEE countries.

Why Has Regional Cooperation in SEE Become Imperative Today?

• All SEE countries have already entered the same stream of political and economic processes and are coping with similar challenges such as: democratisation, economic and institutional reform, and modernisation. Many of the problems encountered at present in the region can be resolved only through cooperating with each other, such as ethnic tensions, organised crime, the return of refugees, and the re-establishment of regional communications. None of the region's countries can ensure a sustainable progress, neither in its national programme of reform nor in the bilateral Association Agreements, so long as our region remains unstable and economically backward.

• Political, economic and cultural intra-regional cooperation appears to be the unique way to overcome mutual historical distrust, to prevent further escalation of conflicts and disintegration, and to ensure the existence of multi-ethnic societies in the region.

• Intra regional cooperation is a natural prerequisite as regards the future integration with Euro-Atlantic Structures.

• The main causes of destabilisation and conflict in the peninsula are of a regional character. Sustainable peace and stability, given that international actors remain involved and committed, can only be achieved and guaranteed in a cooperating environment of all regional factors.

• The countries of the region feature small economies and narrow markets and an increase in their commercial exchanges would surely represent an impulse affecting positively economic growth. Increasingly, growth and development in the Balkan countries will depend on increasing exports.

• Existing interdependence for major transportation/communication lines and energy supplies.

The tendencies and factors that enable and promote a cooperative approach between states in the region are as follows:

• the pre-Cold War ideological, political and military barriers between them have been eliminated;

• Western policies towards the region are no longer motivated by traditional geo-political interests, indeed, it is now the whole region that represents an interest for and attracts attention from the West rather any particular country. A better understanding of this fact could help Balkan countries to start behaving as a "region", accepting regional identities and developing common regional interests;

• numerous wars and conflicts over the past decade have at least resulted in a direct and unprecedented involvement of the EU and USA in regional developments;

• compared to ten years ago, there is of course much greater understanding of and political will for dialogue and cooperation among the region's countries themselves. Despite the modest results so far, an intensification of effort and further cooperative initiatives can be observed, either at a bilateral or multi-lateral level;

• although diplomatic contacts have been limited, cooperation and Balkan dialogue is not starting from scratch. It has continuity and a tradition at least regarding the "low political issues" of cooperation;

• contacts amongst people from different countries in the region have significantly increased in recent years. The pioneers of such exploration have been above all businessmen, artists and people from the civil society.

There are now possibilities and pre-conditions in the region that might allow for an intensification of trade cooperation. Firstly, there are no significant differences in growth rates of the countries in the region, almost all of which have opened up their economies to the world. And secondly, some of the macroeconomic variables such as inflation, unemployment and investment have similar trends.

What are the obstacles and other factors that block better regional cooperation?

• SEE remains the most destabilised region in the continent where conflict potential remains high (Kosovo, B&H, Montenegro, FYR of Macedonia). All states and emerging nations in the region are still hampered by the difficulties of painful political and economic transition. Many are still threatened by economic crisis and political and social instability (Albania, FYROM, Montenegro, Serbia and to lesser extent Bulgaria and Romania).

• Old enmities and traditional distrust rooted in the history of the Balkans itself.

• More recently, the fresh memory of crimes and casualties caused by the dismantling of ex-Yugoslavia, and a range of regional disputes such as the fragility of the Dayton Agreement, the undefined Kosovo status, and the frictional relationship between Greece and Turkey obviously represent barriers to achieving regional cooperation.

• The cultures of Balkan societies are, in general, isolated from one another. Paradoxically enough, it can be observed that these national cultures were in the past more open to and exchangeable with other cultures (mainly oriented towards Western Europe) rather than with each other. The traditional elements in these cultures such as ethnicity, religion, and patrimonial psychology are still quite strong and prevent governments from undertaking integrating initiatives.

• The existence of extremist and aggressive nationalisms that become even more harmful when at the service of populist policies. Unfortunately, Balkan countries do not have visionaries and courageous political leaders able to detach their nations from the psychosis of inter-ethnic hostility and convince them of the necessity for cooperation and integration with former "enemies". (We still don't have Balkan equivalents of Adenauer, Schumann, De Gaulle or De Gasperi.)

• The region lacks power centres able to serve as an initiator and accelerator of integrating processes. None of the Balkan countries can play the historical role that France and Germany took in the integration process of Western Europe. Such a power centre exists only outside the region, i.e. the EU.

• Lack of homogeneity. The Balkans represents one of the most diversified sub-regions of Europe. States differ significantly from each other in size, in their economic development and structure, in their cultural and religious traditions, and in their institutional relations with European structures.

What is the Actual State of Cooperation in SEE?

Today, SEE is even less economically integrated than ten years ago and, as in the past, this is still determined to a large extent by non-economic factors whether these be historical, geopolitical or ideological. All efforts focusing on regional cooperation and integration within the last ten years have been initiated from outside of the region. The region itself, until today, has demonstrated a very low propensity for integration.

Although there has been a little progress with trade and investment, regional trade markets remain embryonic, mutual investments are insignificant, and even bilateral trade relations are still underdeveloped. In fact, many SEE governments have continued to give priority to other extra-regional trade areas or economic cooperation institutions. Within the region, there are still serious trade barriers, including both tariff and non-tariff barriers, inefficient institutions and infrastructures (such as at customs and border crossing points), and transport bottlenecks.

However, bilateral relations and cooperation seem to follow a more positive trend than multi-national cooperation, where progress has been insignificant and largely symbolic. It is obvious that the crisis in ex-Yugoslavia has seriously hampered any progress with multilateral cooperation to the extent that a certain phobia exists about any kind of such cooperation. Until now, cooperation initiatives within the region have been focused mainly on "low political" matters such as trade, energy, transport and environment, rather than - and perhaps in the hope of stimulating - cooperation initiatives focusing on "high political" issues such as political, military, and security problems.

Prospectives for Increased Cooperation in the Region

A concrete and credible prospective (clearly accepted and articulated) of the region's integration into the EU would obviously induce a new dynamic into the political processes in the region. Governments would become more committed and responsible in implementing reform pro-grams; it would create a more competitive environment; support would be given to moderate and reformist politicians in these countries, and it would help to intensify cooperation and regional integration. The international community correctly considers regional integration to be a pre-condition for European integration. This, however, should not necessarily mean that integration in the EU would be a follow-up phase, starting only when measurable progress towards regional cooperation has been made. The perspective of European integration will produce its maximum impact only if it is and is seen to be a parallel and complementary process with regional integration.

If the EU offers the same non-discriminatory opportunities to all countries of the region (of course, by duly respecting its conditionality and performance criteria), it would preserve the coherence of the region and would also increase the beneficial effects of cooperation among the countries concerned. When we speak about the necessity for integration in Europe and its impact upon the stability of the region, this must be understood primarily as concrete forms of political inte-gration. As a matter of fact, what is often being articulated (even in the activities of the Stability Pact) is mainly economic cooperation. Prior to achieving economies of scale in the region, we should develop the politics of scale. Regardless of how far commercial cooperation inten-sifies, it is hard to believe that this would automatically lead to a spillover into political partnership. In fact this indicates an exaggerated estimation of the effects that an intensification and liberalisation of trade relations with the EU would produce in the economic recovery of the region. In any case, regardless of how intensive the trade exchanges with the EU become, they could not address the structural problems of Balkan economies.

It is difficult to believe that regional integration can be substantial when lacking institutionalised and appropriate instruments. This is precisely the crucial problem for the evolution of the process. While willing to renounce bits of sovereignty to Brussels, regional governments remain sceptical and even hostile towards the existence of regional organisations and authorities, even in the form of a simple regional trade organisation (as proposed by the EU Commission in August 1999). In this context, the only acceptable integration pattern for the region would be a pan-European structure, meaning Balkan countries plus West European countries. This fact may lead us to engage in concrete thinking about the most appropriate type and status of a cooperation structure to serve during the period that precedes the full membership of Balkan countries in the EU and other Euro-Atlantic structures.

The integrating structures in our region should ensure partnership not simply among regional countries but also between them and the EU (the WEU could act as a model). The tables and sub-structures of the Stability Pact are still formed according to a donor-beneficiary relationship rather than as a real partnership. A narrowing of sovereignty, as the underlying rationale of any regional integration, does not necessarily result in the parallel erosion of national sovereign states as a source of collective identity. On the contrary, these nation states should continue strengthening their institutional capabilities, since they will be the major actors of this integration process.

THE POLICY FRAMEWORK OF YUGOSLAVIA IN THE BALKAN REGION

Marko Paunovic

*Economic Adviser to the Deputy Prime Minister
of the Federal Republic of Yugoslavia (FRY)*

The Balkan region occupies a distinctive place in all aspects of FRY's general policy framework. Based on historical as well as economic grounds, cooperation among states of this region has become almost inevitable due to national and international reasons. However, turmoil and instability have prevailed with serious global repercussions. Peace, prosperity and stability in the Balkan region are high priority objectives for FRY, which attaches special importance to its relations with this region. However, history has shown that these goals require enhanced and diversified regional cooperation and there is no doubt that improving economic cooperation would also reduce the tensions we have all witnessed in the earlier months and previous years.

Political and economic transformation of the Balkan region will definitely be a complex and long term process, which will last for many generations although its foundations are being laid now. The main problem is the lack of a significant democratic tradition in the countries of SE Europe. There are many old and new conflicts between the countries of the region, especially territorial and ethnical, with animosities and deep distrust. The unique symbol and example of that is Kosovo. The break-up of former Yugoslavia and Yugoslavian wars have deepened that distrust and created new serious quarrels. All political, economic and other negative consequences of these are now hard to judge, but it is clear that the region will suffer because of them for a long time. Regional economic cooperation is on a very low level and even though these countries are oriented one to another, they are more economically connected to the markets outside of the region than within the region. It is true that the Balkans is above all a geographic, not an economic, region. Besides, in the economic aspect, it is lagging more and more behind Western Europe as time passes.

It is very indicative that almost all of the initiatives for regional economic and political cooperation are coming from outside of the Balkans. This fact shows that there is still a lack of consciousness and knowledge about the key significance of good neighbourhood relations, which is often proclaimed by officials of these countries, but more through words than by action. The syndrome of self-sufficiency is still strong in the Balkans and it is very much related to nationalism in these countries. Numerous international initiatives concerning this region are created to secure peace and stability in this part of Europe. Of course, for this to happen, many problems need to be solved, both economic and political. Without that, the region will remain a permanent threat to stability and peace in Europe. It is extremely important that the international community realises that Europe cannot live in peace and prosperity if the countries of the Balkan region are not integrating and are not connected to the network of European institutions. If that does not happen, it is very realistic to assume that the Balkans will continue to be a very risky and insecure place. The negative aspects of this will be hard to keep within the borders of this region.

In the last few years, economic globalisation has shown how countries have become interdependent and, furthermore, how cooperation among them is essential. For FRY as well as for other Balkan countries, a further step to this integration in the global economy is the aspiration to be part of the European integration process. It is a strategic interest of Yugoslavia to integrate in the EU. It is, from one side, a way to get easier access to one of the most important markets in the world, and from the other side, it is a basic precondition to solve the problems of economic development and stable democratic society. It is also the only way for all countries of South-Eastern Europe to fully liberalise flows of international trade and capital, reconstruct and develop their infrastructure and, by accepting European legal and institutional frameworks, to improve their competitiveness in the European and World economies. The European option will enable FRY to strengthen current relations and to re-establish broken connections with ex-Yugoslav republics. Cooperation with countries of Eastern and Central Europe, together with Mediterranean countries, is a natural way to prepare for the highly competitive West European and World markets.

But the starting point for Yugoslavia is very poor. Most quantitative indicators are the worst in the region. Special problems are the arrested process of transition, disbelief in state institutions and the lack of independent market institutions. Also, around 35% of the population is officially or effectively unemployed, 70% live below or close to the regional poverty line, and around 600,000 refugees from Croatia, Bosnia and Kosovo lack basic necessities. People have to live with very low salaries by regional standards. Savings are extremely low and many segments of society have run out of reserves. Any further shock to the standard of living would be devastating for our citizens. Moreover, infrastructure is suffering from many years of decay, mismanagement and the consequences of the NATO 1999 bombing campaign. After being swindled several times by state and private banks in the 1990s, the population has lost trust in the banking sector. Real fiscal revenues and expenditures were much lower than planned because of tax exemptions, rate cuts and the development of the grey economy. Bad debts and inter-enterprise arrears are a permanent threat to macro stability as they represent, according to available estimates, around 80% of GDP. Finally, despite its willingness to honour again its international debts, the country is not in a position to do so, as the level of debt represents approximately 150% of GDP.

All in all, the FRY is facing both transition and post-conflict problems. After leading the transition process at the beginning of the last decade, the country is now lagging behind the most advanced transition economies. Its reform path has to recognise this peculiarity and be very dynamic and ambitious. This is also why the country requires significant external support, both in the form of humanitarian assistance but also technical assistance, training, budgetary support, grants and loans. We will mobilise all our internal resources to overcome this dire starting position and reform rapidly. The FRY certainly does not want to become dependent on foreign assistance. We want to be a self-sustaining country, benefiting mostly from foreign private investment flows and international trade. We recognise the need to restructure deeply our economy. However, given the enormous weight of the past, my country will require significant backing from the international community in the short term to succeed. We hope that the Donors conference, organised by the World Bank, will succeed in mobilising foreign capital that will be used to rehabilitate infrastructure and reduce the negative effects of the transition period.

Macroeconomic reforms and reconstruction of the country to facilitate its return into the international community are difficult jobs that the newly elected democratic government will not be able to finish

113

unless it gets strong support from both the domestic and international publics. To provide a permanent improvement in living standards and to fulfil the great expectations of citizens after the removal of the authoritarian regime, the new government has started immediately with the implementation of radical economic reforms.

So far, most of the work has been done in monetary and fiscal policy, but also in foreign trade regulation and structural price adjustments. The Central Bank of Yugoslavia has already done a great job in keeping the exchange rate of the dinar very stable during the last six months and our foreign exchange reserves are increasing. Regarding fiscal policy, new tax laws have been introduced to establish a transparent and fair system. This should be one of the greatest contributions to the overall economic performance of my country. The government of Serbia has introduced a Gross Budget Principle that should clear the fiscal situation. Also, for the first time, the government has announced an explicit budget deficit. The government of FRY has also accepted new laws concerning international trade. There were many non-tariff constraints to trade, such as licenses, quotas, compulsory applications etc. All of these will be abolished. Second, the government has managed to decrease the average tariff rate from 15% to 9.5% and to reduce the number of tariff rates to six. We feel that it will become much more transparent and that all of this will dramatically reduce corruption that was significant in this field. Also, we expect a great increase in foreign trade, especially with countries in the region.

One of the greatest problems of the new government is structural price adjustment. As I have mentioned before, the standard of living of our people is very low and the former government was "buying" social peace with low prices for the most important products and services. The greatest problems are with electricity, utilities, medicines and basic food products. So far, the prices of food have been liberalised whilst the price of electricity has been increased up by some 60%. They will be increased two more times this year. Concerning privatisation, a new law will encourage the sale of socially owned enterprises to outside core owners. Also, a new law on foreign direct investment is being prepared that will be very liberal. Another thing that is considered to be important is the development of the private sector that should increase employment in the difficult times to come. All of this work has been done to improve the lives of our citizens and to move towards European standards. We recognise the need that all countries in the region should work together towards the fulfilment of

European standards. We must take the lead in the whole course of integration by implementing the basic criteria and by re-shaping the economy.

The Balkans, constituting a bridge between two continents, has to assume a clearly defined and vital role in all aspects of international cooperation. As generally perceived, important developments are expected to happen in this new global millennium. All Balkan countries should contribute extensively to economic cooperation to ensure prosperity and welfare both in this region and in its neighbourhood. We believe that lasting peace and stability in the Balkans can be achieved through regional cooperation. We are convinced that an enhanced and diversified cooperation in this part of the continent will not only help to ease tensions and contribute to stability and peace, but will also reinforce the process of all-European integration. In this context, the Balkan cooperation process offers a very promising prospect to mould the common past of the region into a mutually shared destiny.

THE INTERRELATIONSHIP BETWEEN REGIONAL ECONOMIC COOPERATION, SECURITY AND STABILITY

Rory O'Sullivan

*Special Representative of the World Bank Group
for South East Europe Reconstruction, Brussels*

World Bank Programs in the Balkans

Let me start by giving you a few figures to set the scene. In the Balkans we are talking about 50 million people living in seven countries with a GDP of about US$100bn. If we compare with the European Union, the number of people in the region is equivalent to some 15% of the EU's population but at some US$2,000 per capita GDP, they have only some 15/25% of the average European per capita income. That is a pretty big gap. Of course there are large variations even within the region, with Croatia more than double the regional average and edging close to Hungary in per capita wealth while Albania, Bosnia and now FRY have less than half the average and thus the longest way to go. Poverty remains disturbingly widespread in the region. Some observers classify just over 40% of the Romanian population below a commonly used poverty threshold of US$4.3 a day for example, while new information coming out of FRY indicates similar high levels of poverty in that country. Only Croatia seems to have escaped widespread poverty, with little more than 2% of that population in the category.

Taking the region as a whole it looks as though around 40% of the people should be classified as seriously deprived. This means living in overcrowded poorly maintained dwellings often with rotten walls and leaking roofs, with a diet limited to basic staples such as bread, potatoes and milk. Many people are poorly educated. Unemployment rates among the poor are obviously very high and only a few have savings to buffer their misery. The lucky ones have relatives abroad who send them money. The unlucky, who are in the majority, do not. No wonder then that stirring nationalist speakers have made great headway in the region and found a fertile ground for views which are alien to the ideals of the modern world. The poor want to climb out of their hole and are frustrated because they do not see how to do it. The

117

blue-collar workers earn too little for a reasonable life and are frustrated because wages seem to go down more often than up. The white-collar workers are impatient. And businessmen can't stand the business climate. This is a pretty sorry situation.

So what are we in the World Bank doing about this? Actually quite a lot. We are working closely with the governments of the Region and with other development partners to try to turn the region around economically. And we are collectively making some encouraging progress. But this is not a zero sum game. Things can go awfully wrong. But they can also go "awfully right." Take the case of Yugoslavia in the mid '80's when things started going badly wrong for that economy and no-one was able to take the tough decisions needed to sort it all out. The GDP of Serbia and Montenegro was probably around US$30bn in 1985. A healthy growth rate such as that achieved by Poland and Hungary during the nineties could have ratcheted it up to US$50bn by now. But in fact it is struggling at around US$10bn. That is one fifth of what it could have been. Of course it is easy to be wise after the event but it does illustrate how quickly things can change. Good policies and good economic management can pay huge dividends and transform a country's prospects. Poland and Hungary come to mind on the positive side. The Western Balkans in particular are still on the other side of the equation. We are trying to help them make things go "awfully right" and put them solidly into a path of high growth.

Our work programs in each of the countries are broad ranging yet well targeted. First we provide financial resources for development projects. But each of these projects is carefully designed to achieve a long-range sustainability objective which allows the money that is lent to build more capital and help the economy grow. And we do not just give the money and go away hoping that everything works out OK. World Bank projects are followed carefully by teams of professionals from start to finish to make sure they deliver on their promise. Indeed we spend as much manpower making our projects succeed as we spend in designing them in the first place. This is an unusual use of manpower by an organisation such as ours but we find it pays off in terms of making our projects successful and helping them achieve the long-term objectives sought.

But lending money is only a small part of our work. Critical to the success of our mission is also the work we do advising governments on how to improve their management of the economy. For example, the way funds are allocated in a public investment program. These funds are primarily the scarce funds raised from taxes on people who are seldom very well off and who in most cases have important family needs. Bosnia's tax income from its citizens is over US$1bn a year for example and all of this is spent on various budget items. If you can make this spending twice as effective - certainly possible in most of our countries - the impact can be enormous. It is worth working on. It means accelerating growth rapidly, ensuring better health care, better education, better outcomes all round. That is one example. We are also deeply involved in health and education reform, financial sector reform, civil service reform, private sector development, and anti corruption activities. Indeed, wherever there are priority softspots that need attention and where the government is really prepared to work with us. We spend almost as much on this advisory work as we do handling out investment projects because this work also has a major impact.

Another major area of activity is the mobilisation of financial resources to support the development efforts of the different countries of SE Europe. After the Kosovo crisis of early 1999 the World Bank and the European Commission were given the mandate by the G7 Finance Ministers to mobilise funds for the reconstruction and reform of countries in the Balkans. The two institutions set up a joint office in Brussels to give focus to this work. In the last 18 months or so some Euro6bn has been mobilised for the region in pledges from 25 countries and 10 organisations through donor meetings and conferences. All this has been done in a very transparent way and tracked in the public view of the people of the region through the SEERECON.ORG website, which has 800-1,000 visitors a day indicating a continuing high level of interest and support for Balkan issues. These efforts continue with several new meetings of donors scheduled for 2001.

Where are all these efforts leading? Can we yet point to any successes in work which is by its very nature long term? There is no doubt that the economic climate is at last on the mend after a decade of stagnation. Just two years ago the IMF was recording a continued decline in economic activity of the region partly due to the Kosovo crisis but also because of the lingering effects of the political confusion of the last decade. Things turned sharply better in 2000 and continued growth is foreseen in 2001 and beyond. It is all too slow for the people of the region but progress is certain. The downside risks are still there though. The FRY economy was left in ruins by the departing regime and while excellent efforts are being made by the current authorities to put things back in order, it is a very tough task. Success, and surely there will be a success, will be a major boost for the region. The other risk is of course the situation in Macedonia. This is no great publicity for foreign investors and we can only hope the situation there stabilises as quickly as possible.

But while all these aggregates start moving up and we begin to celebrate a renewed investor confidence in the Region, we return to the start of this paper and remind ourselves that poverty remains widespread and that this will remain a cause of serious instability in the region. The people of this part of the world are in some ways confounded by their situation. They are on the doorstep of Europe and have high expectations that their lot will improve rapidly in the future. Yet most of them remain woefully distant from the kind of standard of living they expect to have. Therein lies a potentially combustible mixture. The donors and the governments need to redouble their efforts to accelerate the adjustment of these economies in a way that protects the poor and helps them move as quickly as possible from their misery. The World Bank is working hard to try to make this happen.

THE LINK BETWEEN SYSTEMIC TRANSFORMATION AND SECURITY: GENERAL ASSESSMENTS OF REGIONAL COOPERATION IN SOUTH EASTERN EUROPE

Katarzyna Zukrowska

Professor, Warsaw School of Economics, Program for European Studies, International Security Department

Definition of Security

Despite the fact that the notion of the security of a state is often used, it is rarely defined by its users. The need for such a definition is indisputable as it deals with relevant and sensitive subjects for each state. Generally speaking, the definition of security usually covers a state's lack of threat or the effectiveness of its guaranteed protection against such a threat.[1] Such an approach can be found in international relations dictionaries. There is no difference in defining this notion in individual countries, which means that there is a common denominator in understanding a state of security. Nevertheless, the same events in international relations are commented on in different ways and can cause, in certain conditions, an overreaction, which on its own can be considered as a threat to the security of the state, such as the conflict between US and Chinese planes in April 2001, the expulsion of Russian diplomats from the US in 2001, or indeed the Polish diplomats accused of espionage and ordered to leave Moscow in January 2000.

Looking closer at the above definition, one should try to define what is understood by threat or a state of threat. This notion has several dimensions, starting with psychological, then becoming real or potential, and finally indicating a subjective or objective element of the threat. This leads us to one important finding, i.e. that perception of a threat can reflect real threats or real potential of threat, either objective or subjective. The subjectivity of threat can be enlarged in specific conditions when people evoke from specific stage of interna-tional relations, which was long enough to route deeply in their minds certain behaviours or reactions. The end of the Cold War can be considered as such a specific state in which subjectivity of perceptions of threats is strongly mixed with an objective approach, when real threats are neglected and unreal dangers are taking over.

Daniel Frei[2] offers a definition of specific conditions under which the size of a threat can be defined more precisely:

• lack of security in conditions which bring real external endangerment of security and when this endangerment is perceived in proper proportions to the real threat;

• state of obsession occurs in conditions when small endangerment is perceived as a big one;

• state of false security is in place when endangerment is big and the perception of it is much smaller and out of proportion;

• state of security occurs in conditions when external threat is not big and the perception of it is seen in accordance to that.

Security in international relations means that needs and interests of the participants in international relations are sufficiently covered and the process is fulfilled on the international stage, while its consequences touch not only interested group of countries but also the whole international system. This is one of the reasons why, for analytical purposes, there is a clear division between international and national security. This division is rather superficial as, generally, the security of states in international relations always has a national dimension as well.

National security defined as needs and interests of a nation are fulfilled by its political organisation, i.e. the state. As the requirement of security is not only defined by the internal structure of society but also results from the evolution of the international environment, it is conducted within the framework of foreign policy. National security is an ability of a nation to protect its internal values against external threats. This definition brings us to the problem of defining aims of such protection and values that should be protected. J. Kukulka defined three such aims: (1) existence, maximisation of chances to survive; (2) coexistence, leading to an improvement in the role in international relations; (3) functional, leading to the high effectiveness of conducted policy in reaching the two formerly mentioned goals.[3] The list of protected values covers: national interests; political institutions, sovereignty, independence, and territorial integrity. All of the mentioned values are still protected although their meaning changes as time passes.

International security is achieved in conjunction between individual security and the collective security of a group of states. This conjunction is effected by participation of the state in the system of international relations.

Old and New Dimensions of Security

In the past, the security model was mainly based on a hard security dimension (military factors), while soft dimensions (non-military) played a secondary role in the system. In the current stage of international relations, the roles of both hard and soft dimensions have changed, which means that the "soft" are now taking the lead. This is happening on two levels - national and international.

The hard dimension of security has not disappeared totally, although its role has changed. The new security system is interdependent and cooperative, which means that states cooperate within a sphere of security. They also start to cooperate in arms production, which stimulates standardisation of arms or even globalisation of arms technology, which in turn follows the pattern of globalisation of civilian technology. This is evidenced by the following occurrences:

• Shrinking internal and external arms markets force international cooperation in arms production, which is accelerated additionally by increasing costs of R&D, asymmetry of sales between US and EU, as well as by the exclusion of competition regarding arms procurement in the EC, which means that the arms market is excluded from the single European market and still continues to work according to specific rules of the game;

• The end of the Cold War created new conditions in international relations, which foster departure from the concept of self-sufficiency in arms supplies and production;

• No longer is there any need to follow the neutrality path of politics by those who wanted to stay neutral in the bipolar world;

- The role of dual-use goods is increasing in international transfers, which is reflected in the organisation of the technology controls system, which now is open for all those who support market rules and democracy.

In the case of "soft" dimensions, the linkages are relatively more complicated because it is difficult to be more precise on the issue as to what exactly are the soft (non-military) dimensions of security.[4] In case of hard dimensions (military), a country is safe when it has enough arms to defend itself within a coalition, as self-defence is impossible in the contemporary world with its stocks of missiles possessed by individual countries and organised institutionally by coalitions of states. Even small coalitions will not possess enough power and potential to protect themselves, especially when this problem is studied in terms of cost-effectiveness. In other words, a country cannot be secure by building-up its military potential on its own or in coalitions formed from a small group of interested states.

This is based on two assumptions: high military expenditures compete with other expenditures within the state budget, if military production is chosen as a way of spending the state's money; and intensive armaments counteract with extensive development of international trade, an important factor which serves to build wealth and stability. There is a list of factors that matter in the context of stabilisation and security. These embrace the following: (1) size of the country; (2) stability of the economy; (3) stability of the political system; (4) relations with neighbours; (5) ability to adjust to changing conditions and their challenges; (6) the problem of national minorities; (7) institutionalisation of external relations; (8) opening up of the economy.

The links between economics, stability and security were defined differently at different stages of development of international relations. This can be exemplified by the period before the Cold War, during the Cold War and afterwards. These differences resulted in different security and economic models. In the past, the security model was based on balanced confrontation between the powers or superpowers and their allies. This was the case both in a multi-power and bipolar world. Currently, security is based on interdependence and cooperation between states and its enhanced by globalisation, liberalisation and established institutional structures, which are not directly linked with security goals.

Economics in the past was based on national, and to a large extent self-sufficient, model, which naturally excluded the possibilities of significant external cooperation. Protection against external competition was considered to be one of the tools of state economic policy. This in turn led to partial isolation and in turn increased susceptibility to economic depression imported from abroad. But with growing international interdependencies of states and their economies, all this has changed. The shape of the economic cycle in the form of sinusoid was replaced by that of a shaky slope, which, with differentiated rates of growth, climbs steadily up. Economists used to call this steady or sustainable growth, with sustainability being achieved by several factors, which include:

• internationalisation of the economy, causing deepened international interdependence;

• opening and liberalisation of the economy internally and externally (on both regional and global scales);

• institutionalisation of external relations, making certain commitments regarding liberalisation that are not reversible in periods of economic slow-down;

• globalisation;

• increasing economisation of the military sector (privatisation, deregulation, internationalisation (mergers), increased effectiveness, and the ending of state aid in supporting exports and arms fairs), which means treating it as a part of the economy that has to follow the same rules of the game as all other branches or sectors (i.e. a departure from Article 223 of the Treaty of Rome which excludes competition in procurement procedure). This process is a long endeavour and it is linked with a very sensitive sector, which additionally can be considered as a factor prolonging reform.

In sum, these findings can be put in a table, giving the parallel development of economic and security systems. The illustration given in **Table 1** below could be additionally enriched by showing the stages involved in the reshaping of global and national financial and monetary systems, which are more sensitive to sovereignty issues than the economic model. Generally, we can show the following three stages of development of financial/exchange rate systems, which go from: (1) multipolarity combining different groups of countries, which try to cooperate in this field together by pegging their currencies to the one which operates in the so-called economic hub or financial centre; (2) through a period of exchange rate coordination and joint interventions; (3) towards the coordination of exchange rate policies; (4) ending with the convergence criteria and a common currency, as with the Euro. This stage could be also viewed as a transition phase in which three financial/currency centres are established around three hubs in New York, Frankfurt and Tokyo which, over the long term, will condense three currencies into one.

This process is stimulated on the one hand by globalisation and on the other by the creation of large free trade zones. The pattern used here follows the experience of the EC as well as of other less advanced forms of integration, such as the Pan-American free trade area from Alaska to Chile, which embraces 34 economies in North and South America and the Caribbean.[5] The EU also has institutionalised relations with organisations located outside Europe, such as ASEAN[6], SAARC[7], Mercosur[8], GCC[9], APEC, ASEM, NAFTA, the Barcelona Process (Countries of Near East), and ACP (the Lome convention, Cotonou Agreement).

Free trade is important for the stabilisation of the economy as well for development. It is a precondition for there to be profit from globalisation, because liberalization is fostered within newly formed or existing free trade organisations. This process also embraces post-communist economies. East-Central European countries in transition founded CEFTA in 1992 (Central European Free Trade Agreement), which initially included Czechoslovakia, Hungary and Poland and was enlarged gradually to 7 members. The number of members grew in two ways: by the division of Czechoslovakia into two separate states and by the enlargement of membership to Slovenia (1995), Romania (1996) and Bulgaria (2000). This formation creates an institutional background for free trade in the region and has resulted in an expansion of trade.

Post-communist countries also create institutional linkages with the EU. This is done by signing asymmetric trade agreements of different types, such as Europe Agreements (leading to membership) or Partnership Agreements introducing liberalisation in trade and leading to association. In the first case, agreements embrace two groups of countries, counting their distance towards membership and advancement in accession negotiations: (1) the Luxembourg Group: Czech Republic, Estonia, Hungary, Poland and Slovenia; and (2) the

Helsinki Group: Bulgaria, Latvia, Lithuania, Romania, Slovakia. Partnership Agreements are concluded between the EU and Russia, Ukraine, Moldova, Armenia, Azerbaijan, Georgia, Kazakhstan, Turkmenistan and Tajikistan.

Finally we have two proposals for free trade arrangements in the former Soviet Union; GUUAM (first letters of Georgia, Uzbekistan, Ukraine, Azerbaijan, Moldavia), and EAEC (Euro-Asian Economic Union) which includes Belarus, Kazakhstan, Kyrgyzstan, Russia and Tajikistan. Both were founded in autumn 2000, although neither has started to function.[10] At the same time, one should expect the launching of a new liberalisation round within the WTO, following failure in Seattle. This failure does not mean the total abandonment of trade liberalisation, which is stimulated on bilateral or regional levels and strongly supported by the EU.

Table 1: The Dependence of the International Security System from Changes in Economic System

SECURITY MODELS	ECONOMIC MODELS
Multipolar model - based on military component in which economy plays a secondary role. Defence doctrine is constructed upon self-sufficiency of defence, which is univocal with self-sufficiency in production. Attempts to create coalitions lead to conflicts, as their construction is based upon temporary common interests, which naturally deprive them of a stable component. Security model as well as model of international relations at this stage is based on power solutions.	**National economy model** - based on the protection of producers and jobs. Developing mechanisms directly engaging the state in the production sphere. This model deviated from the competition mechanism and supported the use of protection measures in periods of recession, thus making the situation worse. It limited the possibilities of building long-term interests internationally. Its ability to stabilise was limited and incorporated a conflicting component.

127

Bipolar model - shaped after WW2, was in force for over 45 years (1945-1989). It led to an increase of the economic component, which in consequence resulted in priority treatment of economics and, later, the take-over of the role formerly fulfilled by the military factor. Security model at this stage is based on deterrence.

Model of slow and gradual departure from protection as well as from (linked) concepts of economic growth stimulation. In practice, this was univocal with departure from protectionist measures by the slow and cautious opening of the economy on national, regional and global levels. This model was fostered by the Bretton Woods system (1944) which established the World Bank, IMF and later GATT. On a regional level, institutions such as the EC, EFTA, OECD and NAFTA were created. Liberalisation was also pushed ahead by bilateral agreements.

Non-polar model - created after the dissolution of the USSR and Warsaw Pact, when relations in the security sphere drifted towards unipolarity (NATO and US playing important role with support of EU, WEU and CSCE) in transition from bipolarity (two pillars : US and USSR) and moving towards non-polarity (cooperative system). This should be followed further by liberalisation of mutual relations. Stabilisation is further guaranteed by the evolution of international organisations, which should be followed by the creation of platforms helping to develop sustainable ties among states supported by common interests.

Liberalised model of the global economy, in which economies tend to be more interdependent, due on the one hand to natural and geographic differences, and on the other to relative differences in size, production factors and levels of development. This does not mean typical dependency relations, but interdependency. Occurring in parallel to this is the intensification of competition and liberalisation.

Source: Own setting.

The cooperative model per se indicates that external threats are diminishing whilst internal threats are increasing:

•   systemic transformation is a process which is characterised by many different types of tensions (political, social, economic, etc);

•   external threats, when they occur, are of a different nature to those familiar only from the pages of history books. External threats can be ascribed more to accidents or terrorism, and less to an external attack.

Looking closer at the differences between old and new security models, one can find that all elements of the so-called values, sovereignty, national interest, strategic goals and so on need to be redefined in the new conditions. They still exist and are still used, but they are far away from the definitions known before WW2 and during the Cold War. Despite the new realities, some still use old definitions and old meanings of those notions, which often results in misleading evaluations of the threat. This can be explained by the existence of two schools of thinking, one of which is in decline whilst the other expands. The former is called the neo-realistic approach; the latter the neo-liberal approach. The characteristic features of the two and the differences between then can be summarised in the following way (Table 2), although this table does not reflect all the differences or characteristics.

Table 2 : Neo-realistic and Neo-liberal Approaches to International Relations and Security

Contents	Neo-realists	Neo-liberals
Subjects in international relations	State	State and institutions
Character of international relations	Anarchic (lack of state government)	Cooperative - Interdependencies
Character of state	Unitary	Pluralistic
Priorities of state functioning	Strength and Security	Economic growth and Social Security.
Ways of conducting policy	Power Politics (realpolitik) and Self-Reliance	Cooperation and Self-Limitation
Attitude towards international cooperation	Pessimistic - Relative Profit - Zero Sum Game	Optimistic - Absolute Profits - "Growing Wedding Cake"
Role of international institutions	Marginal - Arena for States' Self-Interest	Basic - Lowering Costs of Cooperation - Determining the Behaviour of States

Source: J. Czaputowicz, System czy nielad? Bezpieczenstwo europejskie u progu XXI wieku. WNPWN, Centrum Stosunków Miedzynarodowych, 1998, s. 52.

Thus are the differences in approach of neo-realists and neo-liberals regarding international relations, character of the state, attitude towards international cooperation and the role of international institutions clearly indicated. Both approaches have been reflected in international relations at a specific stage of their development, the former during the cold war and the latter subsequently. Nevertheless, not all scientists treat 1989 as a turning point, in that some still support the views which reflect more the former stage of relations than the current one. Such an approach is characteristic of the transitional period, which embraces different four phases:

• majority approves neo-realistic approach;

• neo-realists are in the majority and decide the interpretation of international relations, but as the parallel neo-liberal vision gains ground;

• neo-liberals gain ascendancy and people adjust to their way of thinking and interpretation as, at the same time, neo-realists lose ground;

• neo-liberals are in the clear majority whilst neo-realists become a little exotic in their outdated way of thinking.

This evolution in four stages reflects any evolution of a scientific approach, when practice reflects existing theories. Then gradually reality departs from theory until finally we have a stage where theory starts to reflect reality again. Nevertheless, it should be added that the new setting does not happen per se accidentally. There are abstract theories which are used to formulate the new realities. Decisions on that - in the case of international relations - are undertaken at the highest level of so-called "high politics", while the implementation of those decisions take a longer period and require additional preparations, which is achieved by means of "low politics".

Security Models Against a Background of External and Internal Threats

Generally we can distinguish at least four models of security when we look at the weight of internal and external threats, which change with the passing of time:

• The first shows the balance between external and internal threats. The causes of external threats are territorial expansion, territorial conquest subordinated to gain access to raw materials and other mineral resources, or a form of competition between states of similar power, levels of development and influence. The causes of internal threats are the struggle for power at local or state levels, various calamities (such as disease, hunger, flood, fire), animosity among ruling families, or the clash of interests between different social groups.

• The second model shows the superiority of external threats, when the internal security system works properly. The causes of external threats are the struggle for spheres of influence, the utilisation of weaknesses (economic, political or social) of neighbouring countries, the multipolarity of international relations where the strength of a state is defined by size of its territory and population (military potential), the transfer of conflicts between two states engaged openly against each other onto third countries (Antilles, Vietnam,

Afghanistan), and the progress of decolonisation and the creation of new relations between former dependent territories. The causes of internal threats are economic crises as in the 1930s, natural disasters, mistakes in economic policy, and the struggle for political power, although democracy gradually eliminates this latter factor.

• The third model reveals a relative superiority of internal threats over external threats in the security system. The causes of external threats are too large a dependence on one supply market, an international ecological or environmental crisis similar to the Chernobyl tragedy, or an overreaction to the breaking of a convention or other rules defining ways of co-existence in the international arena (such as the shooting down of a spy plane flying over the territory of another country). The causes of internal threats are related to the costs of restructuring, such as a slow deterioration in the standard of living which in turn leads to social tension. Such threats are concentrated in post-communist states and can lead to conflict when such states are multi-ethnic, multi-lingual or multi-religious as well.

• The fourth model envisages the creation of a cooperative security system. Internal threats are the impoverishment of some transition countries leading to fascist and totalitarian regimes, the inability to introduce successful transformation because of a lack of relevant expertise, and the sheer length and unexpected burdens of transition that can lead to the rejection of change and a renewal of the struggle between new and old political elites. External threats are, inter alia, the possibility that internal instability in one country or region will be transferred elsewhere.

The above described evolution shows that changes in the nature of threats do not eliminate tensions totally but change their weight as factors, which might undermine the existing balance or lack of endangerment. Despite the fact that threats do not disappear, the post war period has been the longest peace period in Europe. Even the Yugoslav conflict did not spread out of the Balkan pen. The most serious danger in the post-communist region can be ascribed to: (1) Externally, the mass exodus of people from one country to another one, which is not prepared to deal with mass emigration; (2) Internally, by mistakes made in transformation or lack of transformation, both bringing problems of a social, economic and political nature; (3) Internally, by increase of religious conflicts ascribed mainly to Muslim Fundamentalism.[11]

Conditions Enabling Systemic Transformation

Systemic transformations were enabled by the end of the Cold War, but this was not the only reason and they could even be considered as a condition of departure from the old rhetoric brought about by over 45 years of mutual accusations as well as specific Cold War rhetoric and politics. The end of the Cold War and transformation was preconditioned by: (1) stabilisation of the pillars of western and democratic security structures; (2) a process of deepening international integration; (3) the process of enlargement in European integration; (4) building bridges of different types (political, economic, cultural) with third parties and external states; (5) political dialogue between East and West, leading to important moves in conventional armaments as well as a reduction in stocks of weapons; (6) confidence building measures and security guarantees; (7) a clear definition of responsibilities among engaged states.

Weaver's European security triangle clearly shows that security is built upon institutional structures, which are supported by some military regimes and organisations as well as by strong interdependencies among states and their economies. The deeper such ties or interlinkages are the stronger impact they have on stability and the irreversibility of the introduced changes. There are numerous new solutions which are being built on top of the emerging security system, these being the European Security and Defence Identity (ESDI), common military troops, and the cooperative use of NATO's infrastructure by EU and NATO. These new solutions show that end of Cold War has strengthened in many ways the existing institutions, which form the core of the security structure in Europe: (1) by closing down non-democratic and non-market oriented organisations; (2) by increasing the number of members or candidates for membership in market democracies; (3) by silent approval of new members in existing organisations, which gathered together countries both further and less advanced in transition. Integration with EuroAtlantic structures are considered here to be the most important ones; (4) by pooling sovereignty in strengthened organisations and supplying them with new functions and powers; (5) by establishing new cooperative institutional solutions which continue to overlap, while other solutions enforce or deepen cooperation (Eurocorp); (6) by introducing solutions which enable cooperation among four groups of countries: NATO members, EU members, members of the two organisations and those which are outside those structures; (7) by establishing common military forces in Europe.

Graphically the existing security system can be shown as follows:

Figure 1 : European Security Triangle

OCSE, Council of Europe, UN
Creation of legal and institutional framework

Stabilization Pact,
Europe Agreement,
European Bank of
Reconstruction and
Development

CFE Treaty (reduction of
conventional arms in Europe)

EuroAtlantic
Partnership Council
(EACP)

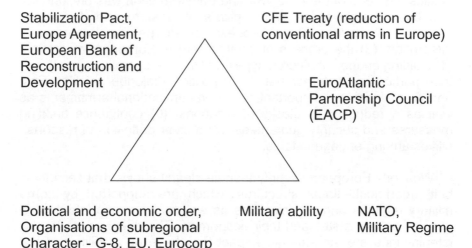

Political and economic order,   Military ability   NATO,
Organisations of subregional   Military Regime
Character - G-8, EU, Eurocorp

Source: O. Weaver, The European Security triangle, Working papers, No.: 12, 1994, COPRI.

Models of Transformation and their Impact on Security

Generally one can distinguish three models of transformation in the sphere of economics, which derive clearly from the practice of post-communist states in the 1990s. All of the models embrace similar or even the same elements but used with different strength and determination. Those differences are mirrored by different sequencing of utilized moves as well as by the degree of opening of the economy. These three models bring different results, measured by depth of transition depression and by the length of time from the starting point to a situation in which the economy starts to grow.

The first model is well known - "shock therapy". This model could be found in Poland and the GDR. In the case of Poland, it resulted in a quick departure from transformation depression and until now this economy has had one of the highest rates of growth. The second model is the "gradual approach". This was applied in most East Central European states. The third model falls into the same category of gradual approach but changes were introduced here at an even slower rate and this group is less advanced. The main difference can be ascribed to the degree of opening of the economy, which in this third model starts after a delay and is pursued at a very slow pace. This model was used in the post-Soviet states. The results of each of the models were clear. With more drastic solutions, higher rates of growth were achieved, which resulted in an improvement in living standards. With lower incomes, there was more frustration, the period of systemic changes was prolonged and it now seems that it will last for a while longer yet.

It should be considered as a philosophical question to say when "shock" ends and "gradualism" starts, or indeed the other way round. There is no sharp partition between the two. Each change is a shock for those concerned as it requires adjustments.

The first model has shown that it is possible to go ahead fast, which is important in the context of a catching-up strategy. The two other models also bring the economy onto a growth path, although this is not sufficient and strong enough to continue in the future. Most of the prognosis speculates that the high rates of growth in 2000 in the post-Soviet Republics are not sustainable. Growth started in 1999 in Russia and spread into the other Republics, achieving a rate of growth averaging 7-8%. This rate of growth is badly needed, but at the same time, economists are starting to believe that shock is a more efficient strategy and also a more secure one as it means quick solutions in restructuring the economy, whilst ending unnecessary production and boosting output of competitive goods. Shock leads to a quick commencement of the transformation depression, a relatively deep fall in production and a short period of departure from depression. This is followed by relatively high rates of growth. Security here can be measured by the number living under the poverty line. Usually, high poverty rates appear in economies that attempt to protect their citizens from intensified competition and external shock.

Table 3: Selected Macroeconomic Indicators in ECE Countries in 2000

COUNTRY	Unemployment - end year (%)	CPI inflation - annual average (%)	Poverty - % of population below US$2a day	Rate of GDP growth	Level of real GDP in 2000 (1989 = 100)
Azerbaijan	13.9*	1.6	68.1#	10.5	52
Bulgaria	17.9	9.9	7.8	5.0	70
Czech Republic	8.8	3.9	<2.0	3.1	98
Hungary	9.9*	9.8	4.0	5.2	105
Poland	15.0	10.1	10.5	4.1	127
Romania	10.5	45.7	27.5	1.6	77
Russia	9.7	20.8	25.1	7.7	62
Tajikistan	2.5	34.0	n.a.	8.3	47
Turkmenistan	n.a.	8.3	59.0	17.6	75
Ukraine	4.2	28.2	23.7	6.0	39
Uzbekistan	0.6	50.0	26.5	1.5	96

* Data for 1999
# National figure, 1995.
Sources: Transition Report Update, April 2001, EBRD, London. Poverty Data - International poverty lines (except Azerbaijan) from World Development Report 2000/2001, World Bank. Table 4, pp.280 & 281.

One can clearly see that from the point of view of catching up, the Polish experience could be evaluated as the best among the group of indicated countries. From the social point of view in the medium term, the best results are recorded by the Czech Republic and Hungary. The slowest progress in both cases is seen in the former Soviet Republics, but also in Bulgaria and Romania, the rate of growth is not high. A catching-up strategy simply requires a rate of growth that is higher than in the countries one is aspiring to catch up. Nevertheless, in the case of former Soviet Republics, the first ten years of transformation were used to create a market environment institutionally and legally, which was followed by the specific education of the population. **Table 3** above is, however, limited as far as indicators for security are concerned.

Only countries with access to oil sources can feel safer with comparison to those who have access to other raw materials. There is a general and accelerating tendency in international trade that prices of raw materials fall in real terms relative to industrial goods prices. In other words, the gap between industrial and raw material prices of goods widens, which diminishes incomes from exports and increases trade deficits. Moreover, those countries often are engaged in a regional conflict, which limits their political and economic relations with other states in the region, thus increasing their autonomy. Countries rich in natural resources often experience a natural cushioning against change, which merely postpones their adjustment.

Conclusions

Security in Europe is currently strongly linked with internal issues, mainly transformation strategies applied in post-communist countries and their respective effectiveness. Ten years of transformation helps us to draw certain conclusions as to what should be applied and how this compares with practice in the newly established market democracies. The main problem is to understand that some strategies are more effective than others and that those less effective can bring about instability and endanger security. This paper brings to light only some of the evidence, but empirical practice supports the simple findings presented here. The second important source of destabilisation can be ascribed to growing tensions among national minorities or religious groups, especially in regions were religion was for long periods considered as "forbidden fruit". Young fundamentalists can be stricter in their beliefs than their elders. Their fundamentalism can be reinforced by difficulties caused by lack of systemic transformation or mistakes made by applying wrongly prepared strategies. These three factors combined (poverty caused by mistakes in transformation or lack of transformation; the heavy burden of systemic change; religious conflicts) form an explosive combination that could be considered as having the greatest potential to both cause and inflame internal and regional conflicts. This could be geographically ascribed to such countries as Tajikistan, Turkmenistan, Azerbaijan and Uzbekistan.

1. R. Zieba, Pojecie i istota bezpieczenstwa panstwa w stosunkach miedzynarodowych, Sprawy Miedzynarodowe, 1989, No.: 10, p. 49-69.

2. Daniel Frei, Sicherheit, Grunfragen der Weltpolitik. Stuttgart 1977, p. 17-21.

3. J. Kukulka, Miedzynarodowe stosunki polityczne. Warszawa 1982, p. 43-44.

4. Approaching the Northern Dimension of the CFSP: Challenges and Opportunities for the EU in Emerging European Security Order. Helsinki, the Finish Institute for International Affairs, 1998.

5. Trade in the Americas. All in the familia. The Economist, April 21-27 2001, p. 19-22.

6. ASEAN - Association of South East Asian Nations (1967). Member states:: Indonesia, Malaysia, Philippines, Singapore, Thailand, Brunei, Vietnam, Laos, Myanmar, Cambodia.

7. SAARC - South Asian Association for Regional Cooperation (1985). Panstwa czlon kowskie: Bangladesh, Bhutan, Maladives, Nepal, Pakistan, Sri Lanka.

8. Southern Common Market (1991). Member states: Argentina, Brazil, Paraguay, Uruguay, Chile, Bolivia.

9. Gulf Cooperation Council (1981). Member states: Bahrain, Kuwait, Oman, Cater, Saudi Arabia, Arab Emirates and Yemen.

10. B. Frumkin, Economic relations of the Russian Federation with Poland and Ukraine in the light of the European Union Extension and Schengen Agreement, paper presented on coneference Poland, Russia, Ukraine in the context of EU integration, Institute for East West Studies, Freidrich Ebert Stiftung, PAN ISP, 26 November 2000, Warsaw.

11. B. Nitecka-Jagiello, Russia vs. Muslim World, Economic Papers No.: 30, Warsaw School of Economics. Institute for International Studies, Warsaw 2000, p. 129-144.

12. R. M. Auty, The IMF Model and resource-Abundant Transition Economies: Kazakhstan and Uzbekistan, The United Nations University. Working Papers no. 169. November 1999.

THE POLITICS AND ECONOMIC GROWTH OF BALKAN COUNTRIES

Ivo Paparela

Professor at the University of Split, Croatia

Introductory Remarks

Economic recovery and cooperation among Balkan "regions" have been slow in giving fruit, for a number of reasons. In other words, poverty is to be the "life companion" for the majority of the population in what is called South Eastern Europe. Conflict is another life companion, with its usual phenomena such as publicly acknowledged crime, corruption, and the wide-spread abuse of drugs and alcohol. Politicians like to address crime/drug/alcohol/corruption issues in order to hide the "politically and business correct" homeopathic dishonesty of the state apparatus and para-governmental bodies.

Therefore, sound political measures are to be effectively introduced, taking into consideration local realities and rejecting an ideological approach. The representatives of the so-called international community do have ideological and socio-political prejudices towards the socio-political realities in the Balkans. Often, the local "fallen angels" (nostalgic for the power they had during the communist regime, second-hand writers or actors in need of TV promotion) do dress up their frustration into cosmic humanistic theories (often foggy).[1] Nevertheless, their influence on the western media and politicians is real.

Thus, political cooperation and political decisions are super-ordinated to economic considerations. The theory that economics is the base and that politics is the superstructure is false. This does not mean that economic elements are not included into political decision-making. The last ten years in the history of the Balkans show that the divorce between politics and economics can also contribute to inappropriate decisions (events in Herzegovina) or smuggling and putrification of political institutions (Yugo-Serbia).

For this and other reasons, in the first part of this paper, a short description of the present political and social situation of the area will be presented, with some prospective elements. Only then shall a model of economic growth be suggested. The main features of future cooperation will be addressed according to the model.

Geo-Politics: Politics and Society in the Balkans - Present and Uncertain Future

This first part addresses the main points of the political and social evolution to be expected over the next 15-20 years. Bearing in mind that many ideological, political and other factors do not allow for the taking of measures that could accelerate "normalisation" of the geo-political landscape, social stabilisation and economic take-off. The area lives in geo-political uncertainty, political weakness, social misery, economic bankrupcy and mismanagement of the international community.

Geo-political uncertainty

De iure, from the geo-political point of view, there are eight countries in the area: Albania, Bosnia-Herzegovina, Bulgaria, Croatia, Greece, Macedonia, Turkey, and Yugoslavia. All are UN members.

Two among them are pro-forma states: Bosnia-Herzegovina and Yugoslavia. Two others need in-depth reconstruction of their internal political organisation: Albania and Macedonia. Two are to act as stabilising factors: Greece and Turkey (if not leaders). Seven are in deep economic and social crisis requiring urgent help from IMF/WB, and/or the EU. (Greece has lived for years with EU subsidies which make up 30% of its budget.) The situation in Greece and Turkey will be mentioned only when necessary for understanding the stabilising action in the area.

Pro-forma states and quasi-states

It is evident that Bosnia-Herzegovina and Yugoslavia are states only de iure. Bosnia-Herzegovina has two "constituent entities": "The Federation of Bosnians and Croats", and the Republika Srpska. Each entity has its own parliament, government, judiciary, armed forces, etc. It also has 3 constituent nations: Bosnians[2], Croats and Serbs. They all have a Presidency in common (in reality another three-man chamber), common passport, central bank, but not banking system. But all is kept together only by SFOR, i.e., NATO.

The other pro-forma state is the Federal Republic of Yugoslavia. The two so-called federal units, Serbia and Montenegro, were, until the fall of Milosevic, on the limits of an armed conflict. Serbia even cut off all commercial and financial relations with Montenegro in 1999. It was a real embargo. Serbians are tired of everything, so nowadays Federal Yugoslavia - as a quasi-state - is supported by western diplomats (always behind the game) and war criminals in both Serbia and Montenegro. (The pro-Serbian units from Montenegro murdered Muslims in Srebrenica, with Arkan and other Serbs; ie. those living in Serbia stricto sensu, those living outside of Serbia stricto sensu are Serbians).

Nowadays (March 2001), Montenegro is preparing for a referendum on independence, with a 60% probability of success.[3] Thus, the Republic of Serbia is the only de facto member state of the Federal Republic of Yugoslavia. This republic has, de iure, two autonomous regions: Kosovo and Vojvodina. De facto, Kosovo is out of Serbia (its situation will be discussed later). Vojvodina, at this stage, is seeking the status of a federal republic. The President of the Regional Government, Mr. Canak, speaks as a President of an independent unity and has strong arguments about Djindic and other leaders of DOS (Democratic Opposition of Serbia).[4] So, the President of Yugoslavia, Kostunica, and the Federal Government of Yugoslavia are irrelevant institutions. President Kostunica has some authority of his own right, as an honest man - very uncommon among politicians - and as a genuine Serbian nationalist - a democratic hegemon. For this reason, he aspires to the Presidency of the future Serbia. But, Djindic wants that job too.

The Federal Armed Forces - or to be precise, the Chief of the Defence Staff, General Pavkovic, a Milosevic appointee, is seated on two chairs. Legally, he is under Kostunica. Factually, Djindic has all the power and the Serbian government. The navy is in Montenegro and the men-of-war are good for scrap. Naval officers who are married in Montenegro have apartments in that country, and their children go to school there. (They do know the sad experience of the Army, Navy and Airforce members who opted for Great Serbia in 1990/91. They left Slovenia, Croatia, Macedonia, Bosnia-Herzegovina - with the hope of coming back as conquerors. They live now in slums around Belgrade - with a high suicide rate.) So, they will opt for an independent Montenegro[5] and for living there in future. The police are more important than the armed forces. The Federal Police Forces are not in any better shape. All the money went for special Serbian security forces that are better equiped and trained than Federal Army Units.[6]

Quasi-states are Montenegro, Republika Srpska, and in a certain sense, the Federation of Bosnia-Herzegovina. Montenegro has, de facto, an independent government and ground forces (militia). The two Bosnian entities have the same - but they are under order of the High Commissioner. Pro-forma states and quasi-states are elements of the future geo-political architecture in the area. More on this later.

Then, there are administrative territories in geo-political limbo. Kosovo under UN/EU, KFOR, etc.; Kosovo's defence forces; Sandjek - an area in Serbia with a Muslim majority; and Vojvodina with important Hungarian and small Croat and other minorities.

Countries That Need Internal Reconstruction

The two countries are Macedonia and Albania. Since 1990, the western part of Macedonia, where there are about 250,000 Albanians (out of the 1,900,000 population in Macedonia as a whole), has been out of Skopje's control. A few years ago, the Tetovo University problem caused an uprising of Albanians. In the spring of 2001, the uprising became more serious, with an embryo of guerilla war. This war has been read as a signal for a need to reconstruct the Macedonian state by the government in Skopje. The "international community" is preparing for the opening of Tetovo University. It seems that Macedonia is heading towards a kind of federal state.

Albania has to set up its shaken state administration and has to set up regions between the Gigs (Albanians from the north) and the Tosci (Albanians from the south).

Governments

The main features of all the governments in the area are that they are coalitions and that they are weak.

Again, the Yugoslav Federal Government is a pro-forma government. The same is true for the government of Bosnia-Herzegovina (this is not the same as the government of Republika Srpska or the government of the Federation of Bosnia-Herzegovina). The government of the Federation of Bosnia-Herzegovina cannot be set up due to the conflicts between the Croats and the Muslims. In Croatia, there is (for the moment) a coalition of six parties. The three

142

major parties are communists, social-liberals (HSLS) and peasants (HSS). The three minor ones are the Liberals (LS), Popular Party (HNS), and Istrians (a regional party from Istria - on the Italian border). This coalition is kept together by immobility.[7] There is a latent conflictuality between the government and the Presidency of the Republic (MESIC). There is open conflict between the Defence Minister and the Chief of General Staff (indirectly with the Presidency). Thus, the measures proposed by the Vice-President of the Government LINIC regarding economic policy are not effective and the country looks "backward". FIAS, an independent agency, found 384 governmental obstacles to economic activities. There is no credible opposition in Croatia, but there are opposition parties.

In Serbia, stricto sensu, the government is a coalition of former opposition parties (five) - DOS (Democratic Opposition of Serbia) - with 52% in opinion polls.[8] The two strongest parties are DSS (Djindic) and DS (Kostunica). DSS being by far the strongest. But Kostunica has a support level of 90%. The most unpopular is the President of Serbia (Milutinovic from the SPS - the party of Milosevic) who is unimportant, but his job will be of the greatest importance in the future. The government is weak, because it cannot stop rapid degradation, due to the mismanagement of the previous government. Neither western public opinion nor western politicians can understand the depth of the Serbian disaster. (The indicators of social illnesses will indirectly show the reality).

The Serbian government has some political capital (political capital means the willingness of the population to accept temporary difficulties without blaming the government), as in Croatia in January of 2000. But, in the spring of 2001, there wasn't any more capital. So, the real political rating of the Djindic government will be seen in the winter of 2001. For the moment, there are no credible opposition parties. In Macedonia, the coalition VMRODPME / Albanian DP - survived the Tetovo crisis. They hold together as they will have to work on the new Macedonian Constitution. The President of the Republic is an ally of the government. But, in Macedonia, there is credible opposition. The signing of a Treaty with the EU is an important point for Macedonia. The Macedonian government has the same social and economic problems as all others - and the same incapacity to change the situation. "Bosnian policy" will have the same effects.

Albania is the Somalia land of the Balkans. Its government, like all others, is important for changing the situation. Albania is a country which moved from the Middle Ages (until 1945) to a Stalin goulag[9] until 1990 - and then from goulag to free market chaos. The Albanians from Kosovo are welcome in Albania only as guests, but their commercial activities are not welcome in Albania. Therefore, the stories of great Albania exist only in the heads of the Albanians who live outside of Albania.[10]

The situation in Turkey is of concern for the Balkan area, as this country is an important stability factor in the area. The same is true for Greece and Italy.

In Bulgaria, the Union of Democratic Forces and the Government succeeded the former Communists. There is a growing movement among public opinion in favour of the return of the King. Bulgaria gave some of its T-55 to the Macedonian Army. There are latent "linguistic" (in reality, socio-historical) unresolved problems in Bulgaria and Macedonia. Albanians should not underestimate the issue. If they say that 6 million Albanians are stronger than 1.7 million Macedonians, Bulgaria, for historical reasons, can answer that there are 10 million Bulgarians (8.4 in Bulgaria and 1.7 in Macedonia).[11] Both Macedonia and Bulgaria have Armed Forces in poor shape.

In all regional countries (with the exception of Greece), the main political objective of their governments is the adhesion to either EU or NATO or both. Kosovo is in the process of creating an embargo of political institutions. Only Serbia and Bosnia-Herzegovina are not members of PFP. Among the former republics of Yugoslavia, Macedonia is the first to have signed a Treaty with the EU. Croatia will follow. On the road towards political (and social) stability, the role of the EU is important. NATO's role is fundamental. Despite all the short-comings and mistakes of the political leadership.

However, both the local governments, the EU and the Non-Governmental agencies failed totally in their basic purpose. They did not introduce law and order in the countries in the area. It is the firm conviction of the author that Parliamentary Democracy is a condition sine qua non for a harmonious society in a peaceful country. But, it has been proved that introducing "democracy" into countries devastated by Bolshevic anarchy appears to be a licence for chaos. The absence of law and order, as important a condition sine qua non as genuine Parliamentary Democracy, postponed the orderly functioning of democracy, state institutions, civil institutions, judiciary, etc... for seve-ral decades, thus aggravating social problems and economic misery.

Poverty Ratio

At this stage, I limit the validity of the poverty index to the social group of urban populations, without any direct contact with rural areas. A four-person family with only a one-salary income per month (bribery excluded) or a small entrepreneur having an equivalent income. Of course, income after taxes. This income is divided by the food basket and minimum health, school expenses for a family of four. Albania: no sufficient data. Kosovo: no sufficient data. Bosnia-Herzegovina: Republika Srpska 0.2; Federation of Bosnia-Herzegovina 0.2; Croatia: 0.55; Bulgaria: 0.45; Serbia: 0.2; Macedonia: 0.45. This means that the average salary represents 20% of family needs - if the salary is regularly paid. About 30% of the workforce does not receive a regular salary.[12]

If one takes people that receive only pensions, then the ratio for Croatia is 0.15. In Serbia, it is less, as in Bulgaria, Bosnia or Macedonia. But, in Bulgaria, 60% of households live with gardens around their houses. In Kosovo, traditional solidarity among members of one family works. Among the elderly people, the result is a fast growing death rate - or budgetary euthanasia. Among the young and bright - emigration.

There is an underground economy, but this contributes nothing towards taxes and hence social security. In Serbia, for every one employed there are three out-of-work and two retired. Thus, one active pays for five people.[13] In Croatia, unemployment is officially 380,000 and there are about one million pensioners. In reality, it is about 500,000. Plus, about 180,000 who are not paid regularly. There are about 750,000 of those who work and are paid. They pay for about one million pensioners, 500,000 unemployed, about 50,000 war veterans, etc. The ratio is about one/two at least. In Macedonia and Bosnia, the ratio is 1/3.

Social Pathology

It is well-known that drug and alcohol abuse are widespread in all these countries. A new trend appears to be alcoholism with drugs amongst children under 15 years. Among bourgeois women, alcoholism is a fast-growing phenomenon. Orthodox Muslims avoid this danger. Thus, Bosnians and Albanians are not under the influences of alcoholism. Others are.[14] This stops the population from working or learning correctly whilst contributing towards suicide and demographic decline. Bosnia now has about 3.5 million people compared to 4.5 million in 1991. Croatia has 4.2 million compared to 4.45 million in 1991.

Along these lines, the abortion rate remains high. For every 1,000 live births, there are roughly an equal number of abortions in Bulgaria, 500 in Croatia, and 700 in Serbia.[15] But not in Albania or Bosnia. In 1953, in former Yugoslavia, for every 100 live births there were: 40 Serbs, 8 Muslims, 7 Albanians, and 20 Croats. In 1989 - 12 Muslims, 18 Albanians, 28 Serbs, and 16 Croats.[16] Demography is the hidden reason for the Serbian genocide of Albanians. Demographic decline and social pathology result in making the Balkans less attractive even for products of mass consumption, thus, foreign direct investment has no interest in the area. The workforce, trained under the socialist regime, prefer not to work rather than to work for small salaries. The conditions, both political and social, are not favourable for an economic take-off. Again, bureaucratic measures rather than market forces will become, on the macro-level, the driving force - at least for as long as poverty persists.

What then are the prospects for favourable economic development?

Serbia, Republika Srpska and Vojvodina will form a Serbian Confederation - to start with. This will be a politically stable entity. Albanians, Macedonians, Kosovars and Montenegrans will create, with Bulgarians, a Black Sea-Adriatic free trade area, assuming that Macedonia agrees to become a federal state. Montenegro shows that this is ethnically, religiously and politically possible. However, Kostunica declared that Serbia was not interested in cooperation with an independent Montenegro.[17] His Interior Minister declared that Montenegrins living in Serbia will be considered as foreign citizens. Croatia and the Federation of Bosnia-Herzegovina will have to find a modus vivendi and create a Confederation - an idea that was in the pipe-line in 1995/96.

The EU and NATO will have to assist this geo-political restructuring, without ideological or other prejudices. The good intentions and ideology à la mode of so-called civil society organizations and NGOs are deadly cocktails. (In countries in transition, human rights groups are often manned by former party and police members who jailed, murdered or destroyed the lives of honest citizens).

146

A firm insistence should be made on introducing law and order, and on promulgating well written laws in harmony with German or French models. They are the European countries legal system by tradition - a tradition that ended in 1945. Financial help should go towards the training of judges, lawyers in general and accountants, as top priority.

The key problem of politics in connection with the economy is the bult-in dishonesty and inefficiency of both governmental and para-governmental institutions.

Balkan Economies and Cooperation Among Balkan States

Balkan economies - a bird's eye view

They are in collapse. Telecom tradings or petroleum pipe-lines (Skopje-Salonique) will not be enough. All assets are out-of-date. The market value of corporations and their assets is negative. Thus, paradoxically, the NATO bombing of some Serbian factories was like shooting at dead animals. In fact, this is a gift to the new political leadership in Serbia. They have no courage to destroy value-consuming assets so that new economically-profitable factories (rather small at this stage) could be built up.

In all countries, the GDP per capita is between US$800-1,300. Albania, Bosnia, Serbia: $800/900; Bulgaria; $1,300; Croatia: about $2,000 (based on added value). Bearing in mind that the average salary in Bulgaria is about US$90 a month, even using PPP, it can hardly be US$4,200.[18] On top of that, the World Bank in its edition of "World Economic Indicators" 2000 revised the GDP calculations for many countries for the year 1998.

Thus, for Bulgaria, the GDP first calculated was US$33bn and the new one was US$40bn, a 20% increase. For Croatia, US$23bn increased by 32% to US$30bn, whilst Romania registered a 41% increase, and so on.[19] The political and financial consequences of such statistical "creativity" are dangerous. This is yet another proof that GDP is a statistical estimation and not an economic phenomenon. Still, with assets having no market price, something is still produced but at the cost of consuming substance and manpower.

More and more small businesses will grow - with a small output/employee ratio, relatively large output/assets ratio (practically no assets), and a small added value/employee ratio. All with minimum or zero share capital. This is effectively self-financing business, leading to slow growth and labour intensive economies. In the sophisticated banking sector, strong non-regional banks will take over local banks and set up subsidiaries. Croatia is a prime example, followed by Bulgaria (Italian banks took over the PRIVREDNA and SPLITSKA banks; Raffeisen bank opened many subsidiaries). Interest rates will remain high due to the risk of failure, most firms being undercapitalised because they cannot get credit. But banks have plenty of money to lend to the government, with the risk of creating unbearable public debt and putting the Parliament devant le fait accompli. The behaviour of local subsidiaries of foreign banks is the continuation of former practices - the non-informing of customers in the household sector as to the real interest rate and, generally speaking, the Shylock type of behaviour. Of course, the risks for them are high. Their customers were used to having easy money under socialism.

All in all, the populations of Serbia, Albania, Croatia, Bosnia lost as much wealth in their dealings with the financial sector as in the war destructions. Governments assisted, or at best did not react when faced with the financial robbery of the population. But, citizens were not careful enough. Local currencies are or will be (in Serbia) the link to the DM (soon to be Euro). Or, as in Montenegro and Kosovo, where the DM is already the currrency.

They are, in many aspects, economies with a predominance of commerce over small industry. Thus, many goods (of poor quality) are imported, and the commercial balance is in deficit. The EBRD plays, more often than not, a positive role. But, due to the desire of fast growth and the desire of the government to slow down the growth of unemployment, the immediate needs for fresh capital are great, as are the risks.

Agriculture needs more help than any other sector. The reason is that agriculture keeps spatial equilibrium, maintains the trade balance and is even important for tourism. Croatia, Serbia, Macedonia, Bulgaria, and Albania have an adequate climate for "ecological" agriculture, but real estate records are still in disorder. Land owner-ship by foreigners is a big issue. In Bulgaria and in Albania, foreigners can buy real estate. Not in other countries. Under patriotic slogans, the ambitious, but broken local "lumpenkapitalistes" want to keep all options open. This is an issue where the EU should be inflexible. Serbs and Croats can buy real estate and land in EU countries.

The legal framework under the slogan of being business-friendly is in reality crime-friendly

The key point is that political instability influences the economy via the rise of risks - and the risks influence the rise of interest rates. The cost of money - i.e. interest rates - which influence the total cost of capital is condensed information within the extant political situation.

The high cost of money, which is the function of the risk born by lenders and by investors, reflects political uncertainty. When rates are high, the actualisation rates (needed for the calculation of the Net Present Value (NPV) and for the Internal Rate of Return (IRR)) are high and the Return on Investments (ROI) and on equity (ROE) need to be even higher, which is difficult in transition economies.[20] Thus, investment is made by public institutions or for money laundering purposes (again, the exception being telecommunications, energy, food and pharmaceuticals), but private direct investment is scarce. This, again, raises both the demand for money and risks. But, expensive borrowing also has negative effects on employment. When heavily indebted firms need to pay their fixed costs, they lay off employees and unemployment rises. This in turn creates political instability.

The Economic Future of the Balkan Countries

From what has been said above, a model of the economic future can be suggested. This is for the next 20-40 years:

• Demography: population decline. High Mortality and emigration: Croatia will have less than 4 million (now 4.2 million). Serbia, less than 9 million (now 10m), and so on. Albanians are the exception, whose number will increase;

• The absence of law and order will become "endemic", like many African and Latin American countries;

• The social structure of the population will stay as it is, viz - very rich (10%), middle class (10-20%), poor (70-80%);

• Government sector: overstaffed and corrupted. In these countries, "civil servants" vote for the government. The government sector is important because it is also a mechanism of wealth distribution;

• Corporate sector: undercapitalised, mostly small enterprises with high mortality. Equity is less than 10% of the balance sheet (should be at least 40%);

• Thus, high unemployment and emigration.

Conclusion

The Balkan economies will be the "Latin America" of the EU for at least the next 20 years. This is not a fatality. But, to introduce law and order, all countries need statesmen. Or they have only politicians.

1. Albert Camus in his magnum opus "L'homme Révolte" writes that all those who want to avoid loving or taking care about people in particular and precisely - love humanity in general. There is no obligation for them in this "love".

2. Until 1997, Bosnians were Muslims - in the sense of NATION - (and that since 1963). After 1997, they decided that they were Bosnians, in order to ease the assimilation of Yugoslavs and Romes.

3. A USA institute, "National Democratic Institute" - in a public opinion poll, found that 60% of the population will vote for the two major political parties asking for inde pendence - March 2001.

4. See: Vreme (Belgrade), 23/III/01.

5. Neither Kostunica, nor Djiudic can give them jobs (Serbia has no sea) and homes (Serbia has no money).

6. This is typical Soviet tradition - NKVD units (interior army) were stronger than many Armed Forces units.

7. "Government facing collapse" - GLOBUS, Zagreb, 13/IV/2001. A government composed of "apathetic" bureaucrats", Nacional, Zagreb, 10/IV/01. Both are considered as pro-governmental. See also Globus, 30/III/01.

8. Vreme, Belgrade, 19/IV/01.

9. This was also a safe haven for the Italian mafia. The SIGURIMI worked with Mafia. The port of Durres has been the basis of the Paraguay (yes, Paraguay, South American country) fleet. Mafia put the Paraguayan flag on its ships in order to do business.

10. This is common in the area. Milosevic and Karadzic are from Montenegro. VUK DRASKOVIC from Herzegovina..., etc.

11. Thus, a commentator of "Slobodna Dalmacija", 3/IV/01 (a Croatian daily), an analysis by Danko Plevnik.

12. See, on poverty index: Ivo Paparela, "Some random reflections, etc." in Reiner Weichhardt editor Colloquim 1966, p.61, Bruxelles, NATO 1997.

13. Djindic - in Vreme, Belgrade, 22/III/01. The Prime Minister speaks only about active employed and unemployed, 1/3.

14. Nedjeljni Telegraf - Belgrade, 28/III/01.

15. Herald Tribune, 16/II/01.

16. Slobodna Dalmacija, 5/IV/01.

17. Radio France Internationale.

18. FT, 24/X/01.

19. Bundesinstitut Köln, now Berlin, research by Roland Götz. The author is grateful to Heinrich Vogel for the information.

20. Except in telecommunications - where the high ROE is the result of cheating customers - when DT/Cronet take 50 cts more than earned, the customer does not see it, and it is $ 3 million monthly in Croatia. On top of other dishonesties.

21. This is specially true of the so-called socialist governments.

SOUTH-EASTERN EUROPE: A SUMMARY OF DEBATE

Christopher Cviic

Senior Political Adviser, EBRD,London

Introduction

Regional cooperation is all the rage at present in South-Eastern Europe. After more than ten years of armed conflict and economic stagnation, many people, particularly in the West, appear to be convinced that the solution to the problems of the region lies in enhanced cooperation among its countries. The assumption behind the concept of regional cooperation seems to be that as local economies become more interdependent, both governments and people will be less likely to resort to violence: everybody will have too much to lose. The idea of regional cooperation was given strong encouragement by the meeting of heads of state and government of South-Eastern Europe in Skopje in February 2001. At this meeting the leaders adopted an Action Plan for Regional Economic Cooperation which identified a number of areas for action including economic and social development and progress in reforms; trade expansion; promotion of foreign direct investment; and improvements in infrastructure. At an earlier meeting, in Geneva in January 2001, organised by the Stability Pact for South-Eastern Europe, representatives of the governments from the region committed themselves to regional free trade and in their Joint Statement of Intent promised to prepare by the end of June a memorandum of understanding on concrete trade liberalisation measures.

In the light of those developments earlier in the year, the decision to devote the May 2001 NATO Economics Colloquium in Bucharest to the interrelationship between regional economic cooperation, security and stability, with particular reference to South Eastern Europe, South Caucasus and Central Asia, was particularly timely.

Discussion in Group I, which concentrated on South-Eastern Europe, probed the rhetoric and the reality of economic cooperation in the region. How much can realistically be expected from economic cooperation in a region such as South-Eastern Europe better known for conflict rather than cooperation? How real is the oft-proclaimed official commitment to regional cooperation by the locals? Does the current political and security situation favour or hinder regional coperation? Those were the main questions addressed in two leading presentations and in the subsequent official statements, the discussion that followed and in the final assessments.

How Much Interdependence?

The most striking fact that emerged from the first comprehensive and detailed paper, on Balkan economic interdependencies, by *Dr Krassen Stanchev,* Director of the Institute for Market Economies in Sofia, was that such interdepenencies were either not there at all or were extremely few. While Balkan economies trade over 60% with the West, they do not trade with one another. According to Dr Stanchev, some of the reasons are:

• regional integration of a low-income economy with other low income economies usually makes an economy poorer;

• demand is weak and relatively unsophisticated and so go-ahead, competitive firms opt for more rewarding markets;

• the countries of the region are not complementary but rather have similar product and quality structure;

• monetary instability of regional markets;

• inefficient contract enforcement and dispute resolution;

• tariff and non-tariff barriers;

• firms' fear of civil conflicts and insurgencies.

He noted the positive factors supporting the search for development and prosperity in the near future, such as the fact that (a) transition to market economy and democracy has become irreversible; and (b) that the international community - particularly the EU - supports the local leaders' express commitment to follow the path of sustainable growth and prosperity. This is clearly more for political and strategic than for economic reasons, in that South-Eastern Europe is not exactly a big market for the EU: in 1998 it accounted for only 1.6% of EU imports and 4.4% of its exports.

154

On the negative side, there was the 'unfinished business in the Balkans'. Political instability, eg. in Kosovo, FYROM, Serbia, Montenegro, Bosnia, undermined the fragile hope that business and trade opportunities would eventually make a difference and scared away foreign investment.

The general picture emerging from Dr Stanchev's paper was sobering, even discouraging:

• foreign direct investment is negligible in both absolute and per capita terms;

• mutual penetration of banking sectors is zero (with the exception of some Turkish and Greek banks); foreign ownership of banks is rare (a common practice is to transfer payments to a neighbouring country via international correspondent banks);

• regional commodity exchanges do not exist or function badly;

• cross-border clusters are an exception.

The real key to the solution, according to Dr Stanchev, does not lie in externally-inspired regional initiatives (though external stimulus may be helpful), but rather in comprehensive domestic reforms aimed at fostering the rise of truly competitive firms, mobile and responsive to demands of a sophisticated market and driven by productivity and quality. They should replace what he calls 'subsistence' and 'survival' firms, still far too numerous in the region and too influential politically, forever demanding subsidies and protectionism and thus blocking reforms. All in all, concluded Dr Stanchev, regional initiatives and policies must not be perceived as a substitute for core market and democratisation reforms.

Nationalism Strikes Back

In the second, also substantial paper on the region's economic and political prospects, *Dr Vladimir Gligorov,* of the Vienna Institute for International Economic Studies, started off with the bad news. The area suffered from high unemployment; fiscal fragility; external imbalances; large black markets, pervasive corruption and significant economic criminality. But he also noted the good news:

• continued price stability (except in Yugoslavia and Romania);

• positive growth rates in 2000;

• accelerated structural reforms in Bulgaria, Croatia, Macedonia; and even Bosnia & Herzegovina and Albania;

• better prospects for foreign direct investment due to greater efforts by the locals to attract it and to improved risk assessments on the part of foreign investors;

• momentous political changes in FR Yugoslavia as well as, less spectacular but modestly encouraging ones in Bosnia.

However the rather hopeful 2000 has given way to a rather less hopeful 2001 with a number of adverse developments, the worst of them being the start of armed conflict in FYR Macedonia. Dr Gligorov postulated as the most likely scenario a localised, low-level but prolonged conflict (possibly even a gradually deteriorating one) but confined to Kosovo and FYR Macedonia, with some negative consequences for Albania, Bulgaria and Serbia.

More fundamentally, Dr Gligorov saw the key problem for South-Eastern Europe as that of weak states - weak constitutionally, politically and economically, with constitutional issues (e.g. in Bosnia, FR Yugoslavia and FYR Macedonia) being the most fundamental ones. The issue of EU integration, to which governments in the region all aspire, will give the EU a lot of opportunity to influence events in a positive way (e.g., FYR Macedonia). But it will not be easy. The process of 'state capture' by a variety of interests (some of them criminal) is well advanced. Local states tend to respond to domestic and international groups rather than to their electorates. The weakness of those states cannot easily be overcome by promises of EU integration, according to Dr Gligorov. But EU integration will not take place without those states and their institutions becoming strong - a long and arduous task.

Dr Gligorov's economic scenario for the short and medium-term was rather gloomy. The 2000 growth, consequence of better export performance by most countries in the region, was due to higher growth in the EU. This cannot be expected in 2001 and beyond and so there will be some uncertainty and nail-biting. For the long-term prospects, the strategies of transition adopted will be crucial. The market and the state, once seen as competitors, are now increasingly seen as partners. Sustainable economic development is vitally important in the continuing confrontation between resurgent nationalism on one side and the rule of law and democracy on the other. The outcome will be to a large extent determined by the way macroeconomic imbalances are handled in the context of steady progress in intra-regional and EU integration, concluded Dr Gligorov.

Concerns About Regional Cooperation Remain

The main themes raised in the two leading presentations were echoed and elaborated upon in the official statements by senior advisers to the governments of Albania *(Genc Ruli,* of the Institute of Contemporary Studies, Tirana); Romania *(Mihnea Constantinescu,* Special Adviser on South-Eastern Europe to the Minister of Foreign Affairs); FR Yugoslavia *(Marko Paunovic,* Economic Adviser to the Deputy Prime Minister of the Federal Republic of Yugoslavia); and *Ukraine (Andrey. V. Nikitov,* Deputy Head of Department, Ministry of Economy). The current preoccupations of at least one of the global financial institutions strongly active in the area were reflected in a statement by *Rory O'Sullivan,* Special Representative of the World Bank Group for South-East Europe Reconstruction in Brussels. Speaking from the Chair, *Christopher Cviic,* touched upon the important role played in the region by the European Bank for Reconstruction and Development (EBRD) in London.

Some of the speakers from the floor expressed doubts about regional cooperation as a panacea for the region's ills and were critical of the results so far achieved by programmes such as the Stability Pact for South Eastern Europe. Some divergent views were also voiced in the general discussion about the role so far played by individual international financial institutions.

Widespread concerns about the foreign policy of the Bush Administration, prompted a statement by *Jonathan B. Rickert,* of the US Department of State. He said he was in a position to impart the good news that the United States remained committed to the region. The United States would carry on with the task of helping the region achieve peace, stability and prosperity and recalled that this approach had been recently confirmed by the Secretary of State, *Colin Powell,* during visits to Paris, Skopje and Sarajevo. During the visit to Skopje, Powell stressed the need for further democratisation and inter-ethnic dialogue: "...the ultimate solution is not how good your army is to defeat extremists, it is how good your political system is to accommodate the beliefs and aspirations of all the people in your society". Rickert confirmed that the United States would during this fiscal year - through the Support for Eastern Europe Democracy Programme - provide US$674m in assistance to South-Eastern Europe. He ended his wide-ranging statement by stressing that the key to progress in the region was the building of political and social conditions to foster peaceful resolution of disputes, adding that this approach was as applicable to the region as it was to Macedonia.

Concluding assessments were given by *Professor Katarzyna Zukrowska,* of the Warsaw School of Economics; *Professor Ivo Paparela,* of the University of Split in Croatia; and by *Thomas Price,* Co-Ordinator of OSCE Economic and Environmental Activities in Vienna.

GROUP II :

SOUTH CAUCASUS AND

CENTRAL ASIA

ON THE FORMING AND REFORMING OF STABILITY PACTS - FROM THE BALKANS TO THE CAUCASUS

Michael Emerson

Senior Researcher, Centre for European Policy Studies (CEPS), Brussels[1]

The term Stability Pact has entered into the lexicon of European international relations over the last decade. It seems to mean an initiative with the following characteristics:

• it covers a region of the EU's borderlands, which calls for conflict prevention or resolution;

• a region fragmented into nationalities and ethnic groupings which overlap state borders;

• the technique is comprehensive, being both multi-sectoral (economic, human, political, security dimensions) and multilateral (all major international actors and institutions);

• the objective is stabilisation, either as a preliminary to EU membership or as an extension of the European zone of stability;

• the initiative might come from either the external powers or the region itself or from both together.

The Stability Pact approach overlaps with other forms of regional organisation and cooperation in the EU's borderlands. In fact the whole of the EU's periphery is now covered by regional initiatives which see the overlapping of EU member states, candidates and non-candidates (for the Barents and Baltic Seas, Arctic, Northern Dimension, Mediterranean, Central European Initiative etc.). Stability Pacts are a sub-set of these regional actions, which critically involve conflict resolution or prevention.

The focus here is on the Balkans and Caucasus as two target regions with much in common, except they are in different 'near abroads' geo-politically.

The Balkan Stability Pact has at best been a temporary expedient, awaiting the maturing of events, in particular the passing of the Tudjman and Milosevic regimes, and thence the confirmation of EU integration perspectives for the whole of the region. However, it was ambiguously conceived from the beginning as to what its real role might be, and has had insufficient substance in practice to become credible. It is now due for reform, or at least down-sizing. Some observers even suggest that the real pact was between the competing international actors and agencies, a concordat for them all to be involved.

For the Caucasus a real Stability Pact is needed, and there could soon be an opportunity to implement a strategic set of actions in the region. Whatever now happens in the Caucasus it will not be called a Stability Pact, because the EU and West do not want to hint at money on the scale of what the Balkans have received. However, the Caucasus invites an initiative which could deserve such a name. An official proposal is, to follow Shevardnardze, a 'Peaceful Caucasus Process'. But here I stick to a Caucasus Stability Pact in the sense already defined.

Restructuring the Stability Pact for South East Europe

The Stability Pact for South East Europe is almost two years old, having been initiated at the Sarajevo Summit of July 1999 after the end of the Kosovo war. There is widespread agreement, at least unofficially, that the Stability Pact is not working well. This is heard in the region, in the EU and among other international actors.

The poor performance of the Stability Pact is not surprising, because of its ambiguity as a political and bureaucratic mechanism. Who owns the Stability Pact? Everybody, yet nobody really. That is one way of summarising the problem. More precisely the problems are:

• the states of the region do not want a serious regional political structure (neither a neo-Yugoslavia, nor a distraction from the priority task of joining Europe);

• the major financiers and international powers do not want some other body to coordinate their aid or strategies for them.

162

There is a role for an international forum for all interested parties, but that does not have to mean a huge number of unproductive committee meetings of 200 or so officials on almost every subject conceivable. A public debate on the future of the Stability Pact has recently been initiated in a report by the EastWest Institute (EWI)[2] and partners (Financial Times, 6 April). This report recommends discontinuing much of the bureaucracy of committees and task forces. A single forum for high level officials might be retained (the 'Regional Table'), but the three sectoral Working Tables would be discontinued. The numerous specialised task forces and expert groups would be left to decide themselves whether to continue a more decentralised and autonomous existence. Some of the most useful groups existed before the Stability Pact adopted them, and will no doubt continue without it. Their value is not to be underestimated. It is desirable for any well-identified region to develop a profusion of official, private sector and civil society networks. But they do not all need central coordination.

It is also argued in the EWI report that the Stability Pact should retain strategic ambitions in a limited number of domains, such as energy markets and the movement of persons, referring to the Monnet method of the European Coal and Steel Community. However the extension of this model to South East Europe looks problematic, since the big guns (EU, World Bank etc.) will not hand over their powers and resources or merge them with the Stability Pact even for a few key policy sectors. Yet without real powers and resources there can be little expectation of strategic action. Pragmatic regional cooperation is of course desirable in many domains, even in the absence of heavy political structures. But here the leadership should pass to the region itself.

Alternative options should therefore be considered to restructure the Stability Pact. A proposal might be as follows.

The successor to the present Special Coordinator of the Stability Pact, Mr Bodo Hombach, would be unambiguously the EU's Special Representative and Ambassador-at-large in the region. Mr Hombach is the EU's nominee, but he is answerable to everybody. He cannot really represent the EU. Yet the EU needs a Special Representative for the region. This post, once internalised into the EU, would help both Chris Patten and Javier Solana deploy all the EU's powers and resources in the region, rather than threaten to take these powers away from them. The EU Special Representative would have the important task to look to the coherence of EU policies as between the accession candidates and other states of the region. This involves key issues, such as trade and monetary (euroisation) policies, infrastructures, and visas and policing for the movement of persons, for which the region is a natural whole. At present EU policies for accession candidates and others are treated as being in different boxes. An early view of how EU policies should be attempting to integrate the whole of South East Europe as full or virtual member states was set out in the "CEPS Plan for the Balkans", [Emerson, Gros and Whyte, 1999].

The EU's future Special Representative would also have the task of thinking through how the whole of the region should best integrate into Europe in the medium to longer term, which is the only strategic option really available. This task will include some fundamental issues not yet being sufficiently addressed. One is how the international protectorate regimes of Bosnia and Kosovo should migrate in due course more fully into the EU's domain, which would need a huge strengthening of the EU's capacities for external action. A related question will be how the EU's emerging security (military and civilian) capabilities can best be used in the region.

The EU's staffing in the region needs serious reinforcement. One just has to observe the powerful US embassies in the region alongside the tiny EU Delegations and the crowd of EU bilateral embassies, all busy duplicating each others' political reportings. Strengthened EU Delegations should be at the service of all the EU institutions, Commission and Council, which would be easier to coordinate with the Special Representative to oversee them. Chris Patten is already decentralising much of the administration of EU aid to these delegations in the field. This is excellent. But next the EU will have to work out how to organise its diplomatic presence in the increasingly operational sectors of security policies

A major rationale of the present Stability Pact has been, with good reason, to retain the continuing and substantial engagement in the region of the other G8 powers - Canada, Japan, Russia, and the US. This might be done better with a lighter Stability Pact structure. The Special Representatives of these non-EU powers could deal directly with a full-time and fully legitimised EU counterpart. The present secretariat of the Stability Pact would be disbanded, giving way to arrangements in Brussels whereby the several Special Representatives (or their staff) would concert. The ministries of finance of G8 already have their High Level Steering Group for the region, co-chaired by the Commission and the World Bank. This also meets at senior official level, and is supported by technical work of a joint Commission-World Bank unit in Brussels. This part of the system functions satisfactorily. Foreign ministers might perhaps structure their work in a more consistent and transparent way, building on the informally called Quint group (a G5, with the big 4 EU and US) and Contact Group for the former Yugoslavia (a G6, the 5 plus Russia). The Stability Pact at present cannot orchestrate these coordination activities on the Western side, and proposals to reform it in this direction are bound to fail.

In the region itself there is already the South East European Cooperative Process (SEECP), which meets regularly at summit and foreign minister level. This includes all those states willing to try to concert together (Albania, Bosnia, Bulgaria, Macedonia, Romania, Serbia/FRY and Turkey together with Greece; with Croatia also as observer). This group has a rotating presidency, which can concert with the EU and other Special Representatives. Javier Solana, Chris Patten and Bodo Hombach already attend some of their meetings. Also the Zagreb summit of November 2000 innovated with a meeting of all the leaders of the EU and Stability Pact states, a form of meeting which may be usefully if sparingly repeated when political circumstances demand it. SEECP states could also designate their own Special Representative, if they so wished, to support the role of their rotating presidency. But that might be going too far for the states of the region, and should not be a pre-condition for restructuring the Stability Pact. SEECP should receive every encouragement to take the lead politically to develop cooperative initiatives, wholly owned or initiated in the region.

This restructuring of the Stability Pact would thus have the following key points:

• the EU's leading role would be more clearly and legitimately organised;

• the continued engagement of other international actors would be encouraged;

• regional leadership for inherently regional business would be enhanced;

• present excesses of bureaucratic committee meetings would be cut out.

Shaping a Caucasus Stability Pact

The South Caucasus is a land of frozen conflicts - of Nagorno Karabakh, Abkhazia and South Ossetia - which have resulted in the proliferation of blockaded frontiers almost everywhere. The frozen conflicts have left huge numbers of refugees or displaced persons stranded, or held political hostages in camps. Voluntary emigration has also been on a huge scale. Overall the region is in a desperately impoverished and demoralised condition. Of course this is not Chechnya in the North Caucasus, where an entire province is being physically destroyed. We concentrate here on the South Caucasus.

At the end of 1999, at an OSCE summit in Istanbul, the leaders of the region began to call for some kind of Stability or Security pact for the Caucasus. This included all three South Caucasus leaders - Aliev, Kocharian, Shevardnardze - as well as Demirel of Turkey. However none of them spelt out what this might mean in operational terms, except that the 3+3+2 formula gained prominence: 3 for the South Caucasus states, + 3 for the big neighbours Russia, Turkey and Iran, +2 big outsiders EU and US.

At CEPS we therefore tried to fill this gap, offering a general blue-print as free staff work for the interested parties, whose policy planning departments were inhibited by political or bureaucratic limitations. We formed a CEPS task force and published two reports in May and October 2000 (see Emerson, Celac and Tocci, 2000, and Emerson, Tocci and Prokhorova, 2000). The second report was a substantial refinement of the first, benefiting from a summer of consulting the leaders of the secessionist regions. This incidentally suggested expanding the game into a 3+3+3+2 formation, adding the three secessionist entities. The proposal was structured as follows:

Three chapters headings for the South Caucasus:

• conflict resolution, with fuzzy constitutional settlements for Nagorno-Karabakh and Abkhazia. Both cases would see political solutions closer to confederalism than federalism for Azerbaijan and Georgia in relation to the secessionist entities. The option of secession would however be excluded. Power structures would be essentially horizontal rather than vertical with only very thin union structures. Asymmetric relations would be provided, notably in the case of Nagorno-Karabakh with co-ethnic Armenia. Refugees (or IDPs) would be able to return to such areas as the Azeri provinces occupied by Armenian forces and the Southern region of Abkhazia;

• a new regional security order, in which the settlements of conflicts would see monitoring and enforcement for a while by military units from OSCE member states, under an OSCE umbrella;

• a South Caucasus Community (SCC) would be initiated, concentrating initially on scrapping the present blockades, then a free trade area and general trade facilitation, and on regional transport and energy infrastructures and networks. The SCC would also offer a distinct role to the autonomous entities (Nagorno Karabak, Abkhazia, South Ossetia) in their fields of competence alongside the three states of the region.

Three chapters would be devoted to wider regional cooperation:

• enhanced cooperation in the Black Sea - Caucasus - Caspian region, strengthening existing organisations such as BSEC;

• development of an EU-Russia 'Southern Dimension' cooperative concept, following the useful launch of the Northern Dimension;

• for the energy sector, completion of missing elements in the international legal environment, such as for the Caspian sea-bed and the Energy Charter Treaty (Russian ratification awaited) and its transit protocol for pipelines.

All together this would amount to a paradigm shift for the region. In our consultations all parties were interested to discuss these ideas. But frequently the response was 'it would be fine, but can it really happen?' More precisely it was questioned whether various vested interests really wanted resolution of the conflicts, both at the level of the secessionist regions, and geo-politically as regards Russia. For the EU and US it was questioned whether they were seriously interested in the region. The EU was preoccupied with the Balkans. The US was seemingly interested mostly in the Baku-Tbilisi-Ceyhan pipeline as a geo-political move to strengthen Western orientations.

In essence, many people judged that the status quo of frozen conflicts and blockaded borders had the properties of a (nasty) political economy equilibrium, with the external powers too divided or disinterested to change that.

As against this sceptical view, there was the unquestioned logic that a settlement of the conflicts and a new cooperative system could improve the welfare of the people of the region, or at least open the way for positive developments and hope for the future.

Around the end of 2000 there were some developments of importance, giving some hope for the Stability Pact advocates, as well as some worries:

• The EU shifted its position from ignoring the Caucasus under the French Presidency to the organisation in February 2001 of a Swedish-led Troika visit, including Chris Patten and Javier Solana as well as the Swedish Foreign Minister, signalling an upgrading of the region in the EU's priorities, and a specific interest in conflict resolution;

• At the same time Turkey succeeded in organising a semi-official seminar in Istanbul bringing together for the first time all the 3+3+2 at senior official level together with independent experts to discuss stabilisation and regional cooperation in the Caucasus;

• Meanwhile, however, Russia's diplomacy towards the region had gone onto the offensive, most sharply by punishing Georgia for alleged uncooperativeness over Chechnyan freedom fighters taking refuge in the Pankisi gorge region. Russian measures included switching gas supplies off and on during the winter, and introducing discriminatory visa requirements for Georgians to enter Russia, except for residents of secessionist Abkhazia and South Ossetia;

• Meetings between Aliev and Kocharian continued throughout last year at frequent intervals in pursuit of agreement over Nagorno-Karabakh. In April 2001 there was a special summit in Florida for the two leaders with the three Minsk Group co-chairs (US, Russia, France). This signalled some activism in this affair by President Bush, and some near break-through. The Minsk Group is now mandated to submit a full peace proposal for a June meeting in Geneva, and it was even suggested that an historic signing ceremony might be arranged in the margins of the G8 summit held in Genoa in July.

This is a new situation. Let us suppose that Nagorno-Karabakh is settled, the indications being that the solution would be rather along the lines suggested in the second CEPS document, with a fuzzy, horizontal solution constitutionally for Nagorno-Karabakh, the return of the occupied territories, and assurances of strategic passages for road transport both over the Lachin corridor for Armenia and through the Megri district connecting Azerbaijan and its exclave province Nakichevan. Then there would surely be a programme of reconstruction and assistance for refugee return, and financial support for restoring the East-West transport axes for road and rail. This would probably extend also to new oil and gas pipelines on the East-West axis.

The next question would then be whether or how a peace settlement and deblockading of Abkhazia might be agreed, so as to transform the whole South Caucasus region into a zone of peace, reconciliation and reconstruction. The problem is that the situation in Abkhazia, and in Georgian-Abkhaz and Georgian-Russian relations are all very bad. The Abkhaz leadership feels no incentive to negotiate with Georgia, since 'Russia is bigger and protects us', to use the wording of the Abkhaz leadership. Russia itself seems divided over its South Caucasus policy. Working cooperatively in the Minsk Group now over Nagorno-Karabakh, the message seems to be that Russia wants a settlement there. For Abkhazia the message seems to be that Russia is happy with a situation of creeping unstated annexation of the territory (already in the rouble area, with Russian military presence, Russian citizenship available, visa regime discrimination against other Georgians etc.). This Abkhazia policy follows old-style geo-political thinking, where the priority is to maximise influence to the point of domination, if not annexation. However for Russian policy makers there are also arguments going the other way. One is that the miserable, de-populated and blockaded economic condition of Abkhazia is itself a policy with no respectable future. Secondly, Russia has itself a clear interest in attaching a North-South axis to the East-West Silk Road, with the latter likely to be reconstructed and modernised following a Nagorno-Karabakh settlement. Russia has interests in connecting by efficient land routes with an improving South Caucasus economy and with the major Turkish and Iranian markets. The tourist economy of Abkhazia, especially if opened up alongside the Ajarian coastline linking through to Turkey, is also of interest for Russian consumers. Finally Russia could see a more successful South Caucasus generating positive economic and political spillover benefits for the Northern Caucasus.

The key therefore is whether Russia can be persuaded to turn its view of its own national interest away from old-style geo-political conceptions towards modern economic, social and political objectives. It is a question of what is to be maximised. Geo-political and military occupation and control of (miserably poor) peripheral territories versus joining in international development programmes, which would yield benefits for the welfare of the citizens of Abkhazia, including returning refugees, as well as for the Russian business sector in its trade beyond its Southern frontier, and for Russia consumers who would have a renewed Black Sea tourist facility to enjoy. If Russia saw advantage to make this paradigm shift in its policy, then the way would open to complete the assembly of a comprehensive programme of recovery for the South Caucasus as sketched in the CEPS Stability Pact document. The pay-off for the rest of Europe would be important also for other reasons. If Russia made this paradigm shift, it would amount to a new learning experience for Russia, the EU and the wider Europe about the value of cooperation versus competition.

Strategies of the EU For Its Near Abroad

However, there are implications for strategic re-thinking of policies not only on the Russian side, but for the EU also. The proliferation of regional initiatives for overlapping border regions of the EU, including Stability Pacts, calls for a clarification of the paradigm governing EU policy towards the wider Europe beyond EU enlargement. These regional initiatives in fact contrast with and challenge the prime paradigm of EU policy towards its neighbours, which stresses:

- the distinction between being in or out as full member states;

- EU multilateralism for the 'ins' and bilateral relations for the 'outs'.

The disadvantage of this model is that it renews the divisions of Europe and through disappointment for the excluded, risks feeding the processes of divergence dynamics. In its starkest form the transition process for the excluded is not sustained. For the small and weak states the process leads rather into ethnic-cleansing conflict, kleptocracies and virtual chaos. For the big excluded state, Russia, the tendency is towards xenophobic nationalism and the drive to reconsolidate its near abroad according to its own Realpolitik rules.

The alternative paradigm would be:

- de-emphasis of the differences between the 'ins' and 'outs';

- greater emphasis on multilateralism in the border regions.

These alternative strategies are of fundamental importance for the future of Europe. The first set pushes the EU increasingly towards a state with clearly delimited territory, citizenship and powers. The second set sees a Europe with fuzzy frontiers, the EU voluntarily offering to export its policies for application to the neighbours, reducing perceptions of exclusion, although still limiting participation in key political bodies. Some call this alternative the neo-medieval empire (although the model would surely include the Greek and Roman empires)[3] , i.e. one with a fuzzy set of peripheral associates, rather than an EU which becomes a clear-cut European neo-Westphalian state. Which of these alternative paradigms is to dominate, since the outcome is surely going to be a blend rather than a pure case? This is a major aspect of the emerging 'future of Europe' debate, but one which is not yet brought out sufficiently clearly. What is clear is that the member states at the periphery - be it Finland to the North or Greece to the South-East - look for substantial regional dimensions to the EU's periphery policies, whereas the institutional status quo of ideas, legal regulations and administrative structures prefer the neo-Westphalian model, leaving the regional initiatives with more symbolism than substance. Maybe this needs to change, if the stability of the European periphery is to be achieved.

Above all, what we observe now is an increasing tendency for the EU and Russian near abroads to come closer together, and even overlap. Will they embrace in cooperation or collide in competition? Some Russia commentators stress the model of symmetry and equal partners between the two big European entities. Such is the precise argument of Dmitri Danilov,[4] who discusses the Stability Pact propositions in terms of the EU setting the rules for the Balkans, and Russia for the Caucasus. An issue here is that the two big European entities are not really symmetrical, with the EU bigger, richer and representing a more attractive political model, whereas Russia is able to deploy energy plus military strengths. With these asymmetries the EU clearly dominates in the Balkans. But could the EU and Russia (and indeed the US which sustains a leading role in the Minsk Group work) find common cause in a cooperative action in the South Caucasus? If so, that would be a pact of substance.

Conclusions

In summary these are four:

• The Stability Pact, as a generic type of international action, has a serious rationale;

• The Balkan Stability Pact served a certain purpose while Milosevic was still there. But now that EU integration becomes the clear destination for the whole of the region, the Stability Pact should be restructured, down-sized and integrated better with the EU;

• A substantial Caucasus Stability Pact is looking increasingly relevant, although if enacted its name will be different;

• There is a case for EU policies for its near abroad to be shifted in balance, with less bilateralism and discrimination between the 'ins' and 'outs', and more emphasis on regional multilateralism for all classes of neighbour.

References:

Emerson, M, D. Gros and N. Whyte [1999], "The CEPS Plan for the Balkans", CEPS, July.

Emerson, M., S. Celac and N.Tocci [2000], "A Stability Pact for the Caucasus", CEPS, May.

Emerson, M., N. Tocci and E. Prokhorova [2000], "A Stability Pact for the Caucasus in Theory and Practice - A Supplementary Note", Working Paper No. 152, CEPS, October.

See also www.ceps.be for further notes on the Balkans and Caucasus.

1. Centre for European Policy Studies (CEPS), 1 Place du Congres, Brussels, B-1000; e-mail michael.emerson@ceps.be; tel 00.32.2.229.3931.

2. EastWest Institute and European Stability Initiative, "Democracy, Security and the Future of the Stability Pact for South Eastern Europe", 4 April 2001.

3. J. Zielonka, "Enlargement and the Finality of European Integration", Jean Monnet Working Paper 7/00, Harvard Law School.

4. See "A Russian view of a Stability Pact for the Caucasus", CEPS Commentary - Borderland Europe No 5, February 2001, on www.ceps.be.

ECONOMIC COOPERATION IN THE SOUTH CAUCASUS AND CENTRAL ASIAN REGIONS WITH A PARTICULAR FOCUS ON ENERGY

Friedemann Müller

Senior Researcher, Stiftung Wissenschaft und Politik, Berlin

Neither Central Asia nor the South Caucasus, still less the two in combination, could be called a "region" when the Soviet Union dissolved. An infrastructure that linked the republics south of Russia with each other or with their neighbours to the south and west was almost totally lacking.

There is now, however, both a need and opportunity for regional cooperation, which may result in the development of some degree of regional identity. A total population of less than 70 million is divided among eight states. These markets are individually too small to be attractive to investors since both infrastructure and legal systems end at national borders, and the average per-capita income remains less than US$1,000 per year. Another reason why regional cooperation is necessary is based on the fact that seven of the eight states are landlocked: any physical communication with the outside world requires transit routes through neighbour countries. Transportation routes, however, are extremely expensive, especially given the very low gross domestic product of the area. Infrastructure projects are vital for each of these relatively small states.

The resources, especially energy, are available for regional cooperation to support a self-financing infrastructure if the right framework conditions are there. Private investors, for example, usually finance pipelines. They require additional infrastructure like roads but also telecommunications or a functioning health system for which credits can be received if these measures are part of a general and successful development strategy. There are, however, many internal and external obstacles to cooperation which is itself the precondition for a credible development strategy, these being ethnic conflicts, the geopolitical interests of outside powers, a lack of tradition and understanding of the role of democracy and the rule of law, and finally the fact that political structures developed after the dissolution of the

173

Soviet Union tend to give national independence and domestic loyalty a higher priority than international networks. Nevertheless, the fact that there is no chance to gain prosperity without regional cooperation may influence the political class. It is, however, still an open question whether the political structure influenced by domestic and international powers gives room for a corresponding policy.

The Requirements for Cooperation Under the Rules of Globalisation

An important effect of globalisation is that capital now moves much easier across borders to where profitability is the highest than it used to. This does not necessarily mean that capital moves only to regions with the highest productivity. Productivity is only one factor that influences profitability, others being the wage level in combination with educational levels, the distance to larger markets, infrastructure, the level of security, and the quality of governance. All these factors are linked with costs that influence the calculation of potential investors. An obvious comparative advantage of the South Caucasus and Central Asian regions is the low wage level. The disadvantages are poor infrastructure, low levels of security (due to the many conflicts and crime) and poor governance (including insecurity regarding the implementation of laws, the competitive disadvantages for foreign capital, and of course corruption).

A special disadvantage is the smallness of the markets. As **Table 1** shows, the combined Gross National Product (GNP) of the three South Caucasus states is US$11bn. This corresponds to the Gross Domestic Product (GDP) of a middle-sized city in Europe. The combined GNP of the whole of South Caucasus and Central Asia corresponds to the GDP of a large city in Europe. If the relatively big markets of Iran and Turkey are added, we have a total GDP still significantly less than in the Netherlands. The Netherlands, however, would never think that their market is large enough to be sufficiently competitive under conditions of globalisation.

**Table 1: GNP of States and Regions in South West Asia -
1999 (US$billion)**

Armenia	1.9	
Azerbaijan	4.4	
Georgia	3.4	
South Caucasus		**9.7**
Kazakhstan	18.9	
Kyrgyz Rep	1.4	
Tajikistan	1.8	
Turkmenistan	3.2	
Uzbekistan	17.6	
Central Asia		**42.9**
Iran		110.5
Turkey		186.3
TOTAL REGION		**349.4**

Source: World Bank, World Development Report 2000/2001.

This means that major efforts need to be taken to open up markets in the South Caucasus. A free trade zone (no customs duties between the states) is the minimum requirement, with a customs union (equal customs towards third countries) being the next stage. It also means, of course, that harmonised rules, norms and standards need to be introduced at the same time. Otherwise one cannot talk about a common enlarged market. It took decades for the EU to create a single market. There was, however, a strong will to go into this direction. It is indispensable for this region to create an atmosphere of a strong will to become a single market. Otherwise even with assistance from outside prosperity cannot arrive in the region.

Energy - the Asset of the Region

The region to both the east and west of the Caspian Sea is in an absolutely unique position among developing countries. The relation between the wealth of the probable oil and natural gas reserves under the ground and the combined GDP of the South Caucasian states on the western side and Kazakhstan and Turkmenistan to the east (approximately US$36bn) is roughly sixty to one. Not even in the Gulf states there is there such a high wealth-income-relation. Of course, there are a number of uncertainties that makes this calculation volatile. One uncertainty is the oil price. The steady shift of world oil supply to OPEC countries makes it, however, probable that the price will not fall as an average below US$25 per barrel again. This is the figure used for the above calculation. Another uncertainty is the amount of reserves. The proven oil reserves of the region are roughly 20 billion barrels. The assumption of 40 billion barrels as probable reserves is a rather conservative estimate, but still not confirmed due to the difficulties of exploring a region that is difficult to supply with oil drilling equipment due to the fact that it is landlocked. The natural gas reserves of the region might be in the same order of magnitude. Since Soviet times, this has been better investigated than the oil reserves.

While the Soviet empire as such was not landlocked and had a widespread transportation network serving first of all the industrial centres in the European Soviet Union, all Central Asian states like Azerbaijan and Armenia are landlocked. This fact forces cooperation with neighbours if the energy wealth is to be transported to the world market. During the Soviet period these countries were not used to cooperate with each other because the political and physical infrastructure excluded a horizontal network and permitted exclusively a centre-periphery relationship. The states of the Central Asian and South Caucasus regions now prefer not to depend on Russia, but they are also not used to cooperating with each other. Furthermore, many territorial conflicts between and within the states (Nagorny Karabakh, Fergana Valley, Abkhasia) and the lack of understanding of how to build up integration just after having reached national independence is a major obstacle to regional cooperation. Therefore, the region is still far from making efficient use of the option to transform energy development into the economic development of the whole region.

Nevertheless, the option for self-accelerating regional development exists. It requires, however, much more foreign investment because of the lack of capital and technology within the region. The most important impediments for attracting more foreign investment are the deficiencies in the implementation of the rule of law, as well as corruption. Both create an incalculable risk for investors that make other regions in the world more attractive. But the various regional conflicts also raise uncertainties about the ability of the region to create a larger market for economic growth. If, however, foreign investors get the impression that over the medium term this region is in a position to solve its major conflicts, to provide framework conditions for a reliable infrastructure and to transport oil and natural gas without interruption, then chances for rapid development certainly exist.

European Energy Interests: An Opportunity for the Region

Europe's interest in Caspian crude oil has not been expressed very explicitly during the 1990s. The major reason might be that after the breakdown of the OPEC mechanism in 1986 to regulate the world market price by a production quota system among its members, the cartel as such stopped working. This held true until March 1999 when the system became effective again. For thirteen years the world crude oil market had been a true market, to some degree a precursor to globalisation. The spot markets in Rotterdam and Singapore had practically identical prices. If there is a truly competitive market the development of a special relationship between producer and consumer is unnecessary. Now, particularly after the reintroduction of the classical OPEC instruments, the EU has had second thoughts due to the changed picture on the crude oil market.

Since the late 1980s, the share of Middle East OPEC - the five Gulf States of Saudi Arabia, Iraq, Iran, Kuwait, and the United Arab Emirates - in the provision of world crude oil supply grew steadily. According to Table 2, this share was 26% in 1996 and will be 47% in 2010. The reason is the limitations on production in other regions. 64% of the proven world crude oil reserves are located in the Gulf region. Europe and North America own only 5.5% of proven world reserves, but have a share of 24% in world production. This indicates that in the medium term further shares in world production will be shifted to the Middle East OPEC.

Table 2: World Crude Oil Production* 1996-2020 (Share of Middle East OPEC and Rest of World in Million Barrels per Day (mbd) and %)

	1996		2010		2020	
	Mbd	%	Mbd	%	mbd	%
Middle East OPEC	18.5	26	43.8	47	49.0	55
Rest of World	52.0	74	48.9	53	40.8	45
TOTAL	70.5		92.7		89.9	

* excluding unconventional oil and gas liquids.
Source: International Energy Agency, World Economic Outlook 1998, p. 101.

While OPEC realised during the mid 1980s that any production reduction meant a loss of market shares but no price increase, in 1999 the point was reached when OPEC could again reduce production quantities without losing market shares, with the effect of price increases that gave them more export income with less production. OPEC, of course, is aware that this is a short or medium term effect. To prevent the situation of losing cartel power as in the 1980s after the extreme price rises in the 1970s, OPEC decided to establish a window for the world market price in the range of US$22-28 per barrel. Nevertheless, the very fact that all large regions in the world will lose market shares in the coming ten to twenty years (see **Table 3**), only the Gulf OPEC and to a much smaller degree the transition countries will gain and, considering an absolute market share which will be much higher than during the 1970s, will hand back an instrument to OPEC that can be used not only in a wise way but also as a short term blackmail instrument.

Table 3: Crude Oil Demand,
Supply and Net Imports 1996 and 2010
(IEA Projection - Million Barrels per Day (mbd))

	1996			2010		
	Demand	Supply	Net Import	Demand	Supply	Net Import
OECD North America	20.3	11.1	9.2	23.4	8.6	14.8
OECD Europe	14.4	6.7	7.7	17.0	4.5	12.5
OECD Pacific	6.7	0.7	6.0	7.7	0.3	7.4
Total OECD	**41.4**	**18.5**	**22.9**	**48.1**	**13.4**	**34.7**
Transition Countries	5.5	7.3	-1.8	7.2	10.2	-3.0
Africa	2.2	7.7	-5.5	3.3	7.8	-4.5
China	3.6	3.1	0.5	7.1	3.2	3.9
Other Asia	8.5	3.7	4.8	14.2	2.9	11.3
Latin America	6.3	9.8	-3.5	9.0	10.4	-1.4
Middle East	4.1	20.4	-16.3	4.9	44.7	-39.8
World	**71.6**	**70.5**	**1.1**	**93.8**	**92.6**	**1.2**

Source: IEA, World Energy Outlook 1998, p. 117

At the end of the 1990s it became obvious that the amount of Caspian crude oil reserves will be at the lower rather than at the upper end of the range given by the US State Department in a study released in 1997 (15.3 to 176 billion barrels). However, the discovery of the Kashagan field in the Caspian Shelf (in spring 2000), which still does not allow a precise estimate of its capacity, provides some evidence that the probable reserves can be assumed in the range of 30 to 40 billion barrels. According to an International Energy Agency (IEA) estimate, the transition countries are the only region besides OPEC with a growing net export potential (see Table 3). Within the transition countries, it is certainly most of all the Caspian region and not Russia that will provide this net export increase. The IEA further estimates that the share of Caspian crude oil production in world production could be 4-5% after 2015 (see Table 4).

Table 4: Crude Oil Production, Consumption and Net Export of the Caspian States (million tons)*

	1990	2000	2010	2020
Kazakhstan				
Production	25.5	42.5	87.5	145.0
Consumption	27.2	17.8	38.5	68.0
net export	-1.7	24.7	49.0	77.0
Azerbaijan				
production	12.3	14.0	57.5	105.0
consumption	8.6	10.2	14.9	23.9
net export	3.7	3.8	42.6	81.1
Turkmenistan				
production	3.4	8.0	9.5	11.0
consumption	4.8	6.5	7.0	8.0
net export	-1.4	1.5	2.5	3.0

* The given data are average values of the "high case" and the "low case" scenario.

Source: International Energy Agency, Caspian Oil and Gas 1998, p. 51.

Considering that already today two-thirds of Gulf crude oil goes to East, Southeast and South Asia and no more than 10% to Europe, the Caspian crude oil that will be available in the second decade of this century - roughly one tenth of Gulf production - could be relevant for the European market. If the infrastructure is there to transport the crude oil directly to Europe, this market would presumably be preferred by the producers. The regions to the North and South of the Caspian Sea are energy producers themselves, whereas the regions to the East and South East of the Caspian are either too remote to build a transportation infrastructure, or their reliability to make payments on their crude oil invoices cannot be assured. Therefore, Europe is the natural market for Caspian crude oil. Europe, on the other hand, must have an increasing interest in fostering any supply side competition during a time of overwhelming OPEC market domination.

World natural gas supplies generally get much less attention than the crude oil market. This applies in spite of the worldwide and longer term higher demand growth profiles for natural gas, its environmental advantages (less CO_2 emission per energy unit, no soil or water pollution), and the larger resources in comparison to current annual production. The reason for this lower attention lies in the regionalisation of the world gas market and in the long-term contracts between producers and buyers which lead to an inflexible market. This regionalisation is necessary because of the more expensive and less flexible transportation in comparison to crude oil. Practically all national and 80% of the international trade in natural gas is linked to pipeline transportation. This restricts transportation to the participants of a given infrastructure. Such transportation lines are limited to a maximum of 3,000 to 4,000 kilometres.

This explains, for instance, why the Clinton Administration did not much care about Caspian natural gas in the mid-1990s. Only when natural gas transportation from Turkmenistan to Turkey via Iran appeared on the agenda did the US government intervene, because of the inclusion of Iran. The US Administration, therefore, commissioned a feasibility study for a Trans Caspian Pipeline (TCP). This was certainly not driven by interest in the energy source, as such. The European position is quite different. Europe is by far the largest natural gas importing region in the world.

Table 5: Net Natural Gas Imports(+) and Exports (-) by World Regions (million tons of oil equivalents)

	1995	2010	2020
OECD North America	-2	-2	-2
OECD Europe	104	230	387
OECD Pacific	42	42	64
Africa	-35	-61	-93
Latin America	0	0	0
South and East Asia (excluding China)	-35	-2	33
China	0	0	0
Transition Countries	-74	-162	-281
Middle East	-5	-49	-114

Source: International Energy Agency, World Economic Outlook 1998, p. 134.

As Table 5 above shows, OECD Europe imported 104 million tons of crude oil equivalents (toe) more than it exported (net imports) in 1995. By comparison, the North American net export of 2 million tons is insignificant. OECD Pacific is the largest net import market behind Europe with only about 40% of the European import volume. The estimates for 2010 and especially for 2020 show that Europe's position as the largest importer will be further increased. While South East Asia as a net exporter will turn into a net importer, the world market will be supplied mainly by three regions: Transition countries (Russia and the Caspian states), Africa (Algeria etc.) and the Middle East (mainly Iran).

These three regions will have to compete on the European market for reasons of both demand and supply. First, due to the expected decline of European natural gas production, Europe is expecting an average import growth of no less than 5.4% annually until 2020. Secondly, the three big producer regions will have no alternative but to compete on the European market. All other region's import demand will be smaller than the export supply of the three big producer regions. This gives Europe a unique chance to establish the only truly competitive market in the world for natural gas. If the liberalisation of the European natural gas market is to be realised and the infrastructure linking Europe with these three regions is available, natural gas will be traded in Europe like a normal product. There will be no more need for a coupling of the natural gas price to the crude oil price. Demand and supply will fix the price.

Taking the political changes after the dissolution of the Soviet Union and geographic proximity into account, it makes sense to differentiate between the three major regions. Turkmenistan and Azerbaijan, the countries with the major Caspian natural gas resources and neighbours of Iran should be included in the South Caspian/ Middle East group, making this the region with the largest share in natural gas reserves with 39% of the world total followed by Russia with 33%. While Europe is linked with pipelines to Russia and North Africa, the only missing transportation line from the three big supplier regions to Europe is the one from South Caspian/Middle East, the region with the largest resources.

Before the discovery of the large off-shore natural gas fields in Azerbaijan and considering that Turkmenistan has no significant infrastructure to export natural gas outside the former Soviet network, the IEA provided in 1998 the following cautious estimate of the

Caspian natural gas production during the next 20 years (see **Table 6** below).

Table 6: Natural Gas Production, Consumption and Net Export of the Caspian States (billion cubic meters)*

	1990	2000	2005	2010	2020
Kazakhstan					
Production	7.0	8.9	13.5	22.0	27.0
Consumption	14.7	13.8	17.2	23.2	27.0
net export	-7.7	-4.9	-3.7	-1.2	0
Azerbaijan					
production	9.9	7.4	14.2	19.2	26.0
consumption	13.6	7.4	9.2	11.0	17.9
net export	-3.7	0	5.0	8.2	8.1
Turkmenistan					
production	84.3	39.8	55.1	80.8	123.7
consumption	14.5	9.5	10.7	12.9	17.0
net export	69.8	30.3	44.4	67.9	106.7

* The given data are average values of the "high case" and the "low case" scenario.

Source: International Energy Agency, Caspian Oil and Gas, Paris 1998, p. 52.

This expected production growth from 56 (in 2000) to 177 billion cubic meters (in 2020) is not limited by production capacities but by the assumed demand. The argument of demand restrictions, however, holds even more for Iran with its 16% share in proven world natural gas reserves.[2] It is obvious that this restrictive situation could change immediately if a large capacity pipeline were constructed from the South Caspian region supplied by natural gas from Turkmenistan, Iran and Azerbaijan.

The idea of providing access for natural gas from this region to the European market is not new. During the 1970s a triangular swap deal

Iran-Soviet Union-Germany was successfully negotiated. However, the Iranian revolution put an abrupt end to this deal. After the dissolution of the Soviet Union the construction of a large diameter pipeline from Turkmenistan via Iran to Turkey was started. However US sanctions against Iran and the option of the TCP favoured by the US Administration delayed this project. Private investors were also reluctant due to several political uncertainties. Nevertheless, the situation seems to demand further progress on this issue:

• The demand/supply dynamic seen in Table 5 makes it obvious to link the largest natural gas reserves to the largest market. The new discoveries of natural gas fields in Azerbaijan strengthen this argument;

• Russia is not equipped to compensate for the expected decline in European natural gas production and its demand growth with increased exports. Natural gas production in Russia is stagnating. Whether new investment will lead to a high export growth potential is doubtful;

• Turkey is growing into one of the largest markets for natural gas. Its increasing dependence on Russian deliveries - the Blue Stream project, one of the most ambitious, linking Russia directly with Turkey via the Black Sea is under construction - demands diversification which could be easily managed by linking Turkey with its Eastern neighbours. If, however, a pipeline is built from the South Caspian region to the centres of demand in Western Turkey, an extension of the pipeline to Europe would be much cheaper than a new pipeline from West Siberia to Europe.

While it makes economic sense to link the South Caspian/Middle East region with a large diameter pipeline via Turkey and South Eastern Europe to Central Europe, political obstacles like the ongoing sanctions imposed on Iran and domestic instabilities in Turkey contribute to the cautious behaviour of potential investors.

Energy is Not Everything - Perhaps Tourism as a Major Challenge

There is no doubt that energy production, transportation and maybe even processing provide an opportunity for major economic growth in the region as a whole. Nevertheless, as some OPEC countries show, this does not produce a sound economic structure if a region is dependent on its oil or natural gas resources exclusively. This is especially relevant here since the Caucasus region never fully relied on energy production in Soviet times when it had a more diversified economic structure. In the age of globalisation, this region must carefully observe where its comparative advantages lie. It is, for instance, not clear whether cotton production in Uzbekistan or Turkmenistan is a comparative advantage considering the disastrous damage done to the water system of the whole region due to gigantic irrigation projects and the related waste of scarce water.

A project that definitely could be seen as a comparative advantage if rightly structured would be the promotion of tourism, at least in the South Caucasus region. Here we can find within a relatively limited space many cultural and natural spots of major interest. If an infrastructure would allow tourists to reach these places and to find there modest accommodation facilities (say similar to US national parks) which could be constructed and managed by local investors[3], this could bring not only money into the region but also people who become acquainted with it. It would, however, require that all three South Caucasian states would accept a common visa treatment and transnational tourism management. This would, indeed, be a healthy experience for the region as a whole.

Conclusion

Among experts on the South Caucasus and Central Asian regions one will always find optimists and pessimists - those who do not believe that these regions can make use of their development options and those who believe they can. It is, however, undisputed that the region holds its future in its own hands. The opportunities are there and can be summarised as follows:

• regional cooperation is indispensable - otherwise the region will not become a bridge between Asia and Europe and will not be competitive in a globalising world because of its inability to attract foreign investors;

• Caspian energy reserves are an asset that puts the region into a unique position in comparison to other developing regions. If the preconditions of good governance are fulfilled, this asset can create a self-accelerating development process not only for the resource rich countries but also for the transit states;

- energy is important but certainly not the only comparative advantage to be employed; another one is tourism. This is especially important not only because it can be a major sector for development (like in Austria) but also because it is a challenge for regional cooperation in infrastructure, standard harmonisation, and administrative adjustment. Tourism would also contribute to the exchange of people and ideas.

The countries of the whole region must themselves take the initiative of gaining prosperity through regional cooperation. Unlike other developing regions without comparative advantages, this Caspian/Caucasian region has all the instruments in its own hands to create a framework within which a process of economic growth would be possible. The governance issue, however, is crucial. To put it into a nutshell, the alternatives are "Nigeria or Norway". Educational standards combined with its geographical and historic proximity to Europe should give this region the power to choose the "Norway" option.

1. Department of State, Caspian Region Energy Development Report, Washington D.C., April 1997, p.4

2. BP Amoco Statistical Review of World Energy 1999, p. 20

3. These facilities would need to have common standards under the control of an international authority that would not accept corruption and illegal activities.

REGIONAL COOPERATION IN CENTRAL ASIA

Shirin Akiner

Lecturer, School of Oriental and African Studies, University of London

Introduction

At the time of writing, slightly less than a decade has passed since the formal disintegration of the Soviet Union. The Central Asian states, in their modern form, are very new entities. Thus, they have no established strategies to guide them in responding to the challenges of an environment that, at the regional level as well as the international level, presents opportunities for development, but also threats to security and stability. Since independence, the Central Asian states have joined a wide range of international and regional organizations. The latter comprise different groupings of member states. This paper will the trace evolution of the key regional groupings and considers their aims and objectives. Most of these formations are still very new and detailed information on structures, programs and content of agreements is not always to be found in the public domain. Nevertheless, despite the fact that it is not as yet possible to undertake a thorough evaluation of these organizations, a descriptive overview of the current situation is useful in that it casts light on emerging trends.

Defining the Region

Historically speaking, 'Central Asia' is an amorphous concept.[1] Since the demise of the Soviet Union, however, in international relations it has gained currency as the designation of the five newly independent states that lie to the east of the Caspian Sea, namely, Kazakhstan, Kyrgyzstan, Tajikistan, Turkmenistan and Uzbekistan. These states are regarded as constituting a natural region, characterised not only by contiguity and interdependence, but also by a dense web of shared socio-cultural characteristics.[2] Central Asians themselves have been enthusiastic proponents of this idea of a common regional identity.

Yet in recent years two contrasting trends have emerged that challenge this idea of Central Asia as a discrete region. On the one hand, these states have adopted markedly divergent political and economic systems. Increasingly, the dissimilarities seem to outweigh the similarities, calling into question the notion of a homogenous 'Central Asian' space. Various explanations can be advanced for such differences, but undoubtedly they owe something to the fact that traditionally, these societies were very diverse. Even today, the ancient divide between the nomad world of the north and the settled communities of the south is reflected in attitudes towards the ordering of society.[3]

On the other hand, there has been a move to strengthening ties with neighbours to the south and east, as well as to the north and west. Again, this is not a new development but rather a revival - or rediscovery - of latent ethnic, cultural and economic linkages. In the context of these wider regional formations, the Central Asian states (in no small measure as a result of their common Soviet experience) currently constitute a distinctive sub-region. However, this situation is by no means immutable: there are already indications that this 'core' could fracture, with the possibility that segments might be absorbed into different politico-economic configurations. Given this fluidity, it is pointless to impose rigid terminological definitions. Hence, 'region' will here be used in a loose sense to refer both to the five Central Asian states (the main focus of this paper) and to more extensive groupings of adjacent, or nearly adjacent, states.

Challenges of Independence

During the Soviet era, the Central Asian republics were largely isolated from the external world. There were almost no direct communications or transport links with neighbouring countries. All foreign relations were handled through Moscow. Consequently, with the exception of a handful of senior officials and eminent academics, very few Central Asians had any firsthand knowledge of life beyond the Soviet borders. At the same time, direct cooperation between the Central Asian republics was also limited, since the planning and organization of regional projects was directed from Moscow. Thus, when the Soviet Union collapsed - unexpectedly, with no transitional period - the governments of these new states were virtual novices in the field of foreign affairs at the international level, and also at the regional, intra-Central Asia level.

The first stage in the development of external relations was the very basic process of establishing an organizational infrastructure.

Remarkably, this was accomplished within a very short period, thanks to a high level of education and of professional training.[4] Functioning Ministries of Foreign Affairs and Foreign Economic Relations were established in all the Central Asian states within some eighteen months. They were soon able to open embassies in the USA and key European and Asian centres, also in the member states of the Commonwealth of Independent States (CIS). By the mid-1990s, each of the Central Asian states had established trade and diplomatic links with over one hundred foreign countries.

Foreign policy planners in these new states were confronted with several tasks simultaneously: finding their bearings in the international arena; defining their national interests; identifying friends and partners; and prioritising objectives. This entailed a steep learning curve. During the first years of independence, understandably, the approach of the new states was mainly exploratory; policies were tentative and largely reactive to external pressures. Within a relatively short period, however, more nuanced positions began to emerge. Also, divergences between these states in priorities and approaches to foreign policy issues became increasingly manifest.

International Organizations

One of the first priorities of the new states was to accede to the main international organizations. Membership of such bodies was a crucial gauge of external recognition and acceptance. This in turn was a means of protecting and consolidating their still fragile independence. Moreover, participation in such organizations provided these small states with a voice in international affairs, and eventually, through the tactical use of voting rights, enabled them to extract benefits from larger, more powerful members. All five Central Asian states were formally accepted as members of the United Nations on 2 March 1992. They subsequently joined the main UN funds, programs and special agencies (including UNDP, UNHCR, UNCTAD, UNESCO, International Civil Aviation Organization, International Labour Organization, the International Monetary Fund and the World Bank); also the Economic and Social Commission for Asia and the Pacific. Kyrgyzstan is to date the only Central Asian state that has been accepted as a member of the World Trade Organization, though Uzbekistan and Kazakhstan are current applicants and Turkmenistan has observer status.

The Central Asian states likewise acceded to several non-UN international governmental organizations. Several of these bodies have a political-ideological bias. The Central Asians have sought to maintain a balance by the diversification of such links. Thus, they have joined inter alia the Commonwealth of Independent States; the Organization for Islamic Conference;[5] the North Atlantic Cooperation Council; the NATO Partnership for Peace programme (except Tajikistan); and the Organization for Security and Cooperation in Europe. Turkmenistan and Uzbekistan are members of the Non-Aligned Movement.[6] All five have joined the Asian Development Bank; the European Bank for Reconstruction; and the Islamic Development Bank.

Regional Organizations

In regional relations, the Central Asian states have followed a multi-track approach, joining a range of organizations. Most of these regional bodies have similar policy aims and objectives, though they differ in political orientation. Moreover, there is a high degree of overlap in the membership of these groupings. Kazakhstan and Kyrgyzstan, for example, belong to six of the regional organizations. Turkmenistan, by contrast, has opted for a stance of 'positive neutrality'[7] and to date has joined only three regional organizations; even in these bodies, it favours the role of passive observer rather than active participant.

These regional organizations may be categorised in various ways, but an obvious difference is that one set comprises CIS members (though they are not necessarily pro-CIS), while the other set combines CIS and non-CIS members. A more tenuous distinction is that some of the CIS groupings, notably the Economic Eurasian Community and the Central Asian Economic Forum, appear to have full integration as their goal, while others emphasise institutional cooperation and limited harmonisation of regulatory frameworks. However, all are still at an early stage of development and in several cases have already undergone structural modifications. These transformations have usually been accompanied by changes of designation. The following sections give a brief account of the evolution of these bodies.

Intra-CIS Organizations

Eurasian Economic Community (EEC)

All the Central Asian states joined the CIS in December 1991, on the eve of the formal disintegration of the Soviet Union.[8] Very soon, however, differences of attitude emerged. Kazakhstan was a vigorous (though not uncritical) supporter of the CIS; Kyrgyzstan, though less outspoken, adopted a similar stance. By contrast, Uzbekistan took an increasingly sceptical approach, while Turkmenistan gradually distanced itself from any collective involvement; Tajikistan, engulfed by civil war 1992-97, was engrossed in its internal affairs.

In March 1994 Kazakh President Nazarbayev mooted the idea of transforming the CIS into a more tightly knit 'Eurasian Union'. This was firmly rejected by Uzbekistan; Turkmen President Niyazov also expressed reservations about the proposal. Nevertheless, President Nazarbayev continued to air his Eurasian concept and gradually, this project gained momentum. In early 1995, a preliminary agreement on a customs union was concluded between Kazakhstan, Kyrgyzstan, Russia and Belarus. This became the basis for the quadripartite agreement on 'The Regulation of Economic and Humanitarian Integration', signed by these states on 29 March 1996 in Moscow. The main aims of the agreement included the creation of a united economic area; the development of common transport, energy and information systems; and the co-ordination of foreign policy. Uzbekistan and Turkmenistan refused to participate in this new bloc, but Tajikistan became a member at the end 1998.

On 10 October 2000, this five-member group of CIS states (i.e. Belarus, Kazakstan, Kyrgyzstan, Russia and Tajikistan) signed a treaty on the formation of the Eurasian Economic Community (EEC), to take effect from 1 April 2001. The new organization's highest policy-making body, the Inter-State Council, is to be located in Moscow. Kazakh President Nazarbayev was elected chairman at the inaugural meeting held in Minsk on May 31. Other organs include the Integration Committee and an Inter-parliamentary Assembly. The primary aim of the EEC is to further economic cooperation (which the CIS signally failed to achieve), while respecting the sovereignty of member states. It is empowered to represent the interests of member states in dis-cussions with other countries and international organizations on matters relating to international trade and customs policy; this includes negotiating special terms for the accession of EEC countries to the WTO.

Critics of the new body see it as a vehicle for reasserting Russian influence; Uzbek President Karimov disdainfully dismissed it as empty posturing.[9] However, the EEC Charter contains provisions designed to minimise the danger of 'great power' domination. A weighted voting system has been adopted. This allocates the lion's share of voting rights to Russia (40 per cent, with 20 per cent each for Belarus and Kazakhstan, 10 per cent each for Kyrgyzstan and Tajikistan),[10] yet major policy decisions require a two-third majority; this can only be obtained by a coalition of three states.[11] The decision of the member states to delegate some decision-making functions is a highly significant development; if it is implemented effectively, it will strengthen the process of integration.

Central Asian Economic Forum (CAEF)

The Central Asian Economic Forum (CAEF) developed in parallel to the Eurasian Economic Union. Initially, it seemed as though moves to create a specifically Central Asian entity might lead to the defection of these states from the CIS, or at least to the formation of a strong sub-regional group within the CIS. However, all but one (Uzbekistan) of the members of what eventually became the CAEF also opted for membership of EEC. This blurred and weakened the focus of the nascent CAEF.

The origins of the CAEF date back to 1993. On 4 January of that year a summit meeting of the presidents of the five Central Asian states was held in Tashkent. The initiative for this event came from Uzbek President Karimov, but there was general agreement amongst the participants on the need for regional cooperation. This was symbolically underlined by the decision to adopt a single collective designation for the region, namely 'Central Asia' (Tsentral'naya Aziya), in place of the Soviet-era formula 'Middle Asia (Srednyaya Aziya) and Kazakhstan', which was felt to be divisive. Agreement was reached on broad principles for the creation of a regional common market, but a formal confederation was not envisaged at this stage. As President Nazarbayev of Kazakhstan commented: 'Everyone wants to live in his own apartment, not in a communal flat. The same goes for sovereign states'.

The first positive step towards intra-Central Asia integration was the establishment of the Central Asian Union, a customs and economic union between Uzbekistan and Kazakhstan, soon augmented by the accession of Kyrgyzstan. This tripartite agreement was underpinned by a pact on military cooperation, signed in February 1994. In 1995, the decision was taken to create an Inter-State Council; President

Nazarbayev was appointed chairman for the first year. Regular working meetings were instituted at ministerial and presidential level. Regional problems were the chief focus of attention, particularly the on-going civil war in Tajikistan. Also, there was agreement on the need for joint action to alleviate environmental problems. The Nukus Declaration on the Aral Sea, signed in September 1995, summed up the common position of the member states on this issue.

Further moves to strengthen regional integration were undertaken the following year. At the tripartite summit held in Almaty in August 1996, documents were signed concerning the formation of the Central Asian Bank for Cooperation and Development. It was also agreed that free economic zones in border regions of the three countries should be created. The three Presidents further approved the formation of a joint Central Asian peacekeeping battalion, Tsentrazbat, to operate under the aegis of the UN. At the end of that year, the Presidents of Kazakhstan, Kyrgyzstan and Uzbekistan put their signatures to a Treaty of Eternal Friendship. It was agreed that Tajikistan and Russia should be granted subsidiary membership status. Tajikistan later became a full member.

In July 1998 the Central Asian Union was transformed into the Central Asian Economic Community. However, although economic issues were still ostensibly the main focus of the organization's activities, security concerns were becoming more prominent. In April 2000, at a summit meeting in Tashkent, a 100-year treaty was signed between the four member states on joint efforts to combat terrorism, extremism, transnational organised crime and other common security threats. These issues were again highlighted at the meeting of the five heads of state held in Almaty on 5 January 2001. Particular emphasis was placed on the dangers of Islamic extremism, likewise on the des-tabilising role played by the Taleban. Uzbek President Karimov used the occasion to castigate member states for the dismal record of the Central Asian Economic Union. He noted that many resolutions had been adopted, but there had been little progress in implementation. It was decided to rename the organization the Central Asian Economic Forum.

GUUAM

The acronym GUUAM designates an organization that comprises Georgia, Ukraine, Uzbekistan, Azerbaijan and Moldova. The founding members were Georgia, Ukraine, Moldova and Azerbaijan. The original intention of this alliance, first established in 1996, was to facilitate the development of a Eurasian TransCaucasus transportation corridor (TRACECA) that would bypass Russia, thereby underpinning the independence of these former Soviet countries. Other aims included the promotion of democracy and the enhancement of regional cooperation in a wide range of sectors, including commerce, financial services, security, science, education and culture. In alignment, it was very definitely pro-Western; in particular, it sought closer links with NATO.[12] The group was subsequently joined by Uzbekistan; this was formally announced on 24 April 1999, at a meeting of the five heads of state in Washington DC, on the occasion of the NATO Golden Jubilee celebrations.

Despite assurances that GUUAM was 'not aimed at any third country or group of countries', it was clearly intended as a counterbalance to Russian influence.[13] However, despite very considerable Western (more specifically, US) support and encouragement,[14] progress towards setting a policy agenda or creating viable working structures was slight. By June 2000, President Karimov was expressing open irritation at the delay in the creation of institutions. Some of the documents that were put forward for joint signature were also unacceptable to Uzbekistan.

A more fundamental problem is that there is little in terms of a genuine community of interests between Uzbekistan and fellow member states. From a regional perspective, GUUAM is firmly oriented towards the Black Sea and Central and Eastern Europe, while Uzbekistan, located much further to the east, is linked to Asia. Moreover, the organization tends to be dominated by the ambitions of its largest component, Ukraine.[15] Other member states, too, often pursue national interests, especially in their dealings with Russia, to the detriment of group solidarity, thereby calling into question the credibility of the organization. Uzbekistan is very much on the periphery of such political manoeuvrings, and is unable to play much part in shaping the outcome. When the GUUAM summit meeting planned for March 2001 failed to materialise it seemed as though the group had finally disintegrated. However, this turned out to be a temporary setback. The event was rescheduled and eventually held on 6-7 June in Yalta. The chief outcome was the signing of the Yalta GUUAM Charter defining the goals and objectives of the organization, the principles of multilateral cooperation, and the format and regularity of summit meetings.

Regional Organizations with CIS and Non-CIS Members

In the early 1990s, there was much speculation as to whether the newly independent Central Asian states would opt for an 'Iranian model' of governance (i.e. Islamic nomocracy) or a 'Turkish model' (i.e. secular democracy), and by extension, whether they would adopt a pro-Western or an anti-Western stance. However, underlying this purported political-ideological rivalry, there was also cultural competition between the Turks, who belong to the same ethno-linguistic family as the Kazakhs, Kyrgyz, Turkmen and Uzbeks, and the Iranians, who share a similar bond with the Tajiks. Yet the Central Asians proved averse to the establishment of exclusive 'special relationships' with either Turkey or Iran. Nevertheless, both these countries have developed conduits through which to exert indirect influence. Thus, Iran has fostered the Economic Cooperation Organization, while Turkey has sponsored regular Turkic Summits.

China did not immediately exhibit a desire to develop institutional links with the Central Asian states. However, by the mid-1990s it became clear that there were a number of issues that required a co-ordinated regional approach. Mechanisms that were created to deal with local concerns (e.g. border regulations) were transformed into regional structures. The establishment of the Shanghai Cooperation Organization in June 2001 provided a basis for the institutionalisation of ties between the member states.

Economic Cooperation Organization

The Economic Cooperation Organization (ECO) developed out of a series of previous regional alliances (dating back to 1955) between Iran, Pakistan, and Turkey. In 1985 it was relaunched, on the initiative of Iran, under its present designation. An intergovernmental organization, it aims to promote economic, technical and cultural cooperation among member states. The principal policy and decision-making organs are based in Tehran. In November 1992, the five Central Asian states, also Azerbaijan and Afghanistan, were admitted, bringing the total membership of the organization to ten. The institutional base was expanded and given new operational impetus. A sustained program of activities has been initiated, including projects to develop transport and communication networks; also to encourage economic, commercial, cultural and scientific cooperation. Summit meetings are convened annually in the capitals of member states and regular working sessions are held between ministers and senior civil servants. The focus is firmly economic, not political (Uzbekistan in particular has taken an unequivocal stance on this point). Lack of capital, however, has been an obstacle to the implementation of large-scale multilateral projects. Some eight regional institutions are being developed (including a Trade and Development Bank, Chamber of Commerce and Cultural Institute) but in most cases these bodies are still at the planning stage. To date, ECO's greatest success has been in facilitating bilateral contacts between member states.

Turkic Summits

Turkey is an active member of ECO, but it has also developed its own direct links with the Turkic states of the CIS (Azerbaijan, Kazakhstan, Kyrgyzstan, Turkmenistan and Uzbekistan). These include regular meetings between the heads of state of these countries. In 1992, Ankara hosted the first Turkic Summit. There was an expectation in Turkey at this time that the crumbling of the Soviet Union heralded the emergence of an integrated pan-Eurasian Turkic bloc. Many Western policy-makers shared this enthusiasm, assuming that Turkey, by virtue of its ethnic and linguistic links with the newly independent Turkic states, likewise its wealth of experience in international organizations, would be the natural leader of this grouping. Moreover, it was believed that Turkish leadership would ensure that these states adhered to a pro-Western orientation, thereby denying Russia and Iran influence in the region.

However, the results of the Ankara Summit did not live up to expectations: the Central Asian leaders were less than enthusiastic about proposals for integration, and rejected plans for such projects as the creation of a Turkic Common Market and a Turkic Development and Investment Bank. However, President Ozal's visit to Central Asia and Azerbaijan in April 1993 (undertaken shortly before his death) was deemed a success. The next Turkic Summit was held in Istanbul in October 1994; the closing 'Istanbul Declaration' reiterated the call for closer ties between the participating states.[16] Subsequent Turkic Summits were held in Bishkek, Tashkent, Astana, Baku, and most recently, Istanbul. A wide range of issues has been discussed at these meetings. Increasing emphasis, however has been placed on the need for economic cooperation (especially in the energy sector), and for joint action to combat terrorism and drug trafficking.

In his address to the Seventh Summit (Istanbul in 26-27 April 2001), Turkish President Sezer spoke of the role of these meetings in promoting bilateral and multilateral cooperation between member states by providing a high-level forum for the exchange of views. However, in the nine years since they were initiated, there has been little structural evolution. To date, the level of institutionalization is minimal. No permanent secretariat has been created, and there are no specific agencies for implementing regional projects. Moreover, the Turkic Summits do not appear to have developed mechanisms for resolving, or defusing, tensions between member states. It was noteworthy that Turkmen President Niyazov did not participate in the Sixth Summit, held 8 April 2000 in Baku, very probably on account of disagreements with Azerbaijan over the Caspian Sea. Uzbek President Karimov failed to attend either the Sixth or the Seventh Summits; there was media speculation that his absence reflected displeasure with Turkey's supposed support for Uzbek dissidents. The strengthening of ethno-linguistic ties has also not proceeded as rapidly as anticipated. Although all the participating states speak warmly of the importance of the Turkic languages, they still feel more comfortable expressing themselves in Russian.[17]

Shanghai Cooperation Organization (SCO)

The Shanghai Cooperation Organization developed out of efforts to resolve bilateral issues between China and adjacent CIS members. The first such priority was border demarcation. China shares long frontiers with Kazakhstan, Kyrgyzstan, Russia and Tajikistan; in the 1990s, several stretches of these borders were either not formally demarcated, or were regarded as disputed territory (a legacy of the 'unfair treaties' of the nineteenth century between the Tsarist empire and China). Following the collapse of the Soviet Union, China initiated moves to resolve these problems through bilateral as well as multilateral negotiations. On 26 April 1996, the five heads of state met in Shanghai to sign the 'Treaty on Deepening Military Trust in Border Regions'.

This event marked the beginning of a series of annual meetings between the leaders of the so-called 'Shanghai Five' group. Regular working meetings were also convened at ministerial level. Subsequently, broader areas of common concern were added to the original agenda. Thus, at the fourth summit meeting, held on 25 August 1999 in Bishkek, a joint declaration was signed on regional security and cooperation, with particular emphasis on practical cooperation to combat international terrorism, narcotics and arms trafficking, illegal immigration and other transnational criminal activities.

By 2000, a more political tone was becoming apparent. At a meeting of the Defence Ministers, held in Astana on 30 March 2000, objections were voiced to US plans for drawing Taiwan into the anti-ballistic missile (ABM) system. A joint communiqué stated that 'the deployment of a regional ABM system in the Asian-Pacific region may result in upsetting stability and security in the region'. The ministers stressed the need to promote nuclear non-proliferation in the area and to facilitate the enactment of the Comprehensive Test Ban Treaty. At the following meeting of the heads of state, held on 5 July 2000 in Dushanbe, there was an even clearer emphasis on political goals. The group collectively declared its support for Beijing's 'One China' policy, also for Moscow's actions in Chechnya. UN efforts for a political settlement of the Afghan conflict were likewise endorsed. The basis for cooperation between the members was clarified by the affirmation of 'each state's true right of choice of their own course of political, economic and social development in line with their realities'. Moreover, 'interference in each other's internal affairs', even on the pretext of 'humanitarian intervention' and 'human rights' was renounced. Uzbek President Karimov was present at this meeting and expressed the view that the security interests of his country coincided with those of the 'Five'; he welcomed the contribution of Russia and China to guaranteeing security in Central Asia. Subsequently, Uzbekistan, and likewise Pakistan, sought membership of the group.

The move from what was essentially an informal forum to a formal regional organization was accomplished in 2001. The Declaration on the Establishment of the Shanghai Cooperation Organization was signed at the sixth summit meeting of the group, held in Shanghai on 14 June. Uzbekistan's application for membership of the organization was approved, and President Karimov, too, became a signatory to the Declaration. Pakistan (with Kyrgyz backing) had also applied for membership, but admission was deferred. However, there were indications that an eventual enlargement of the organization, to include not only Pakistan, but other border states such as India and Mongolia, was a possibility.

The declared aims of the Shanghai Cooperation Organization (SCO) included the creation of 'a new international and political order featuring democracy, justness and rationality'. The need for multipolarity in international relations was stressed. There was reiteration of previous pronouncements regarding the upholding of the 1972 ABM Treaty, and opposition to US plans to deploy a theatre missile defence system in the Asia-Pacific region; also renewed support for UN efforts to seek a peace settlement in Afghanistan. The importance accorded to regional security was underlined by a separate Shanghai Convention on Combating Terrorism, Separatism and Extremism, also signed by the six heads of state during the June summit meeting. This document provides a legal framework for increased regional cooperation in police operations and intelligence gathering. It was confirmed that the anti-terrorism centre, discussed during the previous summit meeting, was to be located in Bishkek (see section on Security Issues below).

Conference on Cooperation and Confidence-Building Measures in Asia (CCCBMA)

An ambitious attempt to create an Asian counterpart to the OSCE was initiated by Kazakh President Nazarbayev in 1995. A loose association of 25 states, it spans the Middle East, South Asia, South East Asia and East Asia. Its aim is to promote regional stability through military and political cooperation. However, to date it has not proceeded far beyond the planning stage. Some preliminary meetings have been held, but by mid-2001 the basic principles of cooperation were still under discussion. China, Pakistan and Uzbekistan showed little enthusiasm for the organization, though there was a more positive reaction from some of the Middle Eastern countries. It was hoped that a meeting, scheduled to be held in Almaty on 8-10 November 2001 would give new impetus to the association.

Obstacles to Central Asian Integration

In the immediate aftermath of independence, the Central Asian states embraced the idea of regional integration - interpreting 'the region' as the five former Soviet republics - as a vital strategy for development and the consolidation of economic independence. This perception was strengthened by the realisation that there were many common social and environmental problems that could only be solved by concerted joint action. Moreover, regional integration was strongly supported by consultants and specialists from donor agencies. They argued that the economies of the Central Asian states, taken separately, were too small and weak to be of interest to foreign investors; only by uniting to create a larger economic space would they attract much needed investment. It was also stressed that training programs and other forms of technical assistance would have greater impact, and be more cost effective, if a regional approach was applied.[18]

However, it soon became clear that there are many obstacles to integration. Firstly, the newly independent states, acutely sensitive in matters of national sovereignty, are reluctant to cede powers of decision-making and control to multi-lateral institutions. (Only the EEC, as mentioned above, has addressed this problem and it is too soon to judge whether or not it will be.) Secondly, there are issues of national dignity and honour that impinge on attitudes to socio-economic questions. Thirdly, there is a lack of confidence in regulatory instruments; this engenders a deep sense of insecurity. These problems are exacerbated by asymmetries between the five states: they differ greatly in size of territory, population, defence capability, resource endowment, and access to arterial transit routes.[19] The smaller states - Kyrgyzstan and Tajikistan - feel vulnerable in negotiations with their larger neighbours. Rightly or wrongly, they fear that 'collective' goods will not be distributed equitably and that in cases of extreme discord, their territorial integrity will be violated.

Other factors that inhibit integration include the calibre of state officials. Many are young, with relatively little administrative experience. Those of the older generation, who worked in the Soviet bureaucracy, often find it difficult to adapt to new conditions. The result is that institutions for inter-state cooperation may be in place, but frequently they do not function effectively. Another adverse factor is the weak tradition of regional cooperation. There is little practical understanding of how to plan and manage multilateral projects. Consequently, such skills must be acquired almost from scratch.

Yet the most serious potential obstacle is the polarisation of the two larger states, Uzbekistan and Kazakhstan. The leaders of these states have adopted very different stances on regional cooperation. Kazakh President Nazarbayev has consistently advocated alignment with Russia within the framework of a Eurasian alliance. Uzbek President Karimov, meanwhile, has emphatically distanced himself from Russia. However, it is not clear whether this posture is motivated by strategic considerations or whether it is an attempt to bolster personal authority and reputation. His criticisms of the various regional organizations (whether or not Uzbekistan is a member) have been both public and forthright. Some such complaints are certainly justified, but the manner in which they are delivered is often provocative and belligerent, revealing little desire for constructive engagement in any form.[20] By contrast, Kazakhstan has pursued a more measured and consistent approach, working steadily towards establishing itself as the central pole of attraction. Undoubtedly this internal dissension weakens prospects for Central Asian integration. To date, Tajikistan and Kyrgyzstan have avoided taking sides and thereby prevented further fragmentation. However, under pressure, the situation could well deteriorate, resulting in serious regional rifts.

Security Issues

In the early 1990s, regional alliances in Central Asia were regarded primarily as a means to achieving economic development. However, as local conflicts became increasingly violent, it was clear that without stability and security there could be no genuine regional cooperation. There was a frightening rise not only in outright fighting, but also in conflict-related problems, such as the mass movement of refugees; trafficking in drugs and arms; and extra-territorial support for rebel groups. This in turn fostered an upsurge in terrorist attacks, often linked to extremist Islamic slogans and/or separatist movements.

Contrary to many predictions, the civil war in Tajikistan (1992-97) did not trigger a 'domino effect' of conflict throughout Central Asia.[21] However, there was a spillover effect of lawlessness and violence that continued long after the signing of the peace agreement. In 1995-96, the rise to power of the Taleban, a militant and ultra-conservative Islamist group, in neighbouring Afghanistan added to the volatility of the situation. Transborder criminal cooperation intensified. The smuggling of drugs and arms increased dramatically. So, too, did the flows of refugees, with all the attendant social and economic costs. At the end of the decade, a long and severe drought caused further problems. Throughout the region, consecutive years of poor harvests intensified popular discontent and anger. This, too, prompted uncontrolled population movements, particularly from Afghanistan into neighbouring countries.

With the deterioration of socio-economic conditions, militant Islamist groups, propagating an uncompromisingly anti-government agenda, have become more active in the Central Asian states.

Allegedly, they are linked to organised crime and are responsible for acts of terrorism. Uzbekistan has been the main target for such activities, but Kyrgyzstan and Tajikistan, too, have suffered heavy insurgencies. Separatist ethnic movements, particularly of Uighurs in Xinjiang, have also been linked to criminal incidents. Official sources insist that they receive assistance from expatriate groups, particularly from transborder communities of the same ethnic origin.

In this highly unstable environment Central Asian governments have become increasingly concerned about regional security. At the same time, there are markedly different threat perceptions. There are suspicions in some quarters that security threats are to some extent being exaggerated in order to legitimise external interference and aggression. Uzbek officials have laid such claims against Russia, but equally, Kyrgyz and Tajiks have voiced similar fears about Uzbekistan. Such actions as Uzbek aerial attacks on Kyrgyz and Tajik villages, and the mining of border areas, supposedly undertaken in self-defence, have been viewed with extreme nervousness by the neighbouring states. There are fears that this is but the start of more concerted attempts to gain territorial control of border regions.

Nevertheless, given the transnational nature of the primary security threats - drug smuggling, militant religious extremism, and separatism - there is a consensus that such problems can only be addressed within a regional framework. Regional alliances not only multiply resources, but also, for the smaller states, they diminish the threat of an abuse of power by the larger states. As indicated above, 'the region' can be defined in a narrow sense, comprising the five Central Asian states, or more widely to include some, or all, of the neighbouring states. Hierarchies of size, and thus of vulnerability, depend on the configuration of this definition. Thus, in the context of the narrow Central Asian region, Tajikistan and Kyrgyzstan are (or share the perception of being exposed to pressure from Uzbekistan. In a wider context, the 'core' states have similar concerns about Russia and China.

Three of the Central Asian states have recently joined two separate, but overlapping, regional security organizations: the SCO anti-terrorist centre (China, Russia, Kazakhstan, Kyrgyzstan, Tajikstan and Uzbekistan) and the CIS anti-terrorist centre (Russia, Kazakhstan, Kyrgyzstan and Tajikstan).[23] Both are to be based in Bishkek. How these two bodies are to interact, either on a political or on an operational level is not clear. Yet there are a number of potential advantages. Firstly, this duplication is in itself a means of containing and balancing the influence of China and Russia. Secondly, it reduces the possibility of one of the 'core' Central Asian states forging an intra-organizational axis with one of the larger powers and thereby gaining a tactical advantage over its neighbours. Thirdly, it raises the possibility of competition between the larger states in providing resources, which could very well be turned to the advantage of the smaller states.

Conclusions

The Central Asian states are still very young. The regional organizations discussed above are also very new. They were created in haste, against a background of political upheaval and rapid social and economic change. Not surprisingly, there was initially little real understanding of the complexity and magnitude of the tasks that lay ahead. Aspirations far outstripped capabilities; consequently declarations of intent rarely coincided with actual performance, resulting in a lack of credibility. Structurally, these bodies are still in flux. They have scarcely had time to consolidate. In most cases, membership has changed; so, too, has internal organization. Aims and objectives have likewise altered, often in response to emerging crises. Levels of activity are also subject to fluctuation (GUUAM, for example, appeared to be moribund in March 2001, but a few months later underwent a vigorous revival). Given these uncertainties, it is impossible to pass definitive judgements on any of the bodies under review. However, some general points can be made.

Firstly, it is always difficult to create effective multilateral organizations. Even when conditions are favourable, progress can be slow (as the history of a body such as the European Union has amply demonstrated). In the developing world, the problems of cooperation are greatly magnified. The experience of the Central Asian states in this respect is reminiscent of the post-colonial world of the 1960s and 1970s. In Asia, as in Africa (and indeed, Latin America), regional organizations encountered very similar difficulties. Thus, plans for economic integration were often derailed by threats to security; disparities in size and resources created tensions between neighbours, causing smaller states to seek external protection (including from the former colonial power); natural disasters triggered social instability; overlapping alliances proliferated. Specific case studies may differ, but the one clear lesson that emerges from these different parts of the globe is that regional structures cannot be created overnight. There must be a genuine convergence of aims, and a critical degree of complementarity. There must also be stability, adequate levels of development and the necessary human and material resources. It is by no means certain that these conditions are yet to be found in Central Asia.

Secondly, the Central Asian states are facing new and unconventional threats. The chief 'enemy' is not an identifiable external aggressor, whose capabilities can be calculated, but a combination of internal opposition and indeterminate transnational networks. Criminal activities blur into ideological struggles. 'Insider' and 'outsider' perceptions of the nature and severity of security threats are frequently at variance. This ambiguity readily gives rise to suspicions of bad faith and political manipulation. Distrust is further fuelled by a historic legacy of fear of neighbouring powers. It will require very considerable political will to overcome these obstacles. There are no existing models for creating effective structures for collective security in these conditions. Thus, the Central Asian states must find new mechanisms for cooperation.

Thirdly (and again as in other parts of the developing world), external rivalries are being projected on to the region. By contrast with the Cold War period, however, the actual level of competition between the major powers has been very much lower than media rhetoric suggests. In the political arena, the West (the US, and to a somewhat lesser degree, the European Union) has tried to promote democratic reform and respect for human rights. Yet the impact has been negligible, with Central Asian governments paying little more than lip service to these values. The primary focus of Russian interest in the region has been the reconstruction of a common economic space - an aim that coincides with the Eurasian vision of the Kazakh leadership. The anticipated struggle for control of Central Asia's natural resources has not materialised; such factors as the high costs of exploitation and transportation, as well as a hostile business culture, have inhibited Western investment. China's involvement in Central Asia was initially low key, directed mainly towards issues of bilateral cooperation.

This situation changed with the founding of the SCO in June 2001. China has now explicitly stated its intention to create a political bloc that will challenge Western (specifically US) ascendancy in world affairs. This development has generated a torrent of speculation.[24] With regard to Central Asia, there has been much discussion as to whether, or why, the West has 'lost' the region. Yet it will take far more than a declaration, however belligerent, to influence the orientation of the Central Asian states. The crucial factor will be the degree of support - financial and technical - that any external sponsor is able to provide. China's capabilities in this respect are still very limited.

The above comments indicate that regional cooperation in Central Asia will not be easy to achieve. This is not, however, entirely owing to internal obstacles. The larger external players have not set a good example. Actors within as well as without the region are in general agreement on several common concerns: the need for economic development, and also the need to combat the major security threats, namely drug trafficking and terrorism. There is likewise agreement that Afghanistan is the fulcrum of regional instability and that a peaceful resolution of the situation there is of vital importance. Yet rather than combining forces to address these problems, each donor/sponsor country (or bloc of countries) has sought to establish its own sphere of influence. Regional cooperation is lauded, but only acceptable if it is 'under our aegis'. This partiality casts doubt on the sincerity of these external advocates for cooperation. It is difficult, therefore, for Central Asians to take their advice seriously. Genuine commitment to regional cooperation will very likely only be possible when the Central Asian states are themselves strong enough and mature enough to understand and accept the full costs and benefits of integration.

Figure 1: Regional Groupings - CIS Members

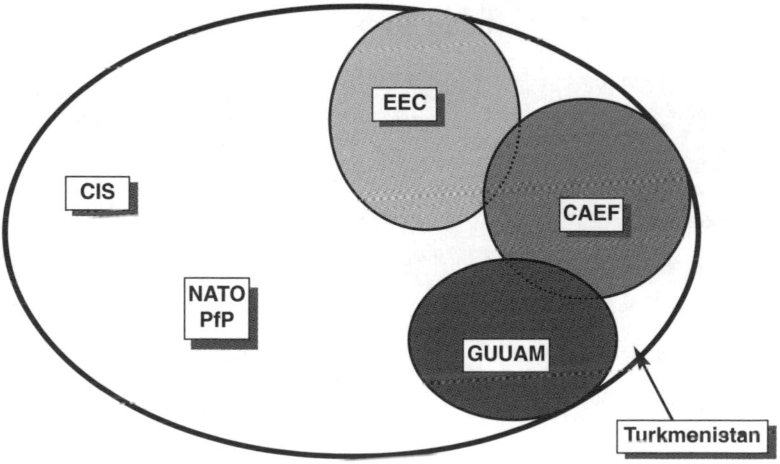

205

Figure 2 : Regional Groupings - CIS and Non-CIS Members

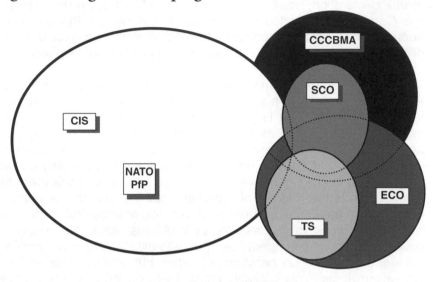

Note : Abbreviations of Regional Organisations

CAEF	Central Asian Economic Forum
CCCBMA	Conference on Cooperation and Confidence-Building Measures in Asia
ECO	Economic Cooperation Organisation
EEC	Eurasian Economic Community
SCO	Shanghai Cooperation Organisation

Table 1 : Selected Data

	Area (sq.km.)	Population (2001 estimate)	Per Capita GNP at PPP in US$ (World Bank 1999)	Per Capita GNP in US$ at official/ market exchange rate (2000)
Kazakhstan	2,717,300	15,000,000	4,408	1,225
Kyrgyzstan	198,500	5,100,000	2,223	275
Tajikistan	143,100	6,600,000	981	158
Turkmenistan	448,100	5,100,000	3,099	415
Uzbekistan	447,400	25,700,000	2,092	298

1. Generations of scholars have grappled, unsuccessfully, to define this term. See further S. Akiner, 'Conceptual Geographies of Central Asia', Sustainable Development in Central Asia (eds S. Akiner, Sander Tideman and Jon Hay), Curzon Press, Richmond, 1998, pp. 3-62.

2. In colloquial international usage these new countries were soon dubbed 'the Stans'.

3. The nomads were predominantly Kazakhs and Kyrgyz. They were forcibly sedentarised in 1930.

4. Diplomatic training was also provided as part of post-Soviet technical assistance programs by donor countries, for example, by the Netherlands, Sweden, Turkey, and the UK.

5. Kyrgyzstan, Tajikistan and Turkmenistan in 1992, Kazakshtan in 1995 and Uzbekistan in 1996.

6. Uzbekistan in 1992, Turkmenistan in 1995.

7. Formally acknowledged by a resolution of the UN General Assembly passed in December 1995.

8. At a summit meeting of the leaders of the ex-Soviet republics, convened by Kazakh President Nazarbayev in Almaty on 21 December 1991.

9. He has described it as 'an initiative to distract people's attention, an attempt on the part of some CIS leaders to claim the laurels of integrationists' (Respublika, no. 22 (89), 7 June 2001, p. 13).

10. Russia is also responsible for 40 per cent of costs of the organization.

11. But Russia does retain the right to exercise a veto on major issues.

12. The document of incorporation stressed that GUUAM would operate within the framework of international organizations such as the Euro-Atlantic Partnership Council and the NATO Partnership for Peace programme.

13. See, for example, T. Valasek, Military Cooperation between Georgia, Ukraine, Uzbekistan Azerbaijan and Moldova in the GUUAM Framework, Cambridge MA, Caspian Studies Program, December 2000.

14. The official GUUAM website (http://www.guuam.org) gives an overview of the extraordinary level of activity that has been generated around this organization. The volume of conferences, media statements and publications could surely not have been maintained without a very high degree of financial and technical support from Western sources.

15. See further Oleksandr Pavliuk, Ukraine's Regional Politics: the Case of GUUAM (presentation delivered at Kennan Institute, 12 February 2001).

16. A good account of Turkish initiatives in Central Asia in the early 1990s is provided by Gareth Winrow, Turkey in Post-Soviet Central Asia, Royal Institute of International Affairs, London, 1995.

17. At the Seventh Summit, for example, the Uzbek representative, Parliamentary Speaker Erkin Halilov, and Kyrgyz President Akayev both addressed the assembly in Russian.

18. It is not only in Central Asia that regionalism is the preferred strategy. Cf the report Central America 2020, commissioned by the European Union and USAID, which advances very similar arguments with regard to the Central American states (The Economist, 11-17 August, 2001, pp. 44-45).

19. See appendix for basic data on the Central Asian states.

20. Thus, for example, within hours of signing up to membership of SCO, President Karimov was stating reservations regarding Uzbek participation. He also stressed the need "to rely on our own strength and power". Interview to Uzbek TV First Channel, reported, partially verbatim, in Turkestan Newsletter, 18 June 2001.

21. For a discussion of the causes of the Tajik war and prospects for peace, see S. Akiner, Tajikistan: Disintegration or Reconciliation? Royal Institute of International Affairs, London 2001.

22. The Central Asian leaders have repeatedly called for renewed international efforts to resolve the Afghan crisis. Most recently, Kazakh President Nazarbayev raised this issue at the inaugural meeting of the Shanghai Cooperation Organization (June 2001).

23. The CIS body is linked to the CIS Joint Programme to Combat International Terrorism and Extremism. Formally entitled the CIS Collective Rapid Reaction Forces, it came into being officially on 1 August 2001. It is to consist of a battalion each from the four member states.

24. Media coverage in the Asia-Pacific region has been especially lively. See, for example, articles in the Times of India, the Straits Times (Singapore) , the Age (Melbourne), in June-July 2001.

PROSPECTS AND PROBLEMS OF CASPIAN REGIONAL SECURITY, STABILITY AND COOPERATION - A PERSPECTIVE FROM AZERBAIJAN

Altai Efendiev

Head, Department of Development and Economic Cooperation, Ministry of Foreign Affairs, Azerbaijan

The purpose of this paper is to reflect on current developments in the region and to share some views and ideas on the most complex issues from the point of view of future security and cooperation developments in the Caspian region. For the sake of clarity, in our analysis the Caspian region embraces all littoral states, e.g. Azerbaijan, Iran, Kazakhstan, Russia and Turkmenistan as well as the broader adjacent territories of Central Asia and South Caucasus.

New Regional Context: Opportunities and Threats

A decade has passed since the dissolution of the USSR, the collapse of the socialist block and consequently the end of global confrontation. New geopolitical realities have appeared in the Caspian region and nine new states have emerged on the political arena: the Russian Federation, Uzbekistan, Kazakhstan, Azerbaijan, Tadjikistan, Turkmenistan, Georgia, Kyrghyzstan and Armenia. It is needless to mention that each country views its own place and role in the world community and in particular in the region differently, has its own interests and tries to pursue them in its own very specific way. Iran and Turkey, due to their geographical proximity to the region as well as historical and ethnic connections to the Caucasus and Central Asia, will also be among the major players influencing developments in the region. Perhaps the interests of big regional powers like Russia, Turkey and Iran will dominate over that of the smaller states. However, matching and shaping a new balance of interests between these states reflecting new realities will be one of the most important tasks facing the future security and cooperation architecture of the region.

There are also other important and significant geopolitical factors that should be taken into consideration when addressing issues of security, stability and cooperation in the region:

• it is located on the strategically important crossroads between West and East and is a natural shortcut between two global economic power centres - Europe and Asia;

• it is vast and rich in natural resources, especially energy, which could serve as a solid basis for fast economic and social development for all the countries and the region as a whole. The resources of the region are of global significance in terms of their reserves and possible contribution to world economic development. These resources can be developed (economically, technically and environmentally) at this crucial historical stage only with massive external assistance. As the countries of the region declare their openness and need for foreign investments and expertise, this has led to competition between the world's major centres for access to the wealth of the region and control over its supplies;

• it is a nexus region for the world's major religions and cultures. Undoubtedly, the competition for ideological influence will play a significant role in shaping societies and have an impact on their development policies.

The above-mentioned has led to new balance of interests in the region with greater international involvement. The Caspian Sea region could also be characterised by it's inherent internal problems:

• practically all the newly independent countries of the region are at the beginning of their transition to democratic societies. So far the process in all the countries has proved not to be smooth but painful and the introduction and establishment of new democratic institutions and the shaping of new societies has a long way to go. Societies are still fragile and volatile, as they are very sensitive and vulnerable to influences from outside. None of the countries of the region could be considered as developed. This factor, as well as the deep economic and social crisis, has inspired centrifugal tendencies in practically all societies. Separatism, terrorism and organised crime in their extreme forms are common throughout the region. To a large extent these tendencies could hypothetically be manipulated from outside the countries;

• stocks of conventional and nuclear armaments are large with no proper mechanisms of control. Their proliferation among Caspian states could be a potential threat to regional stability and security with serious international repercussions;

210

• the foreign military presence in certain smaller countries not only distorts the balance of the region but encourages the formation of new military strategic axes and dividing lines, which is detrimental to such regions as the South Caucasus.

These and other factors make the Caspian region on the one hand highly attractive, but volatile and dangerous on the other. Consequently, events in the region could affect international developments in different ways.

It is clear from the above that security and stability in the Caspian have national, regional and broader international dimensions. Thus have new geopolitical realities created a new international agenda for resolving the complicated political and economic problems of the region, which can be addressed only through coordinated international efforts. Of utmost importance are:

• the preservation of independence, sovereignty and territorial integrity of the newly independent states, thus creating a favourable international environment for the strengthening of their statehood;

• creating international mechanisms to insure political stability and democratic developments inside these countries;

• the peaceful resolution of all military and ethnic conflicts throughout the region on the basis of international law;

• the establishment and development of peaceful bilateral relations and mutually beneficial cooperation between the countries of the region on the basis of internationally acknowledged norms and principles;

• a resolution of Caspian Sea issues relating to the development of a diversified pipeline infrastructure for the export of hydrocarbons;

• the development of a new regional and inter-regional infrastructure that will facilitate closer and better balanced economic integration and political cooperation between the countries of the region whilst also harmoniously integrating them into the world community.

Azerbaijan in the New Regional Context

The Republic of Azerbaijan will soon celebrate its 10th Anniversary. Since independence, this country of 8 million people and 86,600 sq. km of territory experienced probably the most dramatic period in its history. Its development, the strengthening of its statehood, protecting its sovereignty, its territorial integrity and indeed its right to exist, have been under threat. Hardly any NIS has such a record of political upheaval and attempted coups d'etat in the early years of independence. Azerbaijan has been plunged into a most severe and protracted war with neighbouring Armenia. There have also been numerous regional conflicts leading to an almost complete blockade for several years of the major land transportation routes that connected the country with the outer world. Azerbaijan also resisted enormous pressures when it made important decisions on the development of its oil resources and in choosing its partners. It should also be taken into account that Azerbaijan was the only state among the NIS who entered its independence era with no foreign military bases on its territory.

For centuries, due to its advantageous geographical location on the crossroads of continents, Azerbaijan has been the object of conquests as well as attracting merchants, travellers and pilgrims. All major trade routes between West and East passed through its territory, leaving tangible and intangible imprints on the environment, society and individuals. This is reflected in the open, tolerant and friendly character of the people who have inherited the free spirit of entrepreneurship while preserving strong feelings of independence. Openness and the ability to absorb and accommodate new and progressive ideas enabled them to develop an identity characterised by the unique synthesis of real yet different national, religious and cultural values.

Nowadays, independent Azerbaijan is embarked on the route of market-oriented and democratic reforms as well as integration into European and wider international communities. The principles of republicanism, political and economic pluralism, democracy, secularism and openness have been endorsed in the New Constitution by the 1995 Referendum.

Azerbaijan's geographical location, rich natural resources and other comparative advantages offer vast opportunities for economic development and cooperation. Since 1996 the country is enjoying dynamic economic development with average yearly growth rates at

9-10%, with inflation rates subdued at the level of 2-3%. During this period, Azerbaijan managed to attract over US$6bn of FDI. Measured per capita, this is the highest indicator among the CIS and some Central European countries. According to international experts, Azerbaijan has the most promising prospects for dynamic growth among countries of the former Soviet Union and Eastern Europe.

The nation is now entering a new phase of radical administrative and structural reforms, including a large-scale privatisation program, improving standards of public services, ensuring good-governance practices, developing strategies for poverty eradication as well as combating corruption and organised crime. These measures have been undertaken to ensure sustainable social and economic development as well as to enhance the national capacity to address challenges of security and stability. Azerbaijan closely cooperates on the above issues with its major partners and international organisations such as the EU, OSCE, IMF, WB, Council of Europe, and the major industrialised democracies.

To ensure internal reforms and sustainable development, a stable and friendly external environment is of crucial importance to the country. Of vital interest for Azerbaijan is to establish and develop confidence, trust, and good-neighbourly relations in the region and then building on this to create a new security and cooperation architecture in the Caucasus and the Caspian. However, there are major problems and obstacles requiring fair and speedy resolution for the sake of national and regional development. These are Armenia's occupation of part of the territory of Azerbaijan, other ethnic conflicts in the region, the status of the Caspian Sea and the export of energy resources.

The Caspian Sea Region Should be a Zone of Peace, Stability and Cooperation

It is difficult to overestimate the significance of the Caspian Sea for the nations surrounding it. For centuries it played a very important role in their lives and it is just as important now. Therefore, issues arising out of its development and resources are extremely sensitive for all the countries to the extent that it is impossible to address them without a fair and sound consideration of the interests of every state and of the problems facing the Caspian Sea itself.

Given the location and importance of the Caspian Sea, it has for Centuries been an object of struggle for dominance mainly between Russia and Persia. For the last two Centuries it was under practically full Russian and then Soviet control.

Defining new principles and rules of exploitation of the Caspian and preserving the Sea for future generations whilst also reflecting new geopolitical realities in the region are vital for the littoral states. A fair and sound status for the Caspian based on existing practices, international law and experience, which also reflects the interests and responsibilities of the littoral states, will prevent potential tension and conflicts in the future, and lay down a basis for stability, peace and cooperation in the whole region.

After proclaiming independence, Azerbaijan extended its sovereignty over its territory within the existed administrative borders, including the sea sector, which has been internationally recognised. Azerbaijan has pioneered wider international cooperation in the Caspian, however, this does not mean that the interests of the littoral states as well as all other aspects of the Caspian Sea have been ignored. To develop energy resources in its sector of the Caspian, Azerbaijan has invited all major players in the world, including Russian and Iranian companies. So far Azerbaijan has signed 21 production-sharing agreements worth about US$60bn with the participation of oil companies from over 14 countries (USA, UK, Norway, France, Italy, Japan, Germany, Russia, Turkey, Iran, Saudi Arabia and others). New contracts are awaiting their signing ceremonies. We truly believe that a unique opportunity for international cooperation in the resolution of Caspian issues has been created in the region. Wider international involvement in the exploration and development of the Caspian resources and, subsequently, a new balance of interests in Azerbaijan and in the Caspian region in general, are conducive to the stabilisation and development of the country and the region as a whole. This is also a prerequisite for the transformation from the monocentrism in the region and divide and rule policies of the colonial past - to the establishment of civilised relationship of partnerships and cooperation.

Recent years have seen a gradual but significant evolution in the stance of the littoral states towards the sectoral division of the Caspian Sea. A number of bilateral documents have been signed between the littoral states. This is very encouraging indeed. At the same time it is obvious that creating a fair and sound mechanism between littoral states able and capable to address and resolve the profound and acute problems of the Caspian Sea is a long-term perspective. But what is of crucial importance now is that the design and objectives of such a mechanism should be based on the new realities around the Caspian. Demilitarisation of the Sea and the establishment of an atmosphere of confidence and trust, along with cooperation and the delegation of strict responsibility to each state for their respective sectors is essential. Moreover, efficient international control over issues of environmental security and preservation of the unique biological resources should be among main considerations. Ultimately, the Caspian Sea should serve peace, stability and cooperation in the region.

Pipelines and Other Inter-Regional Infrastructure

As the Caspian Sea is landlocked and has no natural outlets, intensive development of its rich energy resources is not possible without proper regional pipeline infrastructure to enable safe and secure export of oil and gas to the international markets.

Proper resolution of this strategic issue could bring about important changes to the geopolitical landscape of the region in terms of its unlocking and integrating into the regional and world economy. The recent experiences of Azerbaijan as well as of other NIS of the Caspian Sea are vivid examples of the vulnerability of states in this respect. Therefore, for the NIS this issue is also a matter of strengthening sovereignty and independence.

Since 1997, two alternative export routes have been put into operation to export the lower volumes of so-called early oil (5-7 million tons a year) from Azerbaijan's offshore fields to international markets. As Azerbaijan enters into the phase of intensive exploration and exploitation of its energy resources, resolution of the export routes has been brought to the top of the international agenda. Agreement on the Baku-Tbilisi-Ceyhan main export pipeline has been signed and ratified by the Parliaments of Azerbaijan, Georgia and Turkey. This project is also enjoying political support from the US Administration. Basic engineering works to assess financial, technical, security and environmental aspects have been completed with detailed studies to be started soon.

Given the enormous energy potential of the Caspian, a number of other pipeline options are under consideration for future export routes as well. Pipelines from Burgas to the Greek port of Alexandropoulos, from Constanca to the Adriatic Sea, and from the Ukrainian port of Odessa to Central Europe are among the options put forward for consideration by groups of countries and companies. To the east, a pipeline route to the Indian Ocean and another to China are also being promoted by some companies involved in developments in Caspian countries. The Persian Gulf alternative through the territory of Iran is also quite an attractive option as it looks to be the most economical one. Practically all these destinations have different interim alternative routes. Other suggestions can be expected.

Different countries of the region are competing to have pipelines through their territory. However, a collision of interests between the big players should not overshadow the vital interests of the NIS. It is quite important for the young Caspian states to ensure safe and secure access of their resources to the world markets. For this reason regional pipeline infrastructure should be diversified and independent of any one particular route. There should also be international guarantees that control over any pipeline will not be used as an instrument of political leverage. Whatever future decisions over pipeline infrastructure are, solid and viable solutions to the export route conundrum will be key elements of the future security and cooperation architecture of the region.

Among other important inter-regional infrastructural projects is TRACECA, a proposed transport corridor linking Europe-Caucasus and Central Asia. Implementation of this multibillion dollar project will provide a direct and independent link between as well as ensuring closer integration of the countries of these regions with Europe. This project could be described as the restoration of the historic Great Silk Road.

Regional Cooperation as a Response to Local and Global Challenges

After the dissolution of the USSR, countries of the region have been engaged in the creation of different regional groupings in order to integrate their transition efforts and to help realise their full potential. Cooperation should allow them to face new challenges as well as to shape the new economic architecture. At least four international economic organisations have been established or expanded and regional initiatives have been developed over the last decade:

• Commonwealth of Independent States (CIS), uniting all former Soviet republics except the Baltic states with the purpose of restoring economic links and developing cooperation, but on a rational economic footing.

• Black Sea Economic Cooperation (BSEC), initiated in the late 1980s under the then Soviet regime has developed into a full-fledged organisation. BSEC stretches from the Mediterranean and the Balkans to the Caspian Sea and at present includes 11 member states with others having observer status.

• Economic Cooperation Organisation (ECO) previously existed with Turkey, Iran and Pakistan as founding members, but is now undergoing a revival with new members - Azerbaijan, Kazakhstan, Kyrghyzstan, Tajikistan, Turkmenistan, Uzbekistan and, remarkably, also Afghanistan.

• GUUAM, uniting Georgia, Ukraine, Uzbekistan, Azerbaijan and Moldova.

• Summits between the Turkic states of Turkey, Azerbaijan, Kazakhstan, Uzbekistan, Turkmenistan and Kyrghyzstan can also be mentioned as a new regional initiative.

All these regional organisations and initiatives are going through their very initial stages of formation, design of organisational structures, defining goals, and determining areas and forms of cooperation. It is too early to speak about their efficiency as these regional structures have yet to prove their viability. It is true that these organisations have different geographical dimensions, and varying economic and political goals. Controversies abound. Nevertheless, Azerbaijan is participating in all of them in the spirit of openness and goodwill, aspiring for mutually beneficial cooperation. One thing that is clear is that dialogue and cooperation within these organisations will be conducive to the establishment of better understanding, confidence and cooperation among member states and play a definite role in the shaping of the future security and cooperation architecture for the region as a whole.

Conclusions

Above I have attempted to draw a diverse and complicated new regional context around the Caspian Sea region which, due to its important location, natural resources and economic potential, will affect in one or another way developments not only in this vast region but far beyond its own frontiers. New realities have on the one hand opened up very good prospects and opportunities for cooperation and the integration of the region into the international community, but on the other, have revealed problems that hamper the process of democratic reforms in the countries of transition, as well as the development of regional cooperation.

The region can be compared with a very dynamic, complex and vulnerable living organism, heavily depended on its environment. The countries in the region are in disarray, overburdened by internal and regional problems, are unable and incapable of effectively addressing and resolving the whole range of the problems they face. In this regard, the international community should perhaps have shared responsibility for their future. The NIS of the region are members and active participants in many international and in particular European political and economic organisations, such as the EU, OSCE, NATO, and COE. This reflects not only their desire to be an integral part of the European peace, security and cooperation architecture, but also their expectations for a more active and constructive role of these institutions in shaping the Caspian region in the new Millennium.

Major international institutions and organisations as well as the industrialised democracies are major donors and investors in the region. It is of crucial importance that, in cooperating with the countries of the region, they use all available means and leverage to endorse and even force compliance with internationally recognised norms and principles in developing relations and cooperation. This is of crucial importance for the development of the wider European security, stability and cooperation architecture in the New Millennium.

SOME ASPECTS OF FOREIGN POLICY IN ARMENIA: AN ARMENIAN VIEW OF REGIONAL ECONOMIC COOPERATION AS A PREREQUISITE FOR THE ESTABLISHMENT OF A STABLE AND SECURE ENVIRONMENT IN THE CAUCASUS

Vladimir Karapetian

Head of Defence Cooperation Division of the Ministry of Foreign Affairs, Armenia

The foreign policy of Armenia has always emphasised and still puts much emphasis upon our immediate environment and regional problems with a view to maintaining stability and long lasting peace. Today, peace in the region is the only guarantee for security and economic development for the Caucasian countries. In this respect, our regional diplomacy is aimed towards spreading and establishing human rights and democracy, supporting regional organisations to becoming prosperous.

Nowadays we, both as a country and the region as a whole, are trying to adjust to the multiple stresses of post Soviet economic, cultural and political transformation. Clearly these problems can strain relations as much within states as between them. Armenia does not see either itself or the region as being permanently condemned to marginalisation, but rather it believes that close cooperation in the region, whether political, economic or security-based, will help to bring lasting stability and prosperity based on a sense of solid and shared emergent values.

The peoples of the Caucasus stand to further benefit if today we reject the polarised labels and definitions of our recent past, and instead embrace the complex interrelationships that are both necessary and possible in the future. Armenia continues to abide by a policy of complementarity, conducting even-handed relations with all countries which have political or economic interests in the Caucasus.

This approach has worked quite effectively over the last several years, as evidenced by a recent chart in the Economist which lists

Armenia's three main allies as Russia, the US and Iran. We believe that this policy has benefited not just Armenia but has also contributed to the reduction of polarisation and tension in the region. We must hope that our neighbours, too, will modify their positions to take advantage of such a policy of inclusion. Five decades of European integration have demonstrated that it is possible to build alliances and mechanisms for cooperation among countries with long-standing friction dividing them.

In creating an atmosphere of mutual confidence, economic factors can in our opinion have a uniting role. This we can obtain only through economic integration. Economic cooperation will support the ongoing process of problem solving and stability enhancement throughout the region. The international community's support in such undertakings is very important for us.

In this context, an observation of successful developments in the Baltic region is very useful. Of course, it is necessary to make a distinction between our two regions, which are comprised of different countries, have different neighbours, and which present a different degree of regional compatibility, not to mention history and religion. At the same time, the results of regional cooperation that we can see in the Baltic states - which were able to transcend differences and various perceptions within their countries - could be very instructive for our countries as well.

It is well known that the region is of much interest as regards economic potential. Both the hydrocarbon resources and the present army of highly qualified specialists are riches of the region. Also the geographic position of the region as an important crossroads is of much interest. Our markets, undoubtedly, would be more attractive for big business if the region were economically integrated. The political elite of the region is coming to this understanding in a slow and gradual way. Equality and mutually profitable cooperation based on the principle of free markets is very important for us. Armenia also cooperates with relevant international organisations proving in practice its adherence to this principle.

Cooperation within the framework of regional economic initiatives such as INOGATE and TRACECA is essential. Armenia is sincerely open to such cooperation, although we have to state with regret that the blockades imposed on Armenia are a serious obstacle to such cooperation. It is obvious that the region's high potential cannot be fully utilised if attempts are made to isolate one of its constituents. Such attempts will adversely affect all economies in the region.

Black Sea Economic Cooperation is another mechanism that could contribute to the region's economic development. The activities of the established Black Sea Trade and Development Bank will considerably contribute to the projects elaborated by the member states of the Black Sea Economic Cooperation. In this regard Armenia fully supports the granting of an Observer Status in the UN General Assembly to the Organisation of the BSEC.

Special meaning is given to regional cooperation within the framework of the Commonwealth of Independent States. It is both shared cultural and spiritual values and a determination to preserve and develop valuable economic integration, which has created the necessary conditions for developing economic cooperation within the CIS. We believe that establishment of a free economic zone within the CIS will help Armenia to ease it's economic difficulties during this time of transition.

Armenia is determined to further develop our successful trilateral cooperation with Greece and Iran. We attach special significance to cooperation in the energy sector. It is well known that Iran is a major producer of oil and gas. And through creation of the necessary mechanisms, we can turn this collaboration into mutually beneficial cooperation. One area where we have made progress is with the construction of the Iran-Armenia gas pipeline, which will, if completed, give new meaning and dimension to this cooperation. Here I would like to highlight the very active participation of the Greek side in the accomplishment of the pre-feasibility study of this project. With welcome assistance from the EU, construction of this pipeline will serve as an important catalyst towards regional economic integration.

Of course, this trilateral cooperation is not limited by collaboration in the energy sector. There are also important agreements linked to the Committee on Transportation and Communication. For Armenia, it is very important that transit freight be freely transported across our three countries and the trilateral corresponding agreement signed recently is very significant in this respect.

Now that Armenia has integrated into all possible organs of regional and economic cooperation, and considering that our region is situated on the intersection of Europe-Central Asia and Russia-Middle

East, a long lasting stability, the unification of interests and their integration in the region takes on a new meaning and importance. But at the moment, our region remains fragmented and lacks universal stability and security mechanisms. Without a solution to these regional antagonisms, there will be no peace or stability.

The reality of regional issues as discussed above suggests some universal principles of regional cooperation, which are presented as follows:

• The projects and programs of regional cooperation should be agreed and implemented not after regional conflicts are resolved but simultaneously with the political resolution process, assuming that there is already a stable cease-fire. It is a question of the synchronisation of political, security and economic dialogues;

• Economic cooperation must not be limited to energy or any other single issue. Nor should oil or gas pipelines become a dominant factor in political talks. A natural resource should not be politicised and used to get a better deal at the negotiation table;

• The security dimension in regional cooperation should not be overlooked or underestimated. A broad security dialogue among parties to the conflict should be essential to any general strategy of cooperation. This dialogue might also include economic and legal elements, such as energy issues, customs regulation, tax policies, joint environmental projects, the fight against terrorism and organised crime, joint anti-corruption campaigns, and joint efforts to stop drug-trafficking and money-laundering. Once a military conflict is over, and given the good will of the parties and mediators involved, all these fields of regional cooperation can be activated. These are more than just concrete confidence building measures but real action that can bear tangible fruit before political conflicts are comprehensively resolved.

• Any model of regional cooperation for countries in a post-military or political conflict situation should take into serious consideration not only the interests of the countries concerned, but also the vital interests of their influential neighbours. In the case of the South Caucasus, this means Russia, Iran, Turkey, and the supra-regional neighbour of the US. If the interests of any of these are neglected or overlooked, this could lead to grave consequences. Unfortunately there are many initiatives for the South Caucasus, Central Asia and

Black Sea countries which ignore this political reality. The Silk Road Act, supported by Georgia, Azerbaijan and the five Central Asian States (although Turkmenistan has a few reservations), though well-intentioned, almost completely leaves out the interests of Russia and Iran, whilst also ignoring some of Armenia's legitimate concerns. It is worth noting that the Silk Sat, a more targeted and simple whilst less ambitious and politicised initiative, causes almost no problems at all and finds a much better response among each and every participant of this project.

• The social sphere is almost always left out when discussions on regional cooperation take place. Democracy-building processes, respect for human rights, and reform of legal infrastructures in all countries previously engaged in regional conflicts - and now moving towards regional cooperation - should be harmonised and synchronised to a consistent level in each of the countries concerned. Discrepancy and discord in this field, which currently exists in many troubled regions undergoing transition, is often overlooked and underrated.

• Along with three-way cooperation (economic; political and security; legal and democracy-building) there should among the parties to regional conflict be launched, immediately after a durable and stable cease-fire is established, a clear-cut and strong collaboration among the international organisations which are entitled to play a mediation role in the given region. The efforts of the UN, the OSCE, the EU, NATO (when it is involved), the World Bank, the IMF and the EBRD must be synchronised. What often happens is that one of the international organisations involved proves to be stronger, quicker to act and more disciplined than the others. A possible result is that the whole rehabilitation effort might be put into question or derailed altogether. Irrespective of how one views and treats the NATO military operations in Bosnia or Kosovo, this organisation proved to be stronger and quicker than those which were responsible for the organisation and monitoring of free and fair elections or for rehabilitation loans. Prior planning not only by but between the responsible international organisations would make a transition breakthrough to much higher levels of regional stability and prosperity more likely.

• The regional economic rehabilitation and development programs in the South Caucasus should have started yesterday. There was a good opportunity to draft and implement them when the cease-fire in Karabakh was established. The same goes for the dynamics of the

Georgian-Abkhazian conflict. But the only international organisation active at that point was the OSCE, which was also mostly responsible for mediating political negotiations to reach a final solution for the Karabakh problem. It was also responsible for monitoring presidential, parliamentary and local elections in the three countries of the Caucasus. The UN was moderately active in the conflict resolution process in Abkhazia. The World Bank, the IMF, the EBRD, other international monetary organisations and donor countries preferred to work with Georgia, Armenia and Azerbaijan only on a bi-lateral basis. There were almost no loans for regional economic cooperation. It is only now that the first signs of collaboration and a joint strategy by the international political, monetary and economic organisations can be discerned.

•   Last but not least, the idea of regional cooperation, just as any other idea, should never become an ideology, a self-seeking goal as is often the case. It should be deemed and viewed as one of the tools necessary to attain regional stability, security and prosperity. It does not have the extra-sensory powers to heal all regional diseases. Yet, if applied properly, it can become an additional remedy to get rid of the indigestible left-overs of the 20th century. We should watch for the side effects though, for any regional change, even a positive one, is painful and hazardous.

INTERNAL STABILITY AND PROBLEMS OF SECURITY DEVELOPMENT IN THE KYRGYZ REPUBLIC

Asel Abylova

Senior Researcher, Economic Analysis Department, IISS, Kyrgyz Republic

A number of radical reforms were carried out with the transition to a market economy in Kyrgyzstan, which have created a base for the formation of a multi-layered economy, a market infrastructure and the achievement of macro-economic stabilisation. These reforms have improved the overall environment for business.

At the same time, during the reform process, economic decline was very evident. Even now with apparent stabilisation of the economy, there remains a potential for crisis. The main reason for this is the inconsistency of the current economic policy of the state. The crisis which threatens to engulf the Kyrgyz economy shows how fragile stabilisation is without an expansion of production and an increase in competitiveness, which in turn provide a balanced development, GDP growth and better finances. Since 1990, there has been a sharp recession in industrial production, which was accompanied by degradation of infrastructure, the destruction of the technological core of the economy, the loss of domestic and export markets, and a growth in imports. Non payments throughout the economy have increased which have further destabilised financial markets. In particular, the devaluation of the national currency has provoked the withdrawal of investors from the Kyrgyz market.

There was also a rapid rise in interest rates, which meant that bank finance was concentrated in the informal, non-tax-paying sector. In such a situation, only raw material industries and shadow enterprises thrive. The tax losses due to the complex and inefficient tax system, the relative absence of direct foreign investment, the growth of the shadow economy and corruption throughout all branches of authority are the main reasons for the negative overall situation in the economy.

In my opinion, the adoption of a new edition of the Tax Code will allow us to reduce the general tax burden on investors and to shift part of it onto consumers. The introduction of a unified rate of income tax, the reduction of the tax on profit, and deductions in non-budget funds will make it possible to increase the tax base and to reduce shadow capital. Moreover, the VAT allowances for new production and investment along with other changes will give a chance to boost foreign capital inflows into the economy of Kyrgyzstan. Such investment is vital for our economy at this moment in time.

The government of Kyrygyzstan carries out a moderate economic policy. It offers a friendly environment for foreign investments and seeks to restructure rather than renege on its external debts. But indecisiveness in actually agreeing and promulgating reform will delay the process of basic socio-economic renewal in the Republic for years to come. The fact that the state lacks control mechanisms combined with the decline in the cultural, moral and ideological potential of society has resulted in the growth of both the shadow economy and corruption.

Low dynamics characterise the real available incomes of the population and investment. The difficult financial position of enterprises in the real sector remains. Our traditional branches of the economy continue to decline due to insufficient funding and the poor state of infrastructure. The competitiveness of what is being sold only remains because of state subsidy. For several years, our shuttle traders have imported goods and taken out mainly US dollars. In this respect the problem of the non-competitiveness of the real sector of the economy has been solved by the invisible hand of the market. Among the countries of the CIS, Kyrgyzstan has the lowest export volumes proportionate to industrial production.

The inadequate development of small and medium-sized business is also an obstacle to economic progress. Given favourable conditions, such businesses can develop very quickly as they are motivated to react rapidly to the requirements of the market. The private sector can be especially effective in the agricultural, tourist and service sectors. The state of small and medium-sized business in Kyrgyzstan is still far from desirable. Under conditions of a transitional economy, such private firms should play a leading role in the national economy. But at present, they only account for one third of GDP rather than the 50-60% of GDP that we believe is necessary and desirable. Moreover, a certain stagnation in general private sector business development has been observed over recent years.

The conclusion remains that it is necessary to create a highly favourable legal, investment, financial, credit and organisational conditions for the rapid growth of small and medium-sized business in Kyrgyzstan, which would also help in the struggle against poverty by creating new jobs for the people of Kyrgyzstan. The economic crisis combined with political mistakes have resulted in stagnation as far as socio-economic reform is concerned. This has manifested itself in a drop in real incomes and further stratification of society. At the present moment, Kyrgyzstan is one of the poorest republics in the CIS, with an official poverty level of 55.3%. Meanwhile, the social crisis continues, unemployment grows, child mortality is high, and life expectancy has fallen. The scale of these social problems makes it increasingly difficult to enact economic reforms.

One consequence of the growth in poverty and the aggravation of social conflicts are the dissemination of religious extremist ideas and the growth of inter-ethnic conflicts that threaten national security. The expense of countering drug trafficking and international terrorism is extremely high and this is another reason why economic growth is stunted. Thus the tasks which our country faces are complex, the most significant being:

- increasing living standards and the development of human potential;

- improving the competitiveness of the economy.

Without a solution to the first task it is impossible to unite Kyrgyz society. Without a solution to the second task, our country would remain on the periphery of global economic development. Therefore we should undertake maximum efforts to boost future economic development.

Ultimately, solutions to these tasks will determine the development of Kyrgyzstan and it will be necessary to solve them simultaneously over the coming years. Moreover, this might only be possible on the basis of constructing a socially-oriented market economy and the consecutive integration of Kyrgyzstan into the World economic system.

In the medium term, Kyrgyzstan must generate a competitive economy, having I believe the longer-term potential of becoming a dynamic growing economy able to increase the living standards of the population, to modernise production, and to guarantee national security. It will be necessary to solve a number of major social problems, to attract investment, to encourage innovation, to reform budget-tax and finance-credit policy, and finally to carry out serious institutional reform. To solve the problem of the external debt - which exceeds 100% of GDP - without resort to default, it will be essential to create and maintain macro-economic stability. This should be the overriding task of the state because it is closely connected to the further stable development of the economy and the improvement of the Kyrgyz Republic's reputation in the global economic arena.

There is a further fundamental dilemma before Kyrgyzstan: development or security? Until recently, the answer was 'development', but events in Batken have shown that spending on security should be increased as well. Security spending in turn makes the resolution of social problems more difficult. Indeed, the success or failure of reform programmes in general are always ultimately judged by the living standards of the population. The hopes that the social problems of the transition period would be eased by fast growth of the economy were not realised. The resolution of these problems will require socio-economic policy reform by the state. First of all, it will be necessary to ensure stabilisation whilst simultaneously creating the preconditions for a gradual increase in the real money incomes of the population.

The achievement of all our goals is possible only under conditions of economic growth, which would in turn enable us to reduce poverty and unemployment, improve social standards, make education and public health services more widely available, increase life expectancy, and reduce the massive income differentials between rich and poor. All these things require more effective government as well as economic growth. This means taking resolute action to achieve macro-economic stabilisation. It also means supporting private business, the creation of new jobs, and making sure that growth is shared throughout all regions of the country.

Kyrgyzstan has chosen the socially-guided model of the market economy, which assumes the harmonious marriage of economic efficiency to social justice. Further market transition should be carried out with a deep and comprehensive consideration of the human factor. In Kyrgyzstan as elsewhere, this is the main "resource" of societal development.

The most important tasks to solve, beginning from today, are:

• maintaining economic growth on the basis of the further development of structural reforms;

• complete institutional reform to enable the effective functioning of a market economy;

• maintain the well-being of society as the economy grows;

• direct resources, including human, for the development of priority sectors, these being:

- hydro-electric power and other non-hydrocarbon forms of energy,
- agriculture and agri-business,
- tourism,
- banking and financial/information technology.

So, the basic purpose of our development should become the steady and stable growth of our economy, with the goal of increasing of well-being of the people. Kyrgyzstan should harmoniously and fully integrate into the World economy, as well as with international and regional economic unions. These links would lift us up onto a higher level of mutually advantageous economic cooperation both with our neighbours and with more distant foreign countries.

Sources:

Koichuev T. "Economic Security", 1998.

Spanov M.U. "Economic security as criterion developing of economy", Sayasat ?6, 1999.

"Economy of Kyrgyzstan last decade XX of century" - Bishkek, 2000.

Abylova G.K. "A problem of the external debt for Kyrgyzstan is that it is more than simply an economic problem", Economic Bulletin ? 4, 2000.

Materials "Complex bases of development of Kyrgyzstan". 2000-2001.

PROBLEMS OF ECONOMIC INTEGRATION IN CENTRAL ASIA

Damir Ramilievici Muzafarov

Institute for Strategic and Regional Studies, Republic of Uzbekistan

The last three decades have seen a rapid boost in the number of multilateral agreements and critical improvements to global financial, transport and information infrastructures. These and other factors have promoted a high pace of global trade and a sharp increase in foreign direct investment (FDI) flows. Thus, regional economic integration is a natural reaction of the Central Asia countries to the new complexities of global economic and political conditions. Such regional security spaces in the form of interstate unions in their turn facilitate integration of the Central Asian countries into the real global economic system.

Tendencies towards regional integration rose sharply following the collapse of the USSR, because from its outset, the Commonwealth of Independent States (CIS) has adopted an amorphous formation. The severance of former economic ties and the lack of real management bodies caused a severe reduction in economic circulation. Tendencies of de-industrialization appeared, as existing and new businesses terminated all inefficient economic relations.

As a result, the role of the CIS in the world economy experienced a nearly two-fold decline: GDP declined from 5% to 2.5 % in 1998; industrial output fell from 7.1% to 3%, whilst exports contracted from 2.6% to 1.6% of the global total. It became obvious that without some alignment of customs, tax, payment, and currency policies it would be very difficult for any Central Asian country to develop its economy.

The economic integration of Central Asian countries is a natural process owing to many factors such as common historical experience, similarities in culture, religion, style of life, mentality of population, and so on. Common threats to the national and regional security of the Central Asian states are important factors in this concern as well. Among them: ecological problems, including the drying up of the Aral Sea, the growth in the activity of religious extremism and terrorism in the Central Asian states, social and economic tensions in

Tajikistan, civil war in Afghanistan and the fact that this state is now the largest centre of political religious extremism and terrorism, drug trafficking and weapon smuggling in Asia, if not the world.

Thus, the new independent states of Central Asia have a lot of common interests in political, social, economic and other fields. Therefore, regional economic integration and cooperation - needed to secure social, economic and political security in Central Asia - must be free from political ambitions of its participants and become a catalyst for integration both at regional and CIS levels.

Real economic integration started in April 1994 when the heads of Uzbekistan, Kazakhstan, and Kirgizstan signed the agreement on the creation of the Common Economic Space (CES). Later, on 17 July 1998, on the suggestion of the Uzbek President Karimov, the CES was transformed into the Central Asian Economic Union (CAEU) to accelerate productive regional economic cooperation. Tajikistan joined the Union in March 1998. In January 2001, the participants of the CAEU supported the suggestion of Karimov to transform CAEU into the forum of CAEU countries.

The CAEU provides for the free movement of goods, capital, and labour and for collaboration regarding payment, budget, monetary, taxation, price, customs and currency policies. For effective coordination of integration processes, the CAEU has created the Interstate Council of Union countries and Central Asian Bank for Cooperation and Development.

Today, the CAEU is a powerful union in the CIS. Its territory covers 3.4 million sq.km. and it has a population of over 50 million people (20% of the CIS population). It occupies a linking location between western and eastern parts of Eurasia and is an intermediate between the advanced North and developing South. Its location combined with an abundance of resources make Central Asia an important theater of global politics. The abundance of mineral resources, including oil and gas, attracts foreign investors. However, one should not consider Central Asia merely as a raw material appendix of advanced states. That is why the CAEU has the task of achieving a principally new international political and economical status as an industrial region capable of playing an important role in the formation of a new world order for the 21st Century.

There is no doubt that the Central Asian countries carry out different strategies of economic development. Nevertheless, Central Asian cooperation is necessary for two reasons, firstly to ensure regional security, and secondly because mutually beneficial economic interdependence is not a precondition for integration, but its output. On the route towards deeper regional integration, the Central Asian countries perceive more and more a need for a critical improvement of the environment policies in each state, the common use of hydro-energy resources in the region, and the taking of common efforts to develop natural resources.

A prime example is the Aral Sea crisis. Even though international donors have provided financial aid, a principal solution of the problem is possible only with the efficient coordination of all Central Asia states. Another example is the water resources problem that is still on the agenda at the moment. This caused a severe imbalance of economic interests between Kirgizstan, Kazakhstan and Uzbekistan that very much impacted on the development of agriculture in Uzbekistan. However, mechanisms of regional economic integration are constantly improving and these have allowed the three Central Asian countries to achieve an accommodation on the problem. These and other examples show that the Central Asian states have open common interests on key positions and hence regional economic cooperation is strongly required for the efficient development of each country.

Uzbekistan and Kazakhstan have been more successful than other states in Central Asia in the economic and political spheres. These countries have a greater potential for expanding their foreign economic sector, have recorded a more dynamic macroeconomic development and are not burdened by a heavy foreign debt. Uzbekistan and Kazakhstan are therefore more successful in attracting FDI.

However, Kirgizstan and Tajikistan do not seek a passive role. These countries are making concerted efforts to be leaders as well. Unfortunately, Turkmenistan with its "neutrality" position still conducts a policy of adapted expectation and chose adjacent Iran and Pakistan as its integration priorities. It seems Turkmenistan will not consider itself as an active player of economic regional integration in the near future.

In transforming their economies, the countries of Central Asia are more actively turning their foreign economic policies into "open door" policies. The countries of the region are becoming today a new favourite of foreign investors. FDI stock in the region has already reached US$9bn (or 30% of the CIS total). Central Asian FDI policies focus on the modernised industrial sectors of the economy. Uzbekistan and Kazakhstan have shown a greater potential in this regard.

Foreign trade has increased in CAEU countries, which show a keen interest in regional trade as well. Uzbekistan conducts its foreign trade policies based on principles elaborated by the President. It has to provide:

- development of trade and economic ties regardless of ideologies;

- equal and mutually beneficial cooperation both on a bilateral and multilateral basis;

- norms of international law must take precedence over national laws, with the principles of the WTO being recognised within the context of the gradual liberalisation of the Uzbek foreign trade regime and with the aim of entering this organisation in the future;

- observance of an optimal balance between competition and cooperation, with the promotion of FDI providing an inflow of modern technologies.

Today, Uzbekistan is a permanent member of 30 prominent world economic organisations. Reforms in Uzbekistan have drastically changed the structure of foreign trade turnover, expanded the reach of foreign trade, and diversified exports. More than 140 states in the world are now foreign trade partners of Uzbekistan. Exports go to 80 of them. A favourable trade regime is provided for 38 countries; agreements "on promotion and mutual protection of investment" have been concluded with 39 countries.

The main tasks to improve the foreign economic sector in 2001 are as follows:

- further development of export potential and achievement of exports growth;

- improvement of promotion system for producers and exporters;

- development of international transport communications;

- attraction of FDI into the industrial sector of the economy.

Central Asian economies are not yet ready to introduce duty free regional trade whilst fixing firm customs tariffs for other competitors. To open foreign trade regimes, all countries in Central Asia have to strengthen their industrial base, develop export potential, increase and diversify export output of secondary industries, and make their national currencies fully convertible.

That is why thorough liberalisation of the foreign sector is a serious step for the transition economies of Central Asia. In particular, entering the WTO means the complete elimination of non-tariff barriers and a constant reduction of import duties. The experience of Kirgizstan has shown that joining the WTO will immediately require a reconsideration of many earlier approved principles. Any careless step would threaten further progress with regional economic integration.

The CAEU should be allowed to develop and evolve gradually. As the experience of the Customs Union between Russia, Belarus, Kazakhstan, Kirgizstan and Tajikistan has shown, efforts to achieve prompt integration at any cost to satisfy political ambitions cause damage to the Union itself. Participants in this Union still change accommodated tariffs not only for production from third countries but also from within the Union itself.

Differences in population, size of market and territory are strong factors that cause the inequality of states and forces in the region. Nevertheless, as the experience of South East Asia has shown, small countries such as Singapore and Malaysia have increased the integration potential of ASEAN. However, these countries have enjoyed successful economic development. The geopolitical structure of Central Asian countries cause difficulties as well. Kazakhstan has comparative advantages in this concern. At the same time, the large central territories of Kazakhstan unfortunately have unfavourable climate and natural conditions that make it difficult to fully develop its economic potential. Kirgizstan and Tajikistan are formed from wide valleys and high mountains, locations that bring about sharp differences in living standards. Uzbekistan is situated in the very centre of Central Asia. Having boundaries with all countries of the region and being a key link between West and East, Uzbekistan has the chance to become a leader of Central Asian integration. At the same time, Uzbekistan suffers from the absence of any direct access to the sea, which causes difficulties for foreign trade.

To improve territorial problems, the Central Asian states seek to attract foreign investment into transportation and communication as a strategic priority of integration. The greatest importance is being paid to the "Great Silk Road" including the realisation of the program TRASECA, which will allow those countries that are abundant with natural resources to get access to world markets. Uzbekistan, for instance, used new transport corridors for 50% of its exports in 2000. Those countries suffering from a lack of resources could receive large profits from transit operations.

The proliferation of religious extremism and terrorism may, due to a number of factors, become a long-lasting problem in the Central Asian region and hinder integration. The countries in the region are undertaking measures to prevent and counteract extremism and terrorism. In particular, they are enforcing borders and strengthening visa and customs regimes.

Despite certain successes, economic integration in Central Asia has spontaneous and contradictory elements as well. Even though integration covers over 50 projects in metallurgy, machine building, light industries, transportation and others, there are no still firm mechanisms to realise projects, whilst many projects are simply not realistic. As a result, nearly 60% of planned measures have not been realised because of various reasons.[1] Today, the countries of Central Asia build up bilateral relations more successfully with third countries. Uzbekistan has already realised over 50 projects with Germany alone.[2] It should be noted in this regard that there is a strong lack of a scientific foundation for integration processes. That is why the present colloquium is deeply welcomed.

The Central Asian countries have failed to achieve mutual convertibility of their national currencies. A legislative foundation for Central Asian economic integration is being created slowly. The coordination between customs, credit, tax, price, and budget policies is not still efficient. There are failures in solving transport communications problems. Interregional private investment flows go slowly as well. The CAEU states do not always consider regional relations as a priority in establishing relations with other countries. Thus, the slowdown in integration is mainly caused by economic problems in all Central Asian countries.

Another main problem that prevents further economic integration between the Central Asian states is finding ways to improve mutual understanding between patricians. It is natural that regional integration should be based on principles of good neighbourhood, observance of a balance between political and economic interests, and non-interference into the affairs of other CAEU states, excepting cases set in the agreement. Uzbekistan does not welcome the creation of any supreme regional management body that would have a right to interfere directly in the integration process and thereby limit its sovereignty and independence.

The economic integration of Central Asian states is open in its nature, and is free from any tendencies towards isolation. It is possible to increase the number of CAEU states - at the expense of Turkmenistan's participation - that would expand the economic potential of the region. At the Bishkek meeting on 24 June 1999, Ukraine, Georgia, and Turkey received observer status in the CAEU. Participation in CAEU does not mean the strict following of only one direction of integration. The CAEU successfully harmonises with other integration formations in the CIS such as GUUAM[3] and the Customs Union. Integration at different levels should follow a principle of mutually beneficial economic cooperation, rather than separation from each other.

Uzbekistan supports the thorough and productive development of economic integration. The Uzbek President, Karimov, has emphasised that the involvement of Uzbekistan into Central Asian integration is not "an integration mode... This is our way of independence and progress in the 21st Century".[4] Furthermore, one should "join efforts to realise concrete economic projects, especially regarding the rich natural resources of the region, energy and water resources, transport communications, construction of gas and oil pipelines, and solving the ecology problems of the region.[5]

Central Asian countries aim to further deepen economic and financial ties, seek civilized solutions to payment problems, and to activate mutual relations at macro and micro levels, in particular SME development. Joining enterprises in the high technology sectors to realise the latest achievements of scientific progress should also serve as a foundation for integration. Moreover, joint forecasts of development in Central Asian economies should also foster economic integration. This may promote the implementation of interstate investment projects developed at the micro or enterprise level.

In conclusion, one could say that ideas of regional integration are being realised. In spite of the many difficulties outlined above, the process of regional economic integration is accelerating. Given efficient macroeconomic policies in every country in Central Asia, their abundant human and natural resources, and the productive coordination of interstate economic efforts, the region will undoubtedly become one of the strongest regions in the world in the 21st Century. Solving economic difficulties alone will encourage integrationalist tendencies.

The main aim for economic integration should be the achievement of balanced economic growth in every country of the region, striving to equal the distribution of productive forces based on principles of comparative advantage. This will provide economic and ecological security for Central Asia. One should also, naturally, pay attention to the monitoring of agreements to help ensure their realisation.

1. Saidazimova G. "Integration in Central Asia: realities, challenges, opportunities". Central Asia and Caucasus, No.3, 2000.

2. Narodnoe slovo No. 64, 2001

3. GUUAM-integration formation consisting of Georgia, Ukraine, Uzbekistan, Azarbaijan and Moldova.

4. Karimov I.A. "Uzbekistan at the eve of XXI century: threats to security, conditions and guarantees of progress". Uzbekistan, volume 6, 1998, (Russian language) p .244.

5. Speech of Karimov at the first session of Olii Majlis of the second calling, "Our supreme aim is independence and prosperity of Nation, freedom and prosperity of the population of Uzbekistan". Uzbekistan, volume 8, 2000, (Uzbek language) p .348-349.

REGIONAL COOPERATION AND STABILITY - A VIEW FROM TAJIKISTAN

Kamol Abdullaev

Senior Researcher, Tajik Centre for Strategic Studies, Dushanbe [1]

Historical Background

Current Central Asia is the product of a colonial dispute between Russia, Great Britain, and to a lesser extent, China. The region has never played a leading role in the political agendas of these empires. The main motive was to secure their backdoors against possible expansion by their neighbours. The Russians defended Siberia and the Caucasus, the British, India, while China defended Mongolia, which in turn protected Peking. Naturally, neither of these Great Game players allowed for the independence and nation-building of ethnic states in Central Asia. Moreover, imperial rule was directed at the prevention of Central Asian unification and development. The borders were defined in such a way so that ethnic and religion groups were dismembered, thereby creating obstacles for their mobilisation. Until now, interrelations of the western world in Central Asia were often considered from a Eurocentrist concept of "modernisation", that is the attack of a "progressive" West upon an archaic East. In this simplistic model, the southern borders of Central Asia (that is the current Tajik-Afghan border) were considered to be the frontier between a capitalist Russia and eastern stronghold of the Christian West, against a feudal Muslim world. The dread of an imagined threat of "Islamic fundamentalism" was created and fanned by the empires that took part in the "Great Game." In the light of this "clash of civilisations "model, Russia appeared to be the defender of the West from the "wild" East.

The implication of this widely held stereotype was that Central Asia was doomed to remain a colony because only through its integration into an imperial system could the political stability of the region be assured. This dependence froze the indigenous development of Central Asians and made them objects of manipulation and experimentation by external forces.

Overview

Formed in 1929, Tajikistan was the poorest post-Soviet republic and the most dependent on aid from Russia. Because of its potential instability, throughout the Soviet era, Tajikistan was regarded by the Kremlin as an important geopolitical area, rather than as a substantial economical unit. While Uzbekistan was treated as a "lighthouse of socialism in the East", Tajikistan served as a sort of a buffer between the USSR and the Muslim world. For that reason, the Soviets did not pay much attention to the economic development of Tajikistan, directing most investments to Uzbekistan (whose border with Afghanistan is ten times shorter than that of Tajikistan). Tajikistan entered the 21st Century at 108th out of 174 countries in the Human Development Index, and with an annual per capita GDP of just US$215. These relatively low figures contrast with a high adult literacy rate of 95-99%.

After gaining independence in 1991, Tajikistan's national economy declined. From 1991 to 1997, GDP decreased by more than 50%. In 1998, the country accounted for 0.3% of total CIS GDP (in 1991, 0.6% of the USSR), occupying last place among former USSR states. Average monthly salary reached US$11 in 2000. According to World Bank estimates, 85% of Tajikistan's population is living below the poverty line.

The structure of the national economy remains as in Soviet times. Agriculture, represented mostly by cotton production, is the most important sector of the national economy in which more then half of the population was engaged in 1991. In 1979, Tajikistan contributed 9.8% of total USSR cotton production, while Uzbekistan produced 62.9%, Turkmenistan 13.3%, Azerbaijan 8.1%, Kazakhstan 3.6% and Kyrgyzstan 2.3%. Since 1996, the state began a gradual phasing out of its monopoly over cotton. Yet because of a shortage of fertilisers, fuel and machinery, a decrease in area sown, and a decline in the market price of cotton, production decreased from more than 800,000 tons in 1990 to 335,421 tons in 2000. Industry comprises 465 enterprises operating in 80 branches, currently working spasmodically yet focusing mainly on non-ferrous metallurgy and power. Institutional reform of the Tajik economy began in 1991, but was postponed by the civil war in 1992. In finance, a two-level bank system was constructed with an independent National Bank at the apex. In 1997, a new tax code was adopted and then amended in November 1998. Privatisation began in 1992 with the sale of housing and small commerce enterprises. Still, the deficit of national capital and foreign investors seriously stunts the economy.

Tajikistan experienced a prolonged monetary crisis after the Soviet collapse. It continued to use the Russian rouble while its neighbours switched to new independent currencies. Tajikistan faced a shortage of roubles and was forced to introduce its own currency (Tajik Rouble) in May 1995. That currency sank very quickly - the exchange rate dropped from US$1=200TR in May 1995 to US$1=2,400TR in October 2000. On 30 October 2000, Tajikistan introduced a new currency called the Somomi, whose exchange rate was set at 1/1,000TR. The Somoni consists of 100 dirams and on the first day of its introduction, the exchange rate was US$1=2.4 Somoni.

Tajikistan has a total area of 143,100 square km, about the size of Wisconsin (USA) or Bangladesh. The country has a population estimated in 2001 at about 6.2 million. The average density of population is 42.2 people per square kilometre. This figure is rather misleading, since the majority of the population live in valleys, which constitute only 7% of the country's territory. Tajikistan has rich water resources, including snow, ice, and glaciers. Its average annual drainage reaches 64 km. cubic, that is 55.4% of the whole drainage of the Aral basin. The country's annual consumption reaches 11.5-12.6 km. cubic (18-20% of the region's total water resources).

Politics

Tajikistan, following the example of other USSR republics, adopted a declaration of state independence and declared a presidential system of government in September 1991. The presidential election of November 1991 led to a contest between an opposition coalition of Islamic groups coupled with newborn secular democratic movements against the old Soviet elites. The struggle turned into open armed confrontation in 1992. Political antagonism for and against communism was gradually eclipsed by region-based group discord. In November 1992, a government led by Emomali Rakhmonov regained control of the state, backed by Russia and Uzbekistan. In 1994-1997, the UN-sponsored intra-Tajik peace-talks led to the General Agreement on Establishment of Peace and National Accord, followed by the incorporation of the United Tajik Opposition into the government on the basis of a 30% quota. The acting Tajikistan Constitution (adopted in 1994) declared an independent, democratic, unified and secular statehood with separated executive, legislative and judicial powers. Although secularity was recognised as a central article of the Constitution, Tajikistan is the only state in post-Soviet Central Asia where an Islamic movement has opted to participate in the political process officially. The supreme legislative body is the parliament, a bicameral Majlisi Oli (Supreme Council). In the November 1999 presidential elections, Emomali Rakhmonov, a leader of the Peoples Democratic Party of Tajikistan from the southern Kulob region won 96.91% of the votes, while his opponent from the Islamic Renaissance Party got only 2.1%.

External Economic Relations

In the past, Tajikistan had mutual relations with most USSR republics. Bilateral links between the republics were developed according to Soviet demands. Great volumes of materials were imported. With these economic links now broken, Tajikistan faces great difficulties in securing supplies of raw materials, consumer goods and food items. The negative consequences of the crash were intensified due to geographic factors. Tajikistan is a mountainous country, the majority of its area is not densely populated, and transport and communication systems with other countries and regions are poorly developed. Today, foreign trade operations are handled with 70 countries (among them 11 in the CIS). Total volume of exports and imports in 2000 reached US$1.45bn. Of this figure, US$927m, or 63.8%, falls to CIS and US$555m, or 41%, to Central Asia countries. In 2000, exports reached US$779m, or 54% of total turnover. Exports comprised mainly aluminium - US$433.6m (55.6% of total exports), cotton fibre - US$91.8m (11.8 %), electric energy - US$86.7m (11.1%), precious stones and metals - US$2.4m (3.1%) and so on. Imported commodities are mineral products worth US$253.3m (37.5%), mainly electric energy and gas from Uzbekistan and oil products from the CIS. Besides, Tajikistan imported machinery and equipment worth US$39.3m. These figures do not include shadow economy operations.

Investment

The adoption of the law "On Foreign Investments" in Tajikistan on 10 March 1992 opened the way for foreign investment. In July 1999, 248 enterprises with foreign investment were registered in Tajikistan (at the end of 1998 the number was 198). Among these enterprises are 164 joint and 84 foreign owned firms. Russia is a partner in 35 joint enterprises, the USA in 16 and Afghanistan in 12. Among investment properties, Russia has 14 enterprises, the USA 11 and Turkey 8. In 1997, the total value of foreign investment in Tajikistan reached US$64.4m and the value of external trade turnover of joint enterprises reached US$171m. In 1999, foreign investment in Tajikistan decreased to US$6.6m, that is 10% of the 1997 level. 71% of this amount was directed to gold and silver mining, 12% to commerce, and only 4% to agriculture and education. Four of the biggest joint ventures are gold mining enterprises: Tajik-British Zarafshon and Darvoz, Tajik-Canadian Aprelevka, and Tajik-Korean Sogchana.

Main Economic Trends and Regional Interaction

Trade and cooperation has always been a substantial feature of Tajik culture. Tajikistan realises that one way for the region to help foster stability and attract foreign investment is through interaction among the states of Central Asia and the Caucasus. Among other Central Asian countries, Tajikistan is a most enthusiastic proponent for greater regional cooperation because it actively participates in all processes of integration within the CIS. In 1998, Tajikistan joined the Central Asian Economic Community in a move that will help ensure an end to the civil war in the country. Within this alliance, Tajikistan regulates the use of water and energy resources. Together with this, Tajikistan develops bilateral economic links with non-Central Asia countries and especially Russia.

Tajikistan pays great attention to hydro-energy, textiles, mining and the development of non-ferrous metals including silver and gold. In 1979, the Norak station, the biggest of its kind in Central Asia, started work in full capacity generating 2,700 megawatt/hour. In addition to the Norak station, in the 1990s, the construction of the Baipazy station (on the Vakhsh river) was completed and the three projects of Rogun, Sangtuda and Shurob stations were launched. Despite extensive energy resources, the country experiences an energy deficiency of up to 600 million kilowatt/hour per year, which becomes a serious problem in winter. Tajikistan meets its electricity needs by imports from neighbouring Turkmenistan, Uzbekistan and Kyrgyzstan. Tajikistan pays between US$0.025 and US$0.05 per one kilowatt/hour. The completion of the Sangtuda station project is expected to solve Tajikistan's energy shortage. The proposed capacity of this station (600 megawatt) would meet Tajikistan's domestic demands and generate surplus electricity for sale abroad. A much more ambitious electro-energy project is the Rogun hydroelectric station, which (in 1999) was in need of US$3bn for its completion. The proposed capacity is 3,600 megawatt and the embankment's planned height is 350 meters. This station is expected to make Tajikistan the biggest exporter of electricity in the region. In 1992, the construction of Rogun was frozen due to financial difficulties and a lack of foreign investment.

Another priority is the development of various inter-country transport links. One of them is a tunnel through Anzob to open a permanent road between Khujand, Dushanbe, Kulob, and Khorugh. Another prominent project is the Murghab-Kulma road, which goes from Murghab (eastern Pamir) eastward to the Kulma pass (4,362 meters above sea level) on the Tajik-Chinese border. Construction started in 1999, with completion planned for 2001. This road will conect Tajikistan with the Karakorum highway in China. It will allow the country to have permanent automobile connection with China, India, Pakistan, and other countries of southern Asia. The Government hopes that this road will help Tajikistan out from a transport "dead-end" and thereby obtain transport and economic independence. Of course, the realisation of Tajikistan's transport projects is dependent upon regional stability.

Barriers That Obstruct Integration

The main obstacle for regional cooperation is of a political nature. This is obvious in the case of the Afghani problem. In the course of this conflict, the regional context became even more polarised. The advance of the militant Taliban aided by Pakistan and Saudi Arabia distressed Russia, Central Asia and Iran, each for rather different motives. Some in the former Soviet republics feared that as the Taliban approached the Tajik border, this could intensify the conflicts in Tajikistan, Kyrgyzstan and Uzbekistan, thus threatening the CIS security border. The Taliban's rise helped Russia indirectly to strengthen its position in Central Asia, whose governments have strengthened their military links with Russia to protect themselves from the perceived threat of militant Islamicist movements.

Diversity in politics causes diversity and incompatibility in the strategy of economic reform. While Uzbekistan prioritises the creation of a free trade zone, Tajikistan remains Russia's closest ally in Central Asia, notwithstanding the fact that the military aspect of cooperation prevails over the economic and cultural dimensions. Since the establishment of Soviet rule in 1921, Russia has maintained military forces in Tajikistan and it was the only country in Central Asia where the government did not demand the withdrawal of Russian troops after independence. Dushanbe delegated the protection of its Afghan and Chinese borders to the Russian Federation until it could develop its own frontier troops. Tajikistan also hosts a Russian military base. If Tajikistan sees Russia as a "main strategic partner", Uzbekistan treats it as the main threat to its sovereignty and to regional stability. Today, Tajikistan and Russia support the anti-Taliban alliance in Afghanistan, while drawing on the experience of the Tajik peace process by advising Karimov to negotiate with the IMU. Uzbekistan and the Kyrgyz Republic denounce the Tajik government for insufficient effort to destroy IMU forces on Tajik territory and have begun to engage directly with the Taliban.

Further obstacles to regional cooperation are the substantial shadow economy and the regional narcotics business. In spite of the efforts of Russian border guards, the Tajik-Afghan border is unreliable and there is a constant flow of illegal trafficking in both directions. Current governments are unable, even sometimes reluctant, to stand firmly against this destructive trend. One of the main reasons for the rise in the narcotics trade is the rapid decline in living standards. As mentioned above, 85% of the Tajik population live below the poverty line. More than a quarter of economically active Tajikistanis are unemployed. Almost a half of million Tajiks are working illegally on a temporary basis in Russia. Substantial finances allow the mafia to recruit the local population, government officials, and border guards, both Russian and Tajik, in illegal trafficking of narcotics. The struggle against illegal narcotic traffic in Tajikistan cannot bear fruit without stopping the war in Afghanistan, where different political and military factions are interested in narcotics production. Surely, no workable regional cooperation and security in Central Asia are possible without a peaceful and stable Afghanistan.

Prognosis

There are three possible options for Central Asian regional cooperation:

Gradual disintegration

The least preferable option that would turn the region into one of total anarchy, turmoil, and constant conflict. The refugee problem would get much worse and the region would become one of the world's biggest centres of narcotics manufacturing and dissemination. Following the Afghani example, separate states failing to maintain their sovereignty could have serious consequenses for peripheral states, such as Russia, Pakistan, China and Turkey. Even so, regional powers and the international community might jointly be prepared and able to extend sufficient support to enable the region to maintain a minimum degree of credibility.

Unbalanced re-integration

This assumes the asymmetrical economic cooperation of Tajikistan with regional neighbours in the framework of bilateral agreements, but even this choice could not provide the degree of desirable security in Central Asia. Bilateral deals will inevitably lead to distortion and rivalries among outside powers and Central Asians themselves. Conflicting Tajikistan-Uzbekistan approaches to the issues of regional militant Muslim movements (Taliban, IMU) and Russia's presence in the region are some of the obvious examples of these emerging discords. The economic situation in Central Asia is expected to remain insecure as the Russian crisis continues.

New model of cooperation

This is the most desirable yet rather idealistic scenario. It assumes the close economic and political cooperation of Tajikistan with all Central Asian states within the Central Asian Economic Community, the Customs Union, the Economic Cooperation Organization (ECO) and other regional associations. Our countries have a common history, culture, and religion. We have common challenges to national and regional security: the Afghan war, the Aral Sea problems, illegal trafficking of drugs and weapons, terrorism, militant Islamic groups and so forth. The difference in economic strategies is not an inescapable obstacle to integration because Central Asian economies can complement each other.

246

Needs

What is needed to make regional integration possible?

• The political will of leaders to approach each other. In spite of episodically emerging arguments at a high level (Karimov vs Rakhmonov for example), there is a ground for optimism. At least none of the leaders have openly denied cooperation, and some observers claim that a real Tajikistan-Uzbekistan rapproachment would be possible after Rakhmonov and Karimov leave their posts.

• The willingness of nations. Here there is more ground for optimism. Indeed, in spite of inter-governmental tensions, sometimes very serious, there are no open interstate conflicts. This is due to the wisdom of the Central Asian masses that for ages used to live in peace and still retain valuable social capital able to sustain peace. For sure, Central Asian states also must be inclined towards the deepening of integration.

• External benevolence. Those foreign governments and international agencies that wish to see an integrated, strong region have to be welcomed in all Central Asia capitals. Only in this case can the region turn into a major supplier of energy and attract regional powers and their investment, above all from China, Iran, Russia, Turkey and, probably, the USA.

Central Asian states today are going in different directions, their political systems are weak and social life is unstable. Most of them, especially Tajikistan, need to submit to outside control. The strengthening of regional cooperation will bring benefits to all. But regional projects have to be in concert with national development plans. At the moment, as far as regional powers such as Russia and Uzbekistan are concerned, Tajikistan is serving as an effective buffer against unstable Afghanistan, just as it did a century ago.

Table 1: Tajikistan Exports & Imports with Central Asian Countries in 1999, in US$

	EXPORTS	IMPORTS	TOTAL	% OF TOTAL TRADE
Kazakhstan	3,594,900	78,788,600	82,383,500	6.1
Kyrgyzstan	3,906,700	7,227,900	11,134,600	0.8
Turkmenistan	1,302,300	15,186.500	16,488,800	1.2
Uzbekistan	180,976,800	264,428,700	445,405,500	32.9
TOTAL	189,780,700	365,631,700	555,412,400	41.0

1.   Written contribution

CAUCASUS AND CENTRAL ASIA: CHALLENGES AND NEW OPPORTUNITIES AFTER TEN YEARS OF INDEPENDENCE

Unal Ceviköz

Deputy Director General for Caucasus and Central Asia
Ministry of Foreign Affairs, Turkey

In the aftermath of the disintegration of the former Soviet Union at the end of 1991, the recent history of the post-Soviet Eurasian space has been marked with efforts for the building of nation-states, developing state structures, creating conditions favourable for the emergence of a civil society with democratic institutions and internalising the concepts and principles of democracy, human rights and a market-oriented economy. In the Caucasus and Central Asia these efforts were also coupled with the struggle to establish, strengthen and secure the sovereignty, independence and territorial integrity of those states which emerged in the international arena as successors of what has been referred to as one of the main actors of the Cold War era. After independence, the immediate task of embarking upon a serious action plan for integration with the international economic and political system dictated membership of these countries in several international organisations, primarily the United Nations (UN) and the Organisation for Security and Cooperation in Europe (OSCE). Today, after a decade of experience as independent actors of international relations, it would be fair to state that the countries in the Caucasus and Central Asia have considerably consolidated their sovereignty and independence. Despite some reported shortcomings, presidential elections and multi-party parliamentary elections have been realised. Measures towards the establishment of market-oriented economies also continue to be taken.

Problems Endangering Security and Stability in the Eurasian Space

Some argue that the countries in the Caucasus and Central Asia have not yet internalised the concept of democracy and that they are mainly governed by authoritarian regimes. Such criticism, however, is

249

marked with the tendency to overlook the problems these countries continue to encounter during their transition.

In the Caucasus, the main conflicts of Nagorno-Karabakh, Abkhazia and South Ossetia have not yet been politically resolved but rather have been conveniently frozen. Approximately 20% of the territory of Azerbaijan is still under the occupation of Armenian forces. The problems of Abkhazia and South Ossetia, on the other hand, continue to pose challenges to the stability of Georgia. In the Caucasus region, these conflicts have left some 1.5 million refugees and displaced persons and this situation aggravates the already poor economic conditions of the countries involved.

The situation in Afghanistan continues to pose challenges to the security and stability of the Central Asian countries. Almost all the refugees flowing into Central Asia originate from Afghanistan and Tajikistan. The Central Asian countries also face the increasing production, trafficking, and use of illegal narcotics. Afghanistan is believed to produce around 30% of global drug output. The region draws the attention of criminal groups smuggling narcotics from Afghanistan, Iran, Pakistan and elsewhere to markets in Russia and Europe via the Caucasus region. Organised crime groups based in producer countries have been able to expand their influence in Central Asia because of poorly patrolled borders, lack of cooperation among the states, lawlessness and corruption among officials, police and border guards.

Slow economic reform and progress, combined with social problems as well as authoritarian rule of the leaderships, have also created a fertile ground for extremist and radical tendencies which may become disastrous for the countries of the region. The Islamic Movement of Uzbekistan (IMU), for example, has reportedly been involved in several terrorist incursions in Uzbekistan. The IMU fighters are believed to have bases in Tajikistan and Afghanistan. The strength of the extremist elements that infiltrated Kyrgyzstan is, reportedly, greater than the total strength of the Kyrgyz armed forces.

The Need for Coordinated International Efforts

The Caucasus and Central Asian regions deserve particular attention of the international community because of their potential for becoming highly unstable, which could affect the whole Eurasian area.

Identifying some of the characteristics of these regions and of the countries there may help develop efficient cooperation with a view to preventing such instability.

First of all, although the countries in the Caucasus and Central Asia appear to have similar problems, their objectives, resources, capabilities and potentials considerably differ. It could be more appropriate not to consider these countries in the same "basket" as if they formed an homogeneous entity. This distinction could be instrumental in understanding the peculiarities of their problems in a regional context but would also contribute to developing appropriate strategies with a view to facilitating their integration with the world community. The countries of the Southern Caucasus region, for example, enjoy the advantage of geographical proximity to Europe. Also, in addition to their membership in the OSCE, they have become members of the Council of Europe. They have developed stronger relations with the European Union and their efforts to participate more actively in the NATO fora by means of EAPC cooperation activities and PfP program are significantly more substantive.

Secondly, countries in the Caucasus and Central Asia have particular and individual problems and offering remedies in a regional context may create difficulties as well. To develop strong bilateral projects with each and every individual country in these geographical regions and to subsequently complement these bilateral approaches with comprehensive multilateral cooperative structures could prove more effective. Appreciation of their individuality and singularity would increase the perception of these countries. A just and equitable approach towards them could enhance their constructive competitiveness.

Although bilateral relations remain an important element of developing international relations, regional and sub-regional cooperation today has also become an important dimension of economic development and proves to be an efficient tool in integrating with other systems and sub-systems. Mutually overlapping cooperative structures, in fact, have become significant components of globalisation. Regional cooperation developed among the countries in the Caucasus and Central Asia themselves would also motivate stronger development strategies in the surrounding systems. This should be particularly encouraged and supported by the international community. The drive for multilateral cooperation, however, should not be imposed by forces outside of the Caucasus and Central Asian regions but should genuinely emerge from within and should be internalised by the countries of the region.

Turkey's New Approach

Turkey's visionary foreign policy approach to the Eurasian region, after ten years of experience in this geographic region as a partner, has also started to go through a responsible and proactive transformation process. Contemporary Turkey aspires to be one of the leading economic and political actors in Eurasia. The fact that Turkey has shared for centuries a common history as well as a common destiny with a majority of the countries in that region provides for solid relationships and a unique platform for cooperation. Turkey, with its relatively dynamic economy and its secular democratic system, also contributes to the stability of Eurasia.

Over the past decade, Turkey's relations with the countries of the Caucasus and Central Asia have matured and a sound basis for political, economic, cultural and military cooperation has been established. At the beginning of the new millenium, regarding its bilateral relations with the countries in Eurasia, Turkey has embarked upon development of a new action plan based on three pillars: enhanced political dialogue and consultations; increased economic cooperation and re-activation of existing mechanisms thereto; increased consultations and cooperation in the field of security, combating terrorism and other contemporary challenges.

As to the enhanced political dialogue and consultations, in addition to frequent presidential and ministerial visits, Turkey has developed an effective political consultation mechanism with the Foreign Ministries of the countries in the region. Also, a thorough analysis and review of the existing bilateral agreements between Turkey and the countries of Central Asia has been launched in order to offer appropriate adjustments as well as to renew the agreements which have already expired. Bilateral political consultations facilitates addressing the key topics on the bilateral agenda of the countries involved, which may not be easily dealt with during the high-level state visits which are generally burdened with protocol.

In order to develop economic cooperation between Turkey and the countries in the Caucasus and Central Asia, existing mechanisms such as Business Councils and Joint Economic Commissions have been re-activated. Enhanced cooperation in the fields of transportation, communications, tourism and agriculture is also under way. The Turkish International Cooperation Agency (TICA), in coordination with the OECD and its counterparts in many western countries promotes projects including private sector development as well as the wider implementation of small and medium sized enterprises. With the new approach, in addition to the above-mentioned traditional and already existing mechanisms, economic bilateral consultations are carried out between the economic departments of the Ministries of Foreign Affairs too.

One of the most important areas of cooperation with Central Asia is security and combating terrorism. Turkey has offered the launching of an effective consultation mechanism with the Central Asian countries both at the military level as well as between the security forces and police officials. Projects to finance the needs for equipment of the Kyrgyz and Uzbek security forces in their combat against terrorism have been developed. The equipment provided is of non-lethal character. Turkey also offers large-scale military education and training facilities to these countries.

A close dialogue and consultation mechanism with the Central Asian countries which would enhance their sense of belonging to the OSCE, as well as a multi-dimensional, comprehensive approach to the problems of the region, would help Central Asian countries to respond positively to the calls of the OSCE as well. The Istanbul OSCE Summit Declaration of November 1999 reiterated the importance of addressing economic and environmental risks in the region, as well as the necessity of joint action by the international community to cope with the threats of international terrorism, violent extremism, organised crime and drug, arms and human trafficking.

Multilateral Cooperation

Turkey's new vision has also prepared the background for launching new cooperation initiatives in the Eurasian area. In 2000, during an official state visit to Tbilisi, Georgia, the ninth President of the Republic of Turkey, Mr. Demirel, together with President Shevardnadze, put forth the idea of working on a Caucasus Stability Pact in order to address the problems faced by the Caucasian countries. Inspired by the model developed under the auspices of the OSCE for the Balkan region, namely Southeast European Stability

Pact, the proposal for the Caucasus Stability Pact (CSP) has immediately drawn the attention of the international community. Although the current situation in the Caucasus region with many unresolved conflicts presents an unfavourable background for implementation, many hold the view that the proposal for the CSP will develop into a viable forum for widening stability and reassuring political, economic, social and military security once the parties involved in those conflicts engage in a responsible commitment to resolve them. An international seminar organised by the Turkish Economic and Social Research Foundation (TESEV) in Istanbul on 17 February 2001 has manifested the shared interest of the three Caucasian countries, namely Georgia, Azerbaijan and Armenia, as well as the potential for contribution of their three neighbours, Turkey, Russia and Iran, to further promote the idea of the CSP more concretely. Participants in the seminar encouraged the optimism of the international community and many creative and innovative ideas were also expressed by potential contributors such as the USA, the European Union and the OSCE.

Another Turkish initiative, namely the Summit of Presidents of the States Speaking Turkic Languages, has marked its 7th meeting in Istanbul on 26-27 April 2001. Launched in 1992 with the first meeting of the Presidents of Azerbaijan, Kazakstan, Kyrgyz Republic, Turkey, Turkmenistan and Uzbekistan in Ankara, this process has had its subsequent meetings in Istanbul (1994), Bishkek (1995), Tashkent (1996), Astana (1998) and Baku (2000). In Istanbul, Presidents agreed to hold the 8th summit meeting in Ashkabad, the capital of Turkmenistan, in the year 2002. They have also agreed that cooperation between their countries has matured significantly and that the summits process should bring out concrete results of cooperation among its members. This view has led to the conclusion that the summit of Ashkabad in 2002 should seek opportunities for the "development of commercial and economic relations" between the participating countries.

Other Initiatives and Mechanisms for Regional Cooperation in Eurasia

Regional cooperation initiatives in Caucasus and Central Asia, as they enhance regional cohesion as well as integration with the global cooperative schemes, deserve appropriate attention too. Here, the focus will rather be on newly appearing initiatives as well as those which may not have significantly drawn the attention of the international community so far. Two regional organisations, namely the Economic Cooperation Organisation (ECO) and the Organisation of Black Sea Economic Cooperation (BSEC), as they have a longer historical existence and established structures, are kept beyond the scope of this study.

One of the most remarkable attempts at integration in Central Asia is the effort to establish the *"Economic Community of Central Asia"* (ECCA) among the regional countries themselves, namely Uzbekistan, Kazakstan, Kyrgyz Republic and Tajikistan. The initiative was first launched as a bilateral effort between Uzbekistan and Kazakstan at the beginning of 1994. The Kyrgyz Republic almost immediately joined whereas Tajikistan waited till 1998. Turkmenistan, in strict compliance with its status of "permanent neutrality", has remained out of this attempt. The Russian Federation acquired observer status at a very early stage. The initiative was named ECCA on 17 July 1998. Turkey, Georgia and Ukraine were granted observer status in this group on 24 June 1999, during the Inter-governmental Council meeting of the members in Bishkek.

The presidents of the four member countries met in Almaty on 5 January 2001, and discussed possibilities of cooperation in the fields of economy, science and technology. They also exchanged opinions on current issues of the region such as peace and stability, the situation in Afghanistan, combating terrorism, organised crime and illegal arms, drug and human trafficking. One of the opinions expressed in the meeting was the establishment of a common economic space between the member countries till 2002. Uzbekistan proposed to transform the community into an "economic forum" in the long run.

Another interesting development is the appearance of *Eurasian Economic Community* (EEC). The founding agreement of this new initiative was signed on 10 October 2000, among the countries which are parties to the CIS Customs Union, namely the Russian Federation, Belarus, Tadjikistan, Kazakstan and the Kyrgyz Republic. The agreement envisages the establishment of an "inter-state council" in which the Presidents and the Prime Ministers of the member countries will take part. In addition to the inter-state council, the initiative will have other bodies such as the "integration committee", the "permanent representatives commission" and a secretariat.

Based on the Customs Union agreement, first signed between the Russian Federation and Belarus on 6 January 1995, and to which the others joined subsequently (Kazakstan in 1995, Kyrgyz Republic in 1996 and Tadjikistan in 1999), the EEC will organise one of its major meetings in Minsk on 1 September 2001. Currently, Kazakh President Nursultan Nazarbayev, as he also maintains the chairmanship of the Customs Union, presides over the new initiative too. The declared purpose of the EEC is to transform the already existing - but mostly inefficient - customs union into a better functioning group by developing infrastructure, as well as the legal and institutional frameworks. Russia still depends on agricultural imports from Kazakstan and Uzbekistan and continues to view Central Asia as a principle source of strategic raw materials. Russian-Central Asian trade turnover, however, was estimated to be US$7bn in 2000, comprising only about 5% of Russia's overall trade. Russia, therefore, could actively promote the EEC to expand its economic position in Central Asia.

The most recent development in the Central Asian region is the formation of the **Shanghai Cooperation Organisation** (SCO). Previously known as the "Shanghai Five", later as "Shanghai Forum", the SCO now comprises China, the Russian Federation, Kazakstan, Kyrgyz Republic, Tadjikistan and Uzbekistan. The latter has joined the group at the latest meeting held in Shanghai on 14-15 June 2001.

The Shanghai Five actually dates back to 1996 when the group, except Uzbekistan, first launched a series of summit meetings with a view to establishing confidence building measures in the border regions. In the fifth summit meeting which took place in Dushanbe, capital of Tadjikistan, on 5 July 2000, the leaders declared their intention to search for a more substantial forum responding to the requirements of globalisation, particularly in terms of combating terrorism in Central Asia. Uzbekistan, by that time, had already unveiled its interest by asking for an observer status. Similar aspirations were also expressed by countries such as Mongolia and Pakistan. After the Dushanbe summit, the initiative has been renamed as the Shanghai Forum.

The summit in Shanghai in June 2001 has further transformed this initiative into the SCO and Uzbekistan has been accepted as the new member. The SCO will adopt its Charter in the next summit meeting due to take place in St. Petersburg in June 2002. Up to then, a meeting to discuss economic cooperation at the level of Prime Ministers in Almaty in September 2001, as well as a meeting of the

Ministers of Culture in Beijing are also planned. With its current configuration, the SCO draws particular attention from the international community.

A more comprehensive initiative in the Eurasian region is the Conference on **Cooperation and Interaction in Central Asia** (CICA), generally accepted as the Asian version of the OSCE, launched by Kazakstan in 1992. Today, the conference gathers many countries in the region.[1] Although the initiative has a long history of almost ten years, it has developed gradually, especially due to the pending bilateral problems among its members. CICA will convene its Summit of the Heads of State in Astana on 8-10 November 2001. At the summit meeting, the Heads of State will consider developing common approaches to the main problems of the region such as terrorism, extremism, illegal trafficking of weapons, etc. The establishment of a permanent secretariat will also be reviewed.

Finally, one should also briefly cite the **GUUAM** as another sub-regional initiative, which brings together Georgia, Ukraine, Uzbekistan, Azerbaijan and Moldova. This initiative also dates back to 1996 when the four countries except Uzbekistan made a joint statement during the CFE Review Conference and hinted that they were considering the formation of a group to identify their common difficulties, particularly vis-a-vis the Russian Federation. Uzbekistan expressed its interest in 1999 and eventually joined the group during the EAPC meetings in Washington on the occasion of the 50th anniversary of NATO. This group, after having frequently postponed its meetings in 2001, finally succeeded in organising a summit meeting in Yalta on 6-7 June 2001 and adopted its Charter, which is considered to be a step forward in the institutionalisation of GUUAM.

The regional and sub-regional initiatives in the Eurasian region constitute favourable cooperation schemes and present exceptional opportunities to consolidate the sovereignty and independence of the countries of the Caucasus and Central Asia as well as enhancing their further integration with the world community by means of overlapping cooperative structures. The OSCE, EAPC and the PfP, by bringing the countries of these regions together under wider umbrellas, should continue to support and encourage such initiatives and play the role of international facilitators in order to contribute to their efforts.

1. Members are; Afghanistan, Azerbaijan, China, Egypt, India, Iran, Israel, Kazakstan, Kyrgyz Republic, Pakistan, Palestine, the Russian Federation, Tadjikistan, Turkey and Uzbekistan.

CAUCASUS AND CENTRAL ASIA THE EURASIAN REGION - TOWARDS A MORE COMPREHENSIVE EU POLICY

Cees Wittebrood

*Head of Unit, External Relations Directorate General,
European Commission, Brussels*

Introduction

The countries of the Caucasus and Central Asia - sometimes also called the Eurasian region - are drawing more and more attention from the international community. After having for a long time been part of the monolithic Soviet Union, the countries of the Eurasian region have embarked on a process of asserting their political independence and national identity. This process gives rise to threats and opportunities in the region. There is good news and bad news: oil and gas, pipelines, investment, resources, trade, but also regional conflicts, Nagorno Karabakh, separatism, terrorism, fundamentalism, Ferghana valley, Afghanistan, illegal trafficking of drugs, migration, transboundary water management, human rights, environment, the Aral Sea, Semipalatinsk, the status of the Caspian Sea, the role of foreign countries and so on.

Policy

At present the EU does not have a comprehensive policy towards the Eurasian region. It rather has a patchwork of assistance instruments and different policies towards the various countries in the area: first of all Caucasus and Central Asia, but also neighbouring countries like Russia, Iran and even Turkey.

It has Partnership and Cooperation Agreements with countries in the region. It has national instruments and various programes like Tacis, food security, ECHO, rehabilitation, democracy, Tempus and so on. As to the region as a whole, it has regional programmes like Traceca for transport, Inogate for oil and gas, environment programmes, a nuclear safety programme, and a programme for fighting drugs.

The EU policy towards the region has been mainly "bottom-up". It was rather the unintentional result of the application of various aid and assistance instruments. The EU is the largest donor of grants. It has granted more than Euro2bn to Russia through its Tacis programme on technical assistance and support to nuclear safety. It has spent roughly Euro1bn to the South Caucasus and Euro500m to Central Asia. This investment has, however, not produced dividends in terms of conflict resolution, political stability and economic development. The question rises - in particular in the Caucasus - whether the EU wants to give its engagement in the region a more political dimension and instead of remaining a paymaster becoming more of a peacemaker.

There is an opportunity to develop a more political "top-down" comprehensive approach, which would be the intentional effect of a deliberate policy. Changes in Europe have opened a window of opportunity: thanks to the settlement of the Balkan conflict and the end of the Chechnya war, the decisions on the process of EU enlargement and the adjustments of its institutional structures as decided by the European Council in Nice. Moreover, the development of new policy instruments under its Common Foreign and Security Policy and European Security and Defence Policy will push the EU to look beyond its own borders and its own backyard and devote more attention to its "new near abroad".

The EU will also be pulled to do so. The countries of the Caucasus turn to Europe for their future development. Very strong requests have been made by practically all players in the region for the EU to become more involved than in the past. The EU is for many of them a beacon of light on the horizon. The countries of the Caucasus are part of Europe. Their accession to the Council of Europe demonstrates their interest in forging closer relations with European institutions. But also Central Asia looks for EU support, even if it were only to counter-balance the heavyweight to the North. Current relations are covered by a Partnership and Cooperation Agreement, the overall objective of which is to support consolidation of democratic and economic reform, provide a basis for economic, social, financial, industrial and cultural cooperation and promote activities of joint interest. But some countries already look beyond the PCA. They have expressed the wish of ultimately joining the EU.

The current Swedish Presidency has soon realised this window of opportunity and taken some fresh initiatives. It decided to send the highest level ever EU mission to the Caucasus in February 2001, including the CFSP Supremo Solana and Commissioner Patten; to start discussions on moving "towards a more effective EU policy on Southern Caucasus"; to strengthen the strategic partnership with Russia; to renew relations with Iran; to help Turkey to prepare for its future accession to the EU; and finally to review relations with Central Asian countries in the framework of the Partnership Agreements.

There are many reasons to use this opportunity. The Union has strategic interests in the region. It is a junction for EU energy interests and an important transport corridor. It gets geographically closer to an enlarged Union since it will border some of the new Member States, including Turkey. It is of strategic importance. Moreover, it is an area where the Union has the potential of playing a constructive role and of making a difference.

Eurasian region

The EU has an overall interest in promoting stability in the Eurasian region. As said before, the region moves politically and economically closer to the heart of Europe, even geographically, as part of it will become a neighbouring region when EU enlargement continues eastward to the Black Sea. The region has abundant energy reserves, a wealth of human resources and a unique richness and diversity of culture and tradition. Its location makes it a potential major crossroads for trade. As a cornerstone of the ancient Silk Road it has invaluable links with the Black Sea countries to its west, Russia to its north, China to its east and Turkey, Iran, Pakistan and India to its south. Future exploitation of the energy reserves in the Caspian region will increase its role as a supplier of energy and a transit zone.

But, at the same time, the region is a sensitive area along some of the major faultlines that condition Europe's stability and security. The diversity of the region's culture and tradition has contributed to complex territorial and ethnic disputes. Some tensions tend to become more acute because of events in North Caucasus (spill over of the Chechnya war), tensions with Russia (visa and gas supply to Georgia), conflict of interests on energy issues (Azerbaijan and Turkmenistan), illegal drugs trafficking, the threat from Taliban in Afghanistan and the rise of fundamentalism and terrorism in the Ferghana valley.

Stability in this sensitive region is essential for developing its potential, in particular its oil and gas resources. No economic development without political stability; but the reverse is also true: no political stability without economic development. They are inter-linked and should be approached as such.

On political stability, the relations between the EU and most of the countries are covered by Partnership and Cooperation Agreements, the overall objective of which is to support consolidation of democratic and economic reform, provide a base for economic, social, financial and cultural cooperation and promote activities of joint interest. Respect for democratic principles and human rights underpin the Agreements. There is no such Agreement with Iran. The EU might decide to start negotiations on a more limited Trade and Cooperation Agreement with this country in order to normalise its economic relationship. On Russia, the European Council has adopted in June 1999 a Common Strategy which aims to reinforce their strategic partnership. On the Caucasus, a Joint Declaration has been adopted by the EU and its partners from South Caucasus (at a Presidential Summit in Luxembourg also in June 1999). The Council recently adopted conclusions and guidelines for the EU's future activities in the Caucasus.

The "frozen conflicts" in the region are a serious impediment to development and cannot be left to fester indefinitely. The EU wants to promote progress in this field, bilaterally, regionally and in international fora. It has committed itself to use its instruments to underpin such progress and to assist the region in post conflict reconstruction and rehabilitation.

On economic development, the region has great potential. Its two main problems are the development of its resources and the access to markets. They are potentially prosperous countries but many are landlocked and far away from world markets. The EU tries to address these issues by carrying out two main programmes, one for resources, oil and gas in particular (Inogate) and the other for transport and transit (Traceca). Let's focus first on oil and gas. This is a sector of strategic importance to the EU. Why?

Europe is the natural market for oil and gas and other natural resources from and through the region. As to gas, the Union is importing 50% of its consumption, out of which about half comes from Russia. The diversification of gas supply through new resources from the Caspian region would be strategically important for the Union. Concerning oil, in spite of reduced estimates of the Caspian reserves, these resources are also of strategic importance. The region provides a crucial link between the Union and its neighbours and Central Asia. The availability of new incremental sources of energy and other basic commodities will be a significant element in the future development of the countries of the Caspian region itself, those around the Black Sea and the present candidates for accession to the EU.

The main instrument to deal with energy supply and cooperation is at present INOGATE, a Tacis regional programme in the area of oil and gas pipelines. Its main achievement was the "Umbrella Agreement" developing rules governing international oil and gas transport activities. Its objectives are to reduce project risks to standard commercial risks and to help introduce international standards and environmental norms in the sector. Inogate is moving away from its initial focus on the Caspian region to the wider Eurasian region, including Turkey and Iran. It will become instrumental in the implementation of an integrated European approach. Political developments call for a greater integration of the East West energy network.

The other main programme of the EU, TRACECA, aims at facilitating the countries' access to world markets by developing a transport and transit corridor. It is in fact the revitalisation of the ancient Silk Road, a concept which is as brilliant as it is simple. The corridor has been narrowed to one specific route on which to focus actions. Participating countries have identified deficiencies in the region's transport systems and translated them into concrete projects. These projects were essential for the diversification of the traditional Moscow-centred trade and transport flows and to open up trade routes to Europe. Traceca assists countries in transport infrastructure, legal and regulatory issues and management training. It has a strong multiplier effect: by granting roughly Euro50m it has mobilized Euro400m from international financial institutions and Euro1bn from private investors. Its main achievement is the signing of the Multilateral Agreement on Transport in Baku at a Presidential Summit in September 1998. This Agreement paves the way for promoting transport and transit in the Eurasian region.

Regarding the countries in the Eurasian region, let us start with the three countries of the Caucasus. The EU is ready to do its part in building a stable, prosperous and peaceful region. See the Joint

Declaration and the new policy paper. The focus is on developing trade and investment links, completing the transition process, sustainable economic development, assisting confidence building and post conflict rehabilitation, and reconstruction. In this way assistance can become an incentive to constructive change. The EU has enhanced its role in the region and announced its willingness to support efforts to resolve the Nagorno Karabakh conflict. In Georgia (Tskinvali region) the EU combines its rehabilitation programme with an effort to promote conflict resolution. The Commission participated in the recent Joint Control Commission in Vladikavkaz. It also supported the Georgian Border Guards to enable them to protect the OSCE monitors on the Chechen part of the Georgian-Russian border. The EU has financed activities to support transport and transit infrastructure and development of pipeline networks. It has also financed an optical cable linking the three countries. The EU hopes that the South Caucasus could become a model of how long-standing animosity can be resolved peacefully through joint cooperation initiatives.

In Central Asia the EU is faced with an increasing difference between the countries. Instead of developing as a region the countries seem to move away from each other. Kazakhstan and Uzbekistan have the potential of playing an important role in developing the region. Kyrgyzstan and Tajikistan are too small and Turkmenistan has effectively isolated itself. Kazakhstan is most of all concerned about its oil and looking for the best outlet to the world market. It has completed the CPC pipeline and considers access to the Baku-Ceyhan pipeline. It would thus improve the BTC project's economics while extending its strategic benefits of strengthened independence, stability and regional integration. Uzbekistan has gas, cotton and troubles. Its efforts to integrate into the regional and world economy have come to a halt. Instead it managed to create problems with all its neighbours because of terrorism, drugs, gas, water and borders. Turkmenistan's role, however, is less clear. Although it would make sense for Turkmenistan to be a part of an energy corridor to the Caucasus and Turkey, a conflicted and clouded decision-making process in Ashgabad over the past year has made, unfortunately, Turkmenistan's access problematic. The country seems to lose out on all three fronts: Russia, Iran and Trans-Caspian.

To reverse the disintegration trend in Central Asia, the EU has started efforts to promote regional cooperation. One of its key objectives is to use its assistance instruments to encourage the peaceful development of the region. The agreements and conventions which the countries of the region have already signed up to offer a useful basis for the development of regional cooperation in areas such as energy, transport, environment and combating illegal activities. The EU has launched assistance programmes in all these areas. The objective is not political: it is to encourage trade and investment on the basis of international norms, to prevent economic hardship owing to the creation of artificial barriers to trade and transit, and to facilitate work on issues such as water management, the war on drugs and maybe pipelines.

The EU has also launched the initiative to develop a strategic partnership with Russia. The initiative to develop a closer dialogue between the EU and Russia will be vigorously pursued. Russia's commitment to economic and political reform is of fundamental importance. Russia is a key player in the region. It is seen to be "part of the problem". It is not known, however, how Russia could become "part of the solution". The role of Russia is complex. Having strong security and economic interests in the region, as well as historic and strategic connections, its leadership has the strategic choice of either fuelling instability - "divide et impera" - or projecting stability and thus contributing to positive developments - "res concordia crescunt". The EU intends to enhance its dialogue and cooperation with Russia so as to stimulate Russia to develop a stability-promoting policy on the region.

Iran should also be engaged in the development of the region. The EU is willing to address the question if and how to engage Iran in a constructive way in EU dialogue and cooperation in the region. Iran has relations with all countries in the region. It is expected to play a key role in deciding the future status of the Caspian Sea and the creation of a multiple network of pipelines. In particular, by constructing a gas pipeline it may play a crucial part in efforts to find alternative sources of energy for Armenia in the framework of the closing down of the Medzamor NPP and to reduce Armenia's dependency on Russian gas and nuclear fuel.

Furthermore we have to add Turkey. Turkey is one of the most dynamic markets. In spite of its current financial crisis, its enormous and continuously growing demand for energy and its strategic location for transit makes it a very attractive partner for cooperation and investment. Turkey has become a candidate for EU membership. It has pledged to reform, modernise and liberalise its economy. One of the most surprising developments is the "thaw" in the relations with Greece, allowing for interesting prospects for cooperation, in particular building a gas pipeline between the two countries, thus creating a "Southern Gas Ring" in Europe.

To complete the Eurasian picture we need to add the United States. The EU and US work closely together. They have a permanent dialogue. Both agree on the same principles and objectives of market economy and pluralistic democracy. In energy they agree on the concept of multiple pipelines. They have adopted a common declaration to that effect at their Presidential Summit in 1998. Both support multiple pipelines because they believe monopolies make neither commercial nor political sense. They do differ however on the role of Iran, less so on the role of Russia. It will be interesting to see what policy the Bush administration will pursue. Will it be driven by the Texas oil lobby or rather by the traditional Republican propensity to limit US intervention to areas of vital strategic interest?

Conclusion

Many wonder whether the Eurasian region will become again the theatre of a "Great Game". Let's use the terminology of game theory from political science: the Great Game at the start of the previous century was in fact "a zero-sum game", where someone's gain (Russia) was some one else's loss (Britain), or vice versa. At the start of this new century we may have a Great Game in the modern sense: current instruments and policies are designed to produce "a positive sum game", where everyone could win and no one should lose. If all the countries and parties cooperate in the region there will be finally a "win-win" situation.

REGIONAL NON-COOPERATION IN CENTRAL ASIA: A PATHOLOGY

Martin C. Spechler[1]

Professor, Indiana University, U.S.

Since independence from the former Soviet Union, Central Asian leaders and economists have always welcomed the prospect of regional cooperation among the five countries.[2] Their rhetoric and joint proclamations have called attention to their common Turkic[3] and Muslim background. In March, 1998, three of them pledged "eternal friendship." They acknowledge the need for a larger regional market permitting division of labor and a better bargaining position with outsiders. They are aware of the arbitrary Soviet-era borders[4] which often cut across natural economic areas and transportation routes. And yet in the main policy arenas, actual regional cooperation has been noticeable by its absence. Neither economic integration nor water regulation nor even security coordination has been a success, despite all the joint communiqués and speeches. This paper explains why.

Soon after the collapse of the rouble zone in 1992-93 and the adoption of national currencies and central banks, the core Central Asian countries (excluding Turkmenistan) adopted a Central Asian Union and a Free Trade Agreement in 1994. Establishment of a coordinating council and a Central Asian Bank soon followed. In principle trade was to be free among the three, later four after Tajikistan adhered in 1998.[5] This grouping is now called the Central Asian Economic Community. However, despite name changes and frequent summit meetings, coordination of trade policy was never achieved, neither for intra-regional commerce nor for the crucial exchange with Russia and the rest of the outside world. In fact, starting in 1994 Kazakstan's President Nursultan Nazarbaev has enthusiastically promoted what is now called an "Eurasian Union" with Russia, Belarus, Kyrgyzstan, and (since 1998) Tajikistan without any clear understanding of how this would be consistent with the former grouping. Overlapping preferential trade agreements are an economic absurdity. In the event, neither grouping became effective owing to internal disagreements.[6] Russia insisted on a higher external tariff than Belarus and Kyrgyzstan, and the latter proceeded with WTO membership, which requires MFN treatment for all partners. Russia also charges a VAT on exports, an unusual practice regionally and internationally.

The Central Asian Bank for Reconstruction and Development has had some modest success, as is also true of a parallel institution in the Black Sea Economic Cooperation. The CABRD has funded several small multi-state enterprises, but its mere US$9m in paid-in capital limits its effectiveness. Although the transportation system of the region was built for trade with Soviet Russia and often traversed union-republican borders without hesitation, the states of the region have done little to improve the poor links with each other. In fact, Uzbekistan is building two roads entirely within its own borders to reach the cities of Samarkand and Andijan from Tashkent. The Kyrgyz have put priority on an all-seasons road from Bishkek, the capital, to Osh in its south. The Tajiks are emphasising a road east to China.

Late in 1996 Uzbekistan made its new currency, the som, inconvertible into hard currency, while the Kazak tenge and the Kyrgyz som were convertible for small transactions and current account trade. The Uzbek action, only partially reversed in mid-2000, has impaired intra-regional trade between that key country - the only one to border all the others - and its neighbours. Tariffs continue to be levied nationally, and ad hoc protectionist measures and outright blockades have marked the last 5 years in the region. As trade in staples, such as cotton, water, natural gas, and oil, are all conducted by state agencies, any failure to pay or other irritation can lead to temporary suspension of deliveries, border closings, or visa-requirements. For example, in 1996 the Kyrgyz cut off water to Kazakstan from the Toktogul reservoir for non-payment of electricity bills.

Riverine water has for centuries been essential to the irrigated agriculture of this semi-arid area. Uzbekistan and to a lesser extent Turkmenistan and Tajikistan could never have become major sources of cotton for Russian industry from the 1860's through Soviet times without the abundant waters of the Amu Darya and Syr Darya, which flow from present day Tajikistan and Kyrgyzstan mountains through the desert valleys to the much depleted Aral Sea far to the west.

Regulation of the flow and allocations is essential to maximize agricultural yields, to avoid desertification, and to avoid open conflict between upstream and downstream powers. The status quo, set in Soviet times, is clearly unstable for a number of reasons. Firstly, the

Kyrgyz and Tajiks wish to exploit the headwaters for hydropower, requiring release of flow from the present and projected dams during winter months. The Kyrgyz Republic, moreover, is demanding the downstream states share in the cost of maintaining the Naryn River dams and reservoirs. Uzbekistan and Turkmenistan require their water mainly in the dry and hot summer months. Both want more water to expand production acreage, but semi-autonomous Karakalpakstan (in Uzbekistan) is the main victim of the notorious destruction of the Aral Sea. Uzbekistani authorities have threatened reprisals if Turkmenistan removes more water from the Amu Darya for the Karakum Canal. What is more, a restored Afghanistan might well want more of the Amu Darya flow, just as China may want up to half of the waters of the Ili and Irtysh rivers, which flow into Kazakstan from the Xinjiang Uigur Autonomous Republic of the PRC.

Several international agencies have set up forums for negotiating these water issues, but both Uzbekistan and Turkmenistan have adamantly refused to take part, preferring a go-it-alone approach of negotiating (or more) with their weaker upstream neighbors. The joint commissions have been underfunded. So far, however, most of the problems have been resolved without violence. And more efficient irrigation techniques, feasible within national borders, could help avoid some of the problems. The Caspian Sea Forum, set up to limit pollution and poaching of the valuable caviar-bearing sturgeon in the common resource, has likewise failed to operate effectively.

During the last five years security cooperation has attracted the most attention from the region's policymakers owing to events in Afghanistan, increased drugs and refugees crossing into Tajikistan, terrorist bombings in Tashkent in early 1999, and the incursions of Islamic forces into the area in spring 1999 and spring 2000. The response by these secular states has been a number of military consultations and coordinated responses, as well as some domestic changes.[7] The Central Asian Battalion (Centrasbat) was formed under the auspices of NATO by the presidents of Kazakstan, Kyrgyzstan, and Uzbekistan. These states have participated in military exercises with American, Russian, and some other CIS troops in recent years.

It should be noted that the principal initiative and force behind these security alliances have been external to Central Asia. Most of the forces in Centrasbat and along the Tajik-Afghan border are Russian. But Centrasbat has not been used to combat the Tajik insurgents. The incursions of the Islamic Movement of Uzbekistan in Batken, Kyrgyz

Republic, in 1999 and again in 2000 have been thrown back by Uzbek forces entering unilaterally into neighbouring states, as well as Kyrgyz army units. In view of the limited numbers of Islamist invaders and their failure to recruit indigenous collaborators, many observers think the Uzbek authorities are exaggerating the external threat for domestic control. Others, however, regard the high youth unemployment in the Ferghana Valley as a fertile ground for future Islamic radicalism. Security fears, whether genuine or exaggerated for domestic political purposes, have led Central Asian politicians to welcome NATO and CIS training, equipment, and forces which they had declined before.[8] Military budgets have increased despite pressing alternative needs in all these countries. Russia signed a new bilateral defense agreement with Uzbekistan in 2000 and has also sponsored regional air defense. Nonetheless, Uzbekistan opposed the idea of Russian air strikes into Afghanistan to support the Massoud forces. The Shanghai Five agreements, which include Russia and are intended to protect the region's borders, have resulted in small arms shipments to Tajikistan from China.

It is not entirely irrational that outside powers would become involved in the security situation of Central Asia. According to some authoritative estimates, about 60% of Afghan opium flows through the region.[9] Since much of the heroin is destined for Russia and Western Europe, not Central Asia itself, such interdiction is similar to that pursued elsewhere. Russia considers that the rebellion in Chechnya is linked to Central Asian fighters and ideologies.

Why has regional cooperation among the Central Asian states been so halting and ineffective despite the salient problems of slow growth, water scarcity, and Islamist hostility?

In all the policy areas, some political factors seem to be working powerfully to diminish the cooperative potential. These are all new states, never before seen on the world stage, and they naturally wish to reinforce the weak national identity by symbolic, administrative, and economic means. All have, to one degree or another, promoted their national languages at the expense of Russian. Nativisation of the bureaucracy is pursued with a resulting massive emigration of Russians, other Slavs, Germans, and even fellow Turkic peoples. This is so despite the disproportionate role of non-natives in the professional and technical roles in these republics.[10]

Absent established parties and in the presence of strong clan, local, or tribal loyalties, Central Asian authoritarianism has become personalistic. This was the historic pattern of oasis potentates, whose rule had a pronounced hierarchical and patrimonial character. In all five states the president is firmly and semi-legally ensconced in office for the indefinite future. Authoritarian politics calls for nationalistic rhetoric, not shared sovereignty. Despite an earlier agreement, many of the Soviet-era borders in the region are in fact disputed, as would be expected with mixed populations on all sides.[11]

Notoriously, authoritarian politicians mismanage the economy by discouraging free entrepreneurship and competition from domestic or foreign companies. Military and prestige expenditures along with budget deficits tend to grow and be financed by shady or off-budget sources. Middle-class taxpayers resist or escape; corruption mounts; the tax base shrinks. Democratic criticism of waste, corruption, and cronyism is suppressed.

Such has been the experience in Peron's Argentina, Saddam Hussein's Iraq, Gaddafi's Libya, and now in most of Central Asia. One major mistake was the previously mentioned inconvertibility of the Uzbek som despite widespread dissatisfaction in Uzbekistan's business and banking community. Regulation of payments has been extremely wasteful of scarce administrative talent, while hampering development of small and medium-sized industrial enterprises in the Republic. But everyone must await the promised decision from the very top to reverse it in favour of convertibility for the current account (at least).[12]

During the first few years of independence, it might be argued, regional cooperation was less attractive than what might be called "export globalism" - that is, multilateral trade and investment without regard to geographical or ethnic affinity. With the breakdown of Soviet markets, the main exportable products of these countries were staples with world markets. Uzbekistan could sell its cotton most profitably in the West; Turkmenistan, its natural gas; Tajikistan, its aluminum and gold; Kyrgyzstan, its gold; and Kazakstan, its oil leases.

The carefully nurtured and subsidised manufactures of Soviet vintage were hardly salable in the West, and erstwhile CIS customers now were unable to pay. So the output of Kyrgyz hay-balers, Uzbek cotton-cultivators and airplanes; Kazak metal products; and so on all declined for lack of a ready market. What is more, with proceeds in hard currency from staples, these countries preferred to buy consumer goods and capital equipment from Western Europe, the USA, and even China, which now entered the lower end of the consumer market with large volumes of shuttle-traded goods. Trade in energy, on the other hand, has been conducted on a bilateral barter basis.

To revive manufacturing markets on a regional basis would require some countries to forego development of product lines or actually close facilities, while expanding others for neighbours' markets. Such regional division of labour has always caused conflict lest a neighbour get the better of the deal. Mercosur in Latin America was delayed years on account of such disagreements. The European Coal and Steel Community went through tough negotiations to close many uneconomic coal mines after World War II.

More than just time is required to develop regional cooperation. Based on experience elsewhere, countries must have high employment growth before they will risk the shutdowns and competition which regional integration might bring. Postwar Western Europe had a strong political impetus as well as a common threat from Communism, and a common protector and patron in the USA.[13] Central Asia has none of these, except perhaps a common threat from Islamic extremists. Russian revanchism is no longer a realistic danger in view of that country's economic frailty, its military weakness, and its preoccupation with the Chechen situation.

The prospects for regional cooperation are dim in Central Asia, and no outside power has a clear incentive to promote it. The interests and/or convenience of Russia, China, Turkey, and the United States are best served by continued state-to-state relations. Any joint Central Asian demarche would only complicate matters. Divide and conquer served the Romans in military matters; it serves present day powers in economic and security affairs.

The most promising agent for regional cooperation would be multi-lateral donors truly interested in economic prosperity in the region, if only to prevent instability and migration. The Asian Development Bank, in which all the Central Asian states are members, has promoted regional cooperation in southeast Asia with its Mekong River plan and has undertaken a number of road projects to connect trans-border areas in Central Asia. These communication and transportation projects have great promise, once the commercial and industrial activity in Central Asia is freed of governmental trammels, like inconvertible currencies, border taxes, and corruption. Free trade zones might perform better, too. If the European Union, World Bank,

UNDP, and the Japanese Overseas Economic Cooperation Fund were to make regional cooperation a condition for major loans and assistance, some positive response might be expected. These donors, unlike the efforts of the major military powers, are not in conflict with each other and are open to joint ventures for the benefit of the Central Asian region.

Private, multinational firms also have an interest in regional cooperation. Agricultural machinery manufacturers, for example, have shown an interest in opening facilities if access to neighbouring markets can be assured. With careful negotiations, these large firms could be persuaded to open facilities in each of the cooperating states to the benefit of all concerned. Eventually, multinational firms - including, eventually, Central Asian equity participation - would provide part of the mortar which would rebuild the region's division of labour on free market principles. The members of NATO have an interest, if not a direct part, in realising this potential.

Bibliography

Allison, Roy, and Jonson, Lena, eds. Central Asian Security. London: RIIA, 2001.

Development Alternatives, Inc. Regional Economic Cooperation in Central Asia. Final Report.

Prepared for the Asian Development Bank. Washington, D.C.: DAI, 1998.

Fairbanks, Charles; Starr, S. Frederick; Nelson, C.; and Weisbrode, K. Strategic Assessment of Central Eurasia. Washington, D.C.: SAIS-Atlantic Council, 2001.

Olcott, M.B.; Åslund, A.; and Garnett, S.W. Getting It Wrong. Regional Cooperation and the Commonwealth of Independent States. Washington, D.C.: Carnegie Endowment, 1999.

Spechler, M.C. "Regional Economic Cooperation in Central Asia: the Middle Road," Analysis of Current Events, vol. 9, number 12 (December, 1997), pp. 1, 3-4.

"Uzbekistan: the Silk Road to Nowhere?" Contemporary Economic Policy, vol. 18, no. 3 (July, 2000), pp. 295-303.

1. Professor of Economics, IUPUI, and faculty affiliate of the Inner Asian and Uralic National Resource Center, Indiana University. 4418 Sheffield Drive, Bloomington, Indiana 47408. All opinions are those of the author and not necessarily those of any sponsoring agency or government. spechler@indiana.edu

2. Kazakstan, Kyrgyz Republic, Tajikistan, Turkmenistan, and Tajikistan.

3. Tajik is a Persian language; the others speak various Turkic languages. Russian is almost universally spoken by the elites.

4. In 1993 a joint communique affirmed these Soviet borders and established diplomatic relations, but some border disputes have arisen nevertheless.

5. It is sometimes forgotten that intra-CIS trade was supposed to be free according to a treaty signed in 1994. M.B. Olcott, A. Åslund, and S.W. Garnett, Getting It Wrong (Washington, D.C.: Carnegie Endowment, 1999), p. 170.

6. Visa-free travel was, however, introduced in the Eurasian Union in April, 2001.

7. Nearly all the presidents, formerly Communist functionaries, have proclaimed their loyalty to Islam, increased accommodation of the established clergy, tried to reduce youth and rural unemployment, and of course increased surveillance and repression of dissidents.

8. The US has given mobile radios, but no arms.   So far, the Partnership for Peace of NATO has confined itself to educational, diplomatic, and peacekeeping exercises. The GUUAM grouping, aligned with NATO, has shown little institutional development and may dissipate soon. The Russians included Uzbeks in their 1999 exercises and recently sold Uzbekistan Ka-50 (Black Shark) helicopters to add to its Russian-made fleet. But the provisions of the 1992 Tashkent Treaty have fallen into desuetude.

9. According to Ralf Mutschle, assistant director of Interpol's Criminal Investigation Division. He added that the IMU itself may be responsible for 70% of that import. Wall Street Journal, May 3, 2001, p. A8. A Bush Administration official was said to agree.

10. Uzbekistan has been the most aggressive in nativisation, the Kyrgyz Republic the least, perhaps reflecting the relative availability of trained native cadres.

11. These borders were deliberately drawn in the 1930's by Stalin to divide Turkestan after the Basmachi revolt, the main historical example of Central Asian military cooperation.

12. For a detailed discussion the problem and recent changes see my "Convertibility of the Uzbek Som," Journal of Central Asian Studies, forthcoming, 2001.

13. Besides the famous Marshall Plan aid, the USA was long willing to overlook the trade diversion inherent in Europe's Common Agricultural Policy and its other protectionist policies. The USA provided a large share of strategic forces for NATO in its earlier years, despite some domestic reluctance to keep American troops at European bases.

274

AN ECONOMIC ANALYSIS OF MILITARY EXPENDITURE LEVELS IN CENTRAL ASIA AND TRANSCAUCASIA

Chris Hill: MOD London
Peter Sutcliffe: NATO Economics Directorate

Where opinions have been expressed in this written contribution, they are those of the authors alone and should NOT be interpreted as either UK or NATO official positions.

An Overview of Transition Progress

Table 1 below extracts selected data from the 2000 EBRD Transition Report, which should be consulted for a fuller description of the classification system used to assemble the transition indicators. Basically, a value of **1** represents little or no progress with structural reform, whereas a score of **4+** suggests a standard or level of performance consistent with advanced industrial economies. Figures in **bold** represent a change from the 1999 rating, with normal type depicting an improvement in performance whilst *italics* reveal a deterioration. The 2000 CPI corruption index relates to perceptions of corruption as seen by business people, risk analysts and the general public. Scores range between 10 (highly clean) and 0 (totally corrupt). For reference, of the 90 countries listed in the index, Finland leads with a perfect score of 10, Japan is awarded 6.4, Brazil 3.9, whilst Nigeria comes in last at 1.2.

Table 1 : Transition Progress in Transcaucasia and Central Asia

COUNTRY (2000 CPI Corruption Perceptions Index)	Popln Million (mid-2000) (mid 2000)	Private sector %age share in GDP (mid 2000)	Enterprises			Markets and Trade			Financial Institutions	
			Large-scale privati-sation	Small-scale privati-sation	Governance and entreprise restructuring	Price liberal-isation	Trade and forex system	Comp-etition policy	Banking reform and interest rate liberalisation	Securities markets and non-bank financial institutions
Armenia 2.5	3.8	60	3	3+	2	3	4	1	2+	2
Azerbaijan 1.5	8.1	45	2-	3+	2	3	3+	2	2	2-
Georgia 2.3 (in 1999)	5.4	60	3+	4	2	3+	4+	2	2+	2-
Kazakhstan 3.0	14.8	60	3	4	2	3	3+	2	2+	2+
Kyrgyzstan 2.2 (in 1999)	4.7	60	3	4	2	3	4	2	2+	2
Tajikistan (no rating)	6.3	40	2+	3+	2-	3	3+	2-	1	1
Turkmenstan (no rating)	5.1	25	2-	2	1	2	1	1	1	1
Uzbekistan 2.4	24.9	45	3-	3	2-	2	1	2	2-	2

Sources: *EBRD Transition Reports for 1999 and 2000; pages 24 and 14 respectively.* 1999 and 2000 CPI from Transparency International/Göttingen University, *www.gwdg.de/~uwvw/2000Data.html*

The data reveals widely varying performance between states, with Georgia, Kazakhstan and Kyrgyzstan emerging as clear leaders whilst Turkmenistan and to a lesser extent Uzbekistan bring up the rear. It is also evident that much more progress has been made in releasing enterprises from state control than in liberalising markets and trade. Least progress of all, not surprisingly, has been made in creating honest and transparent financial institutions. Corporate governance is another area where ratings are universally low and in some cases getting worse. Although examples of an improvement in performance over the past year outnumber examples of regression, overall transition progress appears to be very modest with some states (Uzbekistan, Turkmenistan and Armenia) now heading marginally back towards an even more oppressive level of state control over the economy. It should be added that some of the very positive scores (such as for the Georgian trade and forex system) appear to reflect liberal laws on paper rather than reality on the ground.

An Overview of Macro-Economic Trends

To the limited extent that official statistics reveal true levels of economic activity, the data in **Table 2** below reveals an overall picture of modest - and in a few cases robust - recovery from rock-bottom levels over the past two years. Russia's recovery from the 1998 crisis has aided most economies in the region, as have high prices on global markets for energy, raw materials, and other commodities. Official growth rates could, however, be more than usually suspect given the severe and prolonged drought that afflicted most of these countries for much of the year. Agriculture and related industries comprise a significant proportion of GDP and must have been adversely affected. As in Russia, most states are on course to register a marginally worse macro-economic record in 2001 featuring lower growth and higher inflation, although the picture is mixed. Encouragingly, those FSU states that score higher ratings with transition progress (see again **Table 1**) could experience less of a downturn - or even a slight improvement - in GDP than the reform laggards.

The World Bank per capita GDP figures at Purchasing Power Parity (PPP) in the first column are listed because they give a more accurate appraisal of relative living standards than the GDP data at market exchange rates in column 4, which do not account for the under-valuation - in terms of domestic purchasing power - of local currencies against the US dollar. The data can be compared with PPP per capita GDP figures of US$6,339 for Russia and about US$25,000 on average in the G7.

Table 2 : Selected Macro-Economic Data for Transcaucasia and Central Asia - 1998-2001

FSU Per Capita GDP at PPP World Bank 1999	YEAR	GDP (% growth)	GDP (per cap -US$ at market ex.rate)	GDP (% agri culture)	Unemployment (% year-end)*	CPI (% year-end)	General Govnmt Balance (% of GDP)	Current Account (US$m)	Trade Balance (US$m)	External Debt Stock (US$m)
ARMENIA US$2,210	1998	7.2	498	34	8.9	-1.3	-3.7	-403	-578	828
	1999	3.3	486	31	11.6	2.0	-5.9	-307	-474	855
	2000	6.0	504		10.7	0.4	-6.3	-278	-469	863
	2001	5.0				2.5	-4.7	-302	-516	
AZERBAIJAN US$2,322	1998	10.0	526	20	12.9	-7.6	-4.2	-1,363	-1,046	717
	1999	7.4	499	22	13.9	-0.5	-5.4	-600	-408	1,031
	2000	10.5	507			2.2	-2.6	-64	465	1,190
	2001	8.5				3.7	-2.5	-435	-100	
GEORGIA US$3,606	1998	2.9	644	31	14.7	7.2	-6.5	-389	-685	1,636
	1999	3.0	517	28	14.9	10.9	-6.7	-219	-541	1,754
	2000	2.0	555			7.0	-4.6	-250	-584	1,729
	2001	3.5				9.3	-3.5	-240	-599	
KAZAKHSTAN US$4,408	1998	-1.9	1,452	9	6.6	1.9	-7.7	-1,236	-801	9,932
	1999	1.7	1,123	11	6.3	17.8	-5.3	-233	344	12,051
	2000	9.6	1,225			9.8	-0.8	960	2,641	12,328
	2001	6.0					-1.5	410	2,200	
KYRGYZSTAN US$2,223	1998	2.1	350	36	4.3	18.4	-11.2	-328	-170	1,473
	1999	3.7	264	39	5.4	39.9	-12.8	-200	-84	1,682
	2000	5.1	275			9.5	-7.2	-120	3	1,739
	2001	4.0				12.6	-6.4	-131	-17	
TAJIKISTAN US$981	1998	5.3	218	20	2.9	2.7	-3.8	-120	-139	1,213
	1999	3.7	178	17	2.8	30.1	-3.1	-36	-27	1,214
	2000	8.3	158	17	2.5	60.8	-0.6	-61	-57	1,205
	2001	4.5				16.5	-0.7	-62	-40	
TURKMEN-ISTAN US$3,099	1998	5.0	511	25		19.8	-2.7	-935	-523	1,750
	1999	16.0	374			21.2	0.9	-527	-166	2,050
	2000	17.6	415			7.4	0.4	20	630	2,400
	2001	6.0				23.1	-1.0	-150	500	
UZBEKISTAN US$2,092	1998	4.4	433	26	0.5	26.1	-3.0	-38	171	3,484
	1999	4.1	321	28	0.5	25.2	-2.8	-88	191	4,289
	2000	1.5	298	27	0.6	40.0	-1.2	72	391	4,150
	2001	1.0				40.0	-3.2	241	567	

Sources: *EBRD Transition Report Update 2001.* Data for 2001 are projections.
World Development Report 2000/2001; World Bank - Table 1, pp274 and 275.
* Kazakhstan and Tajikistan are annual average. Official unemployment in Turkmenistan is zero.

Overall, we would assess that sustained regional economic renaissance is unlikely to materialise in the medium and longer terms, although better than average regional performance can ultimately be expected in those states that have made the most progress with structural and economic reform. The presence of rich energy reserves in some of these states may boost economies in the short- to medium-term, but whether this wealth is spent wisely or equitably remains to be seen. Moreover, future cycles of economic boom and bust in Russia are likely to be reflected in the macro-economic data for Transcaucasian and Central Asian states as well.

An Overview of Defence Spending Trends

Defence Spending in 2000

The countries of Transcaucasia and Central Asia provide only limited information on their defence spending. Some, indeed, do not offer even a figure for (supposed) total outlays while most of those that do give no meaningful explanation as to how it has been calculated. Inevitably, there is a suspicion that some items which in the West would be considered part of defence expenditure have been omitted and that the valuation attached to others bears no clear relationship to their true cost. In any case, all of the data is in a currency which is little understood outside the country concerned and cannot be freely converted into western money.[1] Moreover, there can be substantial differences between defence spending in a western context - i.e. the provision of security as a public good - and defence spending in a Central Asian context, where troops can spend a good deal of their time picking cotton, building roads or protecting the commercial interests of their commanders.

It is therefore highly likely that the nominal strength of armed forces in many of these states is substantially larger than the number of combat-ready troops able to counter any military threat. In this respect, military spending in these regions is more a matter of political priority than of affordability. The official budget can play only a small role in military financing, with much larger sums being raised from other, often illegal, activities to fund both the state military apparatus and various ad hoc paramilitary or other armed groups.

We have therefore made our own estimates of defence spending. These are calculated in US dollars,[2] using NATO definitions of what properly constitutes a defence outlay and adjusting for the undervaluation of domestic currencies viv a vis the US dollar. Given both the lack of data and the non-structured nature of armed forces in many of these states, an element of uncertainty in the results is unavoidable. Nonetheless, we are confident that this approach yields more worthwhile data than can be derived through the conventional technique of accepting published defence budgets (where given) as a reliable expression of total defence outlays and then converting these to western currency using the market exchange rate.

Our calculations indicate that, for every country, the traditional procedure understates dramatically the dollar cost of defence spending. (See Table 3 below). For most states true defence outlays are, when measured in dollars, ten times or more the level usually quoted in assessments. Across the whole area, defence spending in 2000 amounted to some US$5.46bn, a rise since 1998 of over 3% in nominal terms but essentially the same once US$ inflation over this period is taken into account. There was some variation between regions. In Central Asia, where Islamic militants continued to pose severe security concerns, the real level of outlays rose sharply in 2000. However, since this followed a reduction in 1999, the growth in Central Asian military outlays over the full two years was, after inflation, less than 4%. In the Transcaucasus, however, spending has declined both in nominal and real terms since 1998 despite the fact that no state has suffered an absolute fall in GDP. Except when unavoidable, governments in the region generally remain reluctant to raise the financial priority of defence, preferring instead to use any additional resources that growth may produce to support standards of living or invest in the civilian economy.

Table 3 : Defence Spending in Central Asia and Transcaucasia - 1998, 1999, 2000[3]

COUNTRY	DEFENCE BUDGET[4] In US$ million - current prices - at official exchange rates (mid year)			DEFENCE EXPENDITURE (NATO definition) In US$ million - current prices - via direct costing		
	1998	*1999*	*2000*	*1998*	*1999*	*2000*
Uzbekistan	170	134	n.a.	1,670	1,600	1,750
Kazakhstan	258	133	83	1,180	1,050	1,250
Kyrgyzstan	30	23	19	170	200	230
Tajikistan	18	13	13	120	120	130
Turkmenistan	102	112	n.a.	250	230	290
Total Central Asia	578	415	n.a.	3,390	3,200	3,650
Armenia	94	74	69	680	710	690
Azerbaijan	194	119	113	820	790	830
Georgia	61	28	22	400	350	290
Total Caucasus	349	221	204	1,900	1,850	1,810

This revised data goes some way towards solving one of the greatest puzzles over the region's defence outlays, namely how in many cases quite large armed forces - in terms of the number of troops - could be maintained on what appeared to be minimal dollar-equivalent spending. It does not, however, mean that the countries' military capabilities are any larger than we had previously thought - on the contrary, they have exactly the same number of men, aircraft, tanks and so forth - nor that they spend more in their domestic currency to secure those capabilities. The real purpose of the dollar cost estimate is to permit reliable defence spending comparisons between nations, thus providing a key input into assessments of the size and scale of any military build-up. The bottom line is that, even with the revised data, outlays are in all states relatively small by international standards. We assess that in 2000 the eight countries of Transcaucasia and Central Asia together spent on defence less than a sixth as much as the United Kingdom or, put another way, sufficient to support the United States' military effort for less than a week.[5]

Table 4 below shows defence spending in 2000 per serviceman (including paramilitaries) and per head of population on NATO definitions. These figures reveal wide differences between countries. In terms of outlays per serviceman, Uzbekistan, determined not only to defend itself from external threat but also to be a leading military power in Central Asia, tops the list. In terms of outlays per head of population, Armenia is the highest followed - a considerable distance behind - by Azerbaijan, two countries still in dispute over Nagorno-Karabakh. Defence outlays per capita in Central Asia and Georgia are by comparison quite low.[6]

Table 4 : Defence Expenditure per Serviceman and per Head of Population in 2000 (NATO definition - in $US at current prices - via direct costing)

COUNTRY	Defence Expenditure per Serviceman (US dollars)	Defence Expenditure per Head of Population (US dollars)
Uzbekistan	22,400	71
Kazakhstan	15,300	84
Kyrgyzstan	16,400	48
Tajikistan	7,900	21
Turkmenistan	10,000	62
Average Central Asia	16,600	66
Armenia	13,500	181
Azerbaijan	9,600	103
Georgia	8,700	54
Average Caucasus	10,800	104

Defence Burden Estimates for 2000

Across the entire region, defence spending last year accounted for a little over 2.5% of GDP, about the same as in NATO and only half that for Russia. There were, as Table 5 below demonstrates, substantial differences between countries but only in Armenia do defence outlays generally seem likely to impinge significantly on the level of funding available for other purposes. Elsewhere, sustainability is probably more a question of the governments' ability to raise revenue than of the overall strength of the economies. Indeed, compared to 1998 the defence burden has fallen in all countries except Kyrgyzstan.

Table 5 : Defence Burdens in 2000 (Milex as % of GDP)

Under 2%	2 - 3%	3 - 4%	4 - 5%	Over 5%
Kazakhstan	Kyrgyzstan	Uzbekistan	Turkmenistan	Armenia
Moldova	Tajikistan		Azerbaijan	

Note: For comparison, Russia and NATO (average) defence burdens in 2000 were roughly 5% and 2.5% respectively.

Military Spending in Central Asia

Kazakhstan

After lengthy debate and the discussion of sums varying between 8 and 16.5 billion tenge, Kazakhstan's defence budget for 2000 was finally set at 11.896 billion tenge. In cash terms this was about the same amount as had been spent the previous year but after inflation represented a marked reduction. The military outcry was strong and within two months President Nazarbayev had agreed to increase funding for the second half of the year by 20%. Then, over the summer, as the security situation in Central Asia deteriorated, the Kazakhs decided to bolster their forces by calling up significant numbers of reservists, particularly specialists in areas such as engineering and telecommunications. The budget allocation for the year eventually topped 17 billion tenge. If price rises for the military sector were the same as for consumer goods, outlays of this magnitude would have been worth around a quarter more in real terms than those for 1999.

Some defence spending falls outside the official defence budget. For example, the science budget, which in 2000 was increased by 260 million tenge to around 1.3 billion tenge, funds most of Kazakhstan's limited military R&D programmes. Internal security forces are also not paid from the defence budget. In 2000 it was agreed that the maritime border guards needed strengthening, but with the Ministry of Finance ill-placed to find any additional funding, businesses were asked to contribute on a voluntary basis. Enterprises are in fact a significant source of funds for the military; in November 2000, the commander of the Atyrau border detachment in western Kazakhstan spoke freely of the assistance given to his unit by companies such as Kazakhoil-Emba, Irbis-Servis and Ofis-Servis.

International barter can provide a significant boost to defence funding. Under an agreement signed in February 2000, Kazakhstan was to receive Russian defence equipment, including transport aircraft and helicopters, rather than hard currency as payment for Moscow's lease of the space facilities at Baykonur.[7] It is also getting large numbers of aircraft (mainly Su-27, L-39 and Tu-154) and two SA-10 air defence systems to replace material taken by Russian troops when they left Kazakhstan after the break-up of the Soviet Union. Overall, we judge that on western definitions of military spending, out-lays in 2000 were probably around 40 billion tenge, just under 2% of GDP.

This sum was inadequate to meet all of the requirements of the armed forces. One general, lamenting the poor conditions in the Kazakh army compared to those in the Chinese military(!), claimed that because the 2000 budget provided only 250 million of the 750 million tenge needed to purchase personal accessories, the typical lieutenant could spend up to one third of his wages on such things. Self provision of shoulder straps, long-service stripes, cap badges and the like seems to have become standard in the Kazakh army and there have even been references to soldiers having to buy their own foot-wear. Efforts underway since early 1999 to increase the proportion of contract servicemen in the forces appear, temporarily at least, almost to have stalled due to lack of funds; the latest figures suggest that there are still only 10,000 such individuals.[8] Despite a fall in the number of desertions in 2000, the life of conscripts remains unenvia-ble. The Ministry of Defence also regularly complains about their quality and motivation. Legislation is apparently now being prepared under which individuals wishing to avoid conscription will be able to do so in return for a fixed payment.

The defence budget for 2001 has been set at 25 billion tenge, an increase after inflation on the sum finally spent in 2000 of about a third. There is, of course, no guarantee that all of the promised extra cash will materialise although the 2001 defence budget was confirmed at a meeting of the National Security Council in March 2001. Whatever actual outlays turn out to be, we assess that their real level will show some significant growth in 2001. There is little detailed information on how this will be spent. The government has, however, said that training will be enhanced and that there is a requirement for more mobile forces. Servicemen's salaries were supposed to be raised by around 30% from the start of the year though for many no extra money had been received by the end of March.[9] There is so far no evidence of negotiations to buy new or upgraded weapons though these are probably taking place. In February 2001 deputy defence minister Gosman Amrin said that he hoped new military equipment would begin to arrive with the forces from 2002; deployment of a modern air defence system is apparently planned for 2005.

There are also plans to increase other parts of the state budget where defence spending is located. Outlays on public order and security have been fixed at 30 billion tenge, a substantial rise on 2000. However, because this allocation also includes money for the police and judiciary, it is difficult to assess exactly how the paramilitaries will fare. The science budget is scheduled to rise from 1.3 to 1.5 billion tenge, though most, if not all, of this is likely to be needed to fund the 30% pay boost given to all budget funded civilian staff from 1 January 2001. Not surprisingly, there have been calls for a further increase in resources, perhaps to 2.3 billion tenge.

Uzbekistan

Uzbekistan's armed forces are the strongest in former Soviet Central Asia. The government last released information on the defence spending needed to support these forces in 1999 and even then the figure (34.9 billion som) had to be treated with caution. All outlays on troops belonging to the Ministry of Internal Affairs, the State Border Service, the Ministry of Emergency Services and the National Security Service were excluded because they were met from outside the defence budget. Expenditure on the research, development and testing of weapons was also omitted as were any subsidies to defence industries. Until the end of last year military pensions were probably paid by the Ministry of Social Security; since then responsibility has been transferred to a non-budgetary pensions fund. Finally, many transactions were completed by barter and it was unclear how, if at all, the value of these was reflected in expenditure figures.

We judge that, if all of these items together with Ministry of Defence debts incurred during the year were included, total defence spending in Uzbekistan in 2000 was probably around 65 billion som, equivalent to just over 3% of GDP. Of the nine-tenths of outlays which are allocable to particular branches of services we assess that about two thirds went to the ground forces with the remainder split roughly equally between, on the one hand, the air and air defence forces and, on the other, the various paramilitaries.

In real terms outlays appear to have risen quite significantly last year, primarily in response to incursions by the militant IMU whose stated aim is the overthrow of the government in Tashkent. Significant numbers of troops had to be deployed to the mountainous border region where fighting was often fairly intense. Substantial quantities of small arms and ammunition were purchased, where possible by barter, and there seem to have been efforts to service and renovate some larger equipment. The importance of the latter can be seen in the comment by Air Force commander Kashimov last November that 90% of the Mi-8 (Hip) helicopter fleet was then in need of repair, that only a third of Mi-24 (Hind) helicopters were operational and that all 12 Su-27 (Flanker) fighters at Chirchik airbase required depot-level work. The authorities also appear to be pressing ahead with plans for a new military airport at Uchkuduk.

"Reinforcing the country's military potential" has been named as one of the priority sectors for budget outlays in 2001 and it seems likely that, despite a relatively gloomy economic prognosis, a further rise in defence spending is planned. We expect part of this extra money to be devoted to modernising the helicopter fleet; in March 2001 Uzbek Defence Minister Qodir Ghulomov reportedly reached an accord with a visiting Russian military delegation for the delivery of an unspecified number of Ka-50 (Black Shark). In May 2001, according to Russian press reports, President Putin agreed to supply substantial quantities of weaponry in exchange for cotton, gas, fruit and vegetables. Beyond that, even if the fundamentalists are suppressed, military outlays may continue to grow as attempts are made to progress President Karimov's vision of a better paid, better organised, all-professional force, albeit with smaller numbers than at present.

Turkmenistan

The Turkmenistan defence budget for 2000 was not published, though it probably provided for a large increase in funds over the

582 billion manats approved for 1999. Salaries for regulars were, for example, typically doubled from the start of the year, a rise several times that needed to match inflation. Plans announced at the end of 1998 to cut the size of the armed forces also appear to have been implemented only slowly and, because of the redundancy package, may not in any case have saved much money in the short term. There is, however, no evidence of any upsurge in arms imports: in May 2000 President Niyazov said the forces already had enough equipment for the next 10-15 years.

The published budget probably includes most outlays on border and internal security troops as well as those on the regular services. Nevertheless, its coverage is still unlikely to be as comprehensive as those of NATO countries. For example, Georgia, which is currently refurbishing 46 Su-25 (FROGFOOT) aircraft for the Turkmen air force, will probably not be paid for this out of the defence budget but rather will have the debts it has incurred for natural gas supplies reduced. According to the press, the cost of the work being undertaken in Georgia is around US$1m per plane, a significant sum even if spread over more than one year when the total published defence and law enforcement budget for 1999 was worth only US$112m at market exchange rates. Turkmenistan is also not always prompt in settling bills that should be paid in cash. For instance, as of October 2000 it owed Russia R5.7m, the most of any former Soviet state, for training its citizens at higher education establishments of the Russian Federal Border Guard Service. Part of the debt apparently dated back to 1996. Allowing for these and other likely omissions (e.g. military pensions and housing benefits for discharged servicemen) we assess that in 2000 total defence spending on NATO definitions was in the region of 1,100 billion manats, some 4.5% of GNP.

No figures for defence spending in 2001 have yet been announced. However, all military pay and pensions rose by 50% on 1 March. But since most salaries across the economy were doubled on that date it seems likely that inflation will rapidly eliminate the benefits to the military of their pay hike and, indeed, real standards of living could fall. The forces will also be required to make themselves fully self-sufficient in certain types of food in 2001. Although no further cuts in personnel numbers are planned for this year, President Niyazov has announced that contract service will eventually be abolished. He said that this was being done with the aim both of cutting costs and rooting out fraud.

Kyrgyzstan

The Kyrgyz defence and security budget is not comparable in coverage to a western defence budget. On the one hand, it is believed to fund not only the Ministry of Defence and internal security forces but also perhaps the police and judiciary. On the other, it probably excludes military pensions and a number of other defence-related items. Furthermore, it is doubtful if an accurate - or perhaps any - allowance is made for goods obtained by barter, either from domestic or overseas sources, while the price attached to many other products probably does not reflect their true cost. Nonetheless, it is worth noting that the budget for 2000 was (probably) initially fixed at 900 million som, a cut of just over 5% in cash terms compared to the previous year. Out of this sum around 460 million som appears to have been directed to the Ministry of Defence.[10]

It was soon apparent that such sums were not enough to meet military requirements. In the first six months of last year the Ministry of Defence received 300 million som, well above the planned amount, and other parts of the security apparatus probably also obtained substantial additional funding. A major incursion by Islamic extremists into southern Kyrgyzstan over the summer - similar to one that took place in 1999 - dramatically added to the problem, with large numbers of troops being once again despatched to fight them. In August alone the Defence Ministry and other security organs received an extra 100 million som while late the following month Marat Sultanov, chairman of the Parliamentary Committee on Budget and Finances, claimed that the total additional cost to the budget of military operations since the start of the fighting had been 400 million som. The money, he said disarmingly, had been found from sums originally set aside to meet Kyrgyzstan's foreign debts.

With military engagements continuing in earnest into October before the militants were finally declared beaten, the financial cost to Kyrgyzstan was doubtless eventually well beyond that figure. Various sources suggest that the Ministry of defence received some 810-830 million som for the year as a whole while relatively substantial extra resources also went to the Ministry of Internal Affairs, the National Security Ministry and the National Guard. Overall, we estimate that on NATO definitions total defence outlays in 2000 might have been in the region of 1,500 million som, that is about 2.5% of GDP.

Despite the increased defence spending and help from abroad Kyrgyz forces remained weak. One report claimed that in early 2001 the air force had only 3 fully operational aircraft (2 subsonic L-39 trainers and an obsolete Mig-21 fighter) and 2 military pilots! The ongoing crisis with Islamic extremism has now pushed the authorities into drafting better mobilisation regulations and a new operations plan. The latter envisages major changes, including the establishment of a Southern Group of Forces with a number of battalion sized sub-divisions. Negotiations have started with Russia for the purchase of Mi-8 helicopter gunships and a defence co-operation agreement has been signed with Kazakhstan. The government has also decided to speed up the process of replacing conscripts with contract personnel but, as with the other developments, the financial consequences will be significant. Contract servicemen are said already to receive salaries on average twice the national average and further increases have been mooted.

The official defence budget for 2001 has been set at 535 million som, a rise in nominal terms of around 16% compared to the allocation initially approved for last year. If inflation in the defence sector is comparable to that in the rest of the economy, the real increase should be around 5%. However, as in 2000, it is doubtful whether the planned sums will be sufficient. Figures for first quarter outlays imply that the Ministry of Defence is already heading for an overspend of 20-25% and this is certain to worsen dramatically if, as expected, the militants renew their attacks. Both the Ministry of Defence and the Kyrgyz parliament have demanded extra funds for the armed forces though, as of mid-April, the Ministry of Finance was still resisting this.

Tajikistan

On the basis of limited information we estimate that, on NATO definitions, total defence outlays in 2000 were probably in the region of 35-40 million somoni and accounted for about 2% of GDP, significantly less than half that at the height of the civil war. Spending at this level was inadequate to overcome serious shortfalls in Tajik military capability. Moscow is, however, trying to help and in 2000 provided some 5.1 billion (Russian) roubles out of its own budget to restore Tajik air defences. Russia also deploys in Tajikistan a motorised rifle division and supplies many of the officers in the internal security forces. Tajikistan has no air force of its own and in a conflict would be entirely dependent on Russia for aerial cover. In February 2001 Defence Minister Sherali Khairulloev visited Moscow where he discussed with the then Russian Defence Minister Igor Sergeyev the possibility of securing for his country unspecified weapons and ammunition at reduced prices, but the outcome is unknown. China, also keen to promote its interests in the region, agreed in July 2000 to grant 5 million yuan (about US$0.7m at the official exchange rate) to enable the Tajik Ministry of Defence to pay for language training for some of its officers in Shanghai and to obtain some minor equipment.

A key decision in 2000 was the axing of contract military service, a promise being made that some of the money saved would be used to increase the salary of remaining servicemen and to purchase new weapons. In August several thousand men apparently left the Defence Ministry, Internal Affairs Ministry, Presidential Guard, Emergency Situations Ministry and State Border Guard, each provided with at least five months' pay. Most allegedly went into farming. President Rahmonov tried to present the move as an attack on crime, claiming that contract servicemen were selling their weapons or using them to carry out robberies. It was probably designed more to rid the forces of former guerrillas who had been allowed to join on contract as part of the 1997 peace deal with the United Tajik Opposition. There is no evidence that the remaining servicemen have yet obtained their pay rise nor have there been any major equipment imports, though fighter aircraft are believed to top the Ministry of Defence's wish-list.

There is as yet no information on the amount of defence spending planned for 2001. However, Finance Minister Safarali Najmuddinov said last December that the major priority was to reduce poverty through a tripling of the minimum wage and salary increases of 40% for workers in education, health and government administration. If these aims are met, we believe that there will not be sufficient money in the state budget also to provide any major boost to the military.

Military Spending in Transcaucasia

Georgia

The armed forces in Georgia suffer from chronic and worsening underfunding. In 2000 the state budget included an allocation of 43.7 million lari for the Ministry of Defence. This was well under half the sum originally requested and, even after allowance for the transfer of military pensions out of the defence budget, an estimated 15% less in real terms than had been approved for the previous year. By comparison with 1997, planned budget outlays had fallen after inflation by well over a half. The military were unsurprisingly adamant that it was impossible to operate efficiently on the promised level of funding, which was in fact equivalent to just 0.5% of GDP. However, the government, far from offering concessions, then decided that it could not fund the defence budget even as it stood. It therefore formally sequestered almost half of the vote, leaving the Ministry of Defence with just 23.5 million lari.

As in other countries in the region, significant amounts of what the West would call defence spending are met from outside the Defence Ministry budget. The State Border Guard appears initially to have been allocated 12.5 million lari (though some sources claim this was cut to 11.1 million lari) while the Internal Security troops were promised 10.1 million lari and the Government Guard Service 7 million lari. Spending on military pensions might, on our estimates, have been set at around 6-7 million lari. However, as with the Ministry of Defence, budget allocations are not necessarily a reliable guide to actual sums paid out and there have been many complaints of grossly inadequate funding.

The authorities argued that large amounts of money could be saved by cutting personnel numbers. In June 2000, at the insistence of President Shevardnadze, the Georgian parliament agreed to cut by year-end the number of Defence Ministry troops from 27,000 to 20,000, of Internal Security troops from 7,900 to 6,400 and of Border Guards from 9,500 to 8,700. The size of the Government Guard Service was, however, increased from 3,000 to 3,300 largely to provide increased protection for oil pipelines. As far as we can judge, the forces met or came fairly close to meeting these targets. Plans to move towards fully professional services were put on hold. The Ministry of Defence said that it alone would need an additional 20 million lari just to replace conscripts with contract staff. Senior officials talked of cutting short the autumn conscription round since many units could not find the resources to absorb more men.

Savings from force reductions were hopelessly inadequate to offset budget reductions, particularly since the law required dismissed servicemen to be given substantial redundancy payments and other benefits. As a result, military salaries were left unpaid for large parts of the year and, even when they did reach soldiers' pockets, were due to inflation worth less in real terms than in the previous year. Allowances were also often left unpaid while most military pensions were months in arrears. Thirty per cent of officers were said to have taken outside jobs, usually menial ones, in an attempt to secure some cash while others were noted selling their blood. There were no uniforms for large numbers of new recruits and those with longer service came to look increasingly shabby. Food supplies fell to alarming levels, with the typical soldier in some units reportedly receiving on average only 1,500 calories a day.[11] In mid-November 2000 Colonel Akia Barbbakadze, head of the Main Rear Logistics Directorate, claimed gloomily that "starvation is beginning in the army".

Overall, we assess that, on NATO definitions and including the value of goods and services received but not paid for, the Georgian defence effort in 2000 cost around 90 million lari, still only 1% of GDP. Despite the likelihood of continued economic growth, the situation seems unlikely to improve this year. The Defence Ministry budget has been set at just 33.06 million lari, a reduction of about a quarter in real terms compared to that originally fixed for 2000. Within that sum, just over 7 million lari has been allocated for the purchase of food, little more than half the amount said by the Ministry of Defence to be necessary to meet requirements. The salary and equipment maintenance bids have also been cut sharply while there is no provision at all in the final budget for either new weapons procurement or for the maintenance of Ministry buildings. The Internal Security Troops, Border Guards and the Government Guard Service are also promised less money than last year. Moreover, as with previous years, it is doubtful whether the promised sums will ever materialise. During the first quarter, for example, the Border Guards received only 88% of the amount authorised for that period. Soldiers belonging to the Interior Ministry's Tqibuli battalion simply went on strike, declaring that they had not been paid for 13 months. Although friendly states are providing some assistance,[12] a further decline in capability seems inevitable.

Armenia

The Armenian defence effort continues to be driven by the as yet unresolved dispute with Azerbaijan over Nagorno-Karabakh. The budget allocation for 2000 was officially fixed at around 38 billion dram, less than 4% of GDP, but this omits a number of items which NATO countries would consider part of their military expenditure.

These include internal security, which last year was expected to cost 5 billion dram, military pensions, which we estimate to require outlays of about 6 billion dram per annum, and numerous smaller elements. Armenia also obtains financial aid from Russia, particularly for border protection. In our view total defence outlays in 2000 (including the value of unpaid bills) probably topped 60 billion dram. At almost 6% of GDP, this defence burden is the highest in the former Soviet Union.

Despite this, Armenia has not been able to meet the requirements of its forces. The number of conscripts called up in 2000 was, at 23,000, about 7% less than in the previous year. Moreover, almost half of those who were conscripted did not have a full secondary education and many were in poor physical shape. Once inducted, large numbers found conditions of service so bad that they routinely went absent without leave. Beginning in June 2000, the number of patrols despatched to apprehend offenders was virtually trebled. This situation is unlikely to improve in the short term. In 2001 the official defence budget is scheduled to decline to 37 billion dram. A pay rise for either servicemen or Ministry of Defence civilians has been ruled out even though inflation will probably be around 4-5%. There are also unlikely to be any major equipment purchases though Defence Minister Sarkisyan has promised to try and improve training, notably by holding in June 2001 the country's first all forces exercise.

Azerbaijan

The Azeri defence budget for 2000 was fixed at 494 billion manats, an increase of 4.8% in nominal terms and perhaps 3% after inflation compared to the previous year. This was not enough to pay off the large Ministry of Defence debt nor significantly to improve the very poor conditions of service prevalent within the forces. Money was, however, found to arm a coastal patrol craft. Corruption is widespread: a check on Defence Ministry spending, completed in October 2000, apparently found irregularities sufficiently serious to be reported to the President though no details as to their precise nature have yet been released. Critics have referred publicly to cases where senior officers have demanded money from soldiers who have completed their military service and, when this has not been paid, have extended their term in the forces.

Many items of defence spending are, as elsewhere in the former Soviet Union, met from outside the defence budget. These include border guards and internal security forces, both of which report to the Ministry of the Interior. Ammunition acquired from Ukraine during 2000 appears to have been paid for, at least initially, in diesel fuel from central stocks rather than with money from the Ministry of Defence. Other goods have also been obtained internally by barter. However, the Azeris have so far been unable to secure payment from Russia of a bill for using the Gabala radar station. Overall, we assess that, on NATO definitions, Azerbaijan spent over 1,000 billion manats on defence in 2000, equivalent to almost 5% of GDP.

The defence budget for 2001 has been set at 539 billion manats, a 9% nominal increase over 2000 and well ahead of expected 3% annual inflation. The science budget, which probably provides most of the limited funding needed for military R&D projects, will grow by 13%. With its economy outperforming, and over the next few years expected to go on outperforming, that of Armenia, Azerbaijan seems likely to be the better placed of the two countries to fund any major build up of armed forces.

1. Further information on published defence budgets is given in the individual country sections.

2. The non-Russian FSU states do not, of course, normally "spend" dollars, except on imports. A more precise description of our measure might be "dollar-equivalent cost of the resources devoted to defence" but this is gramatically cumbersome and we have pre ferred to stick with a simpler, if slightly less accurate, term.

3. Russian defence expenditure in 2000, computed on a similar basis, is estimated at about $50bn - fully nine times more than the Central Asian and Transcaucasian regions together.

4. As initially approved by the relevant parliament. The defence budgets in some countries were revised during the course of the year.

5. At official exchange rates, total Central Asian and Transcaucasian MILEX in 2000 would have funded US armed forces for less than one day.

6. By comparison in 2000 the United States spent c.US$210,000 per serviceman and US$1,060 per head of population. For Russia the estimated figures were US$29,600 and US$340 respectively.

7. Some press reporting suggests that, despite this agreement, Russia may eventually have paid the Baykonur rental fee in currency rather than goods. If so, this presumably reflects its much improved financial position following the rise in the international price of oil.

8. Defence Minister Sat Tokpakbayev has said that he hopes that, over seven or eight years, the proportion of the armed forces made up by conscripts can be reduced to no more than a half. He has acknowledged, however, that this depends both on sufficient funding and on an adequate number of volunteers.

9. The MOD had, however, by then imposed extra accommodation charges on officers and abolished their free food rations.

10. Other sources suggest that the Defence Ministry was allocated either 212 or 350 million som. The MOD's own estimate of its requirement was apparently 674 million som.

11. Despite inflation, the official norm for spending on food has been fixed at 59 lari a month per serviceman since 1996.

12. Bulgaria has, for instance, agreed to supply two amphibious warfare ships free of charge.

PLENARY SESSION

CONCLUSION

WHAT HARMS REGIONAL COOPERATION[1] AND SECURITY?

Daniel Daianu[2]

Professor, Academy of Economic Studies, Bucharest

The linkage between regional cooperation and security is quite obvious. However, what seems to be a conspicuous incentive nexus for both individual and collective players does not always work in reality. Frequently, for reasons which I will try to revisit very briefly, regional cooperation remains - deep down - an elusive goal and, thereby, security is impaired.

At the start of my remarks let me underline a series of factors (circumstances) which are presumed to enhance regional cooperation and cooperation in general. The driving power of these factors/ circumstances should likely get stronger in a world which, supposedly, is increasingly interconnected under the spell of fast technological progress and economic liberalization. First come economic incentives - trade and overseas investment/production. When these operate according to the logic of a non-zero sum game, losers, should they be numerous, can be compensated one way or another. Less ideological confrontation would also work to the same end. Following diminished confrontation, governments would show more restraint in using economic means (including sanctions) as instruments of foreign policy. The diminution (disappearance) of ethnic and religious enmity, where that exists, would be another favorable factor, as would be the reduction of border conflicts. I would range among these factors, also, a convergence of Weltanschaung outlooks, of values and principles which can foster trust and mutual respect. I should say that this convergence would not necessarily mean the acceptance of a sort of Western cultural supremacy. And finally, I would list the power of "attractors", of big players who can exert an "ordering" influence on events with international repercussions and on the conduct of smaller actors.

On this line of reasoning and as an intellectual exercise I would suggest to apply the matrix sketched above to world political and economic dynamics as the latter evolved during the last decade, in the wake of the exceptional year of 1989. To this end one can use different perspectives. One perspective, which is imbued with a western thinking of a prevalent flavor, I would describe as "examining the post-1989 period through rosy lenses". Its main pillars would be:

• the expected effects of the collapse of communism, in the vein of what Fukuyama called "The End of History"[3], including the spread of democracy (of western values) throughout the world, and the setting up of a "new world order"; relatively easy to undertake market reforms and ensuing economic prosperity could be mentioned among the expected effects;

• globalization, driven by information technologies and market forces, which would help disseminate democratic values worldwide[4];

• the pressure towards a "border-less world"[5], with many nation-states under economic siege and relinquishing economic policy prerogatives under the pressure of world financial markets; this would, presumably, help discipline economic policies;

• the gravitational power of NATO and the EU at a time when most European post-communist countries wish to join these two clubs;

• the modernizing impact of the Acquis Communautaire for the institutional reforms under way in Central and Eastern Europe;

• massive trade reorientation of Central and Eastern European countries, which, currently, carry on more than 60% of their overall trade with the EU.

I would turn now to a less optimistic outlook. Evaluating the post-1989 years from a less sanguine perspective would highlight a series of worrying phenomena. One such is represented by the powerful forces of fragmentation, which intensify "cognitive dissonance" and friction (conflicts) among groups of people (communities/countries). These conflicts can involve land disputes (when borders are contested, or multi-ethnic countries disintegrate), or can take place along ethnic and religious lines; they breed resentment and fuel extremism and fundamentalism, which shows up in the form of domestic and international terrorism. Samuel Huntington[6] and Robert Kaplan[7], respectively, provide sobering interpretations of possible future dynamics in this respect - quite opposite to the euphoria of the early 1990s.

Financial and economic crises, which have proliferated during the last decade and confounded the zealots of unrestrained globalisation, have brought about tremendous pains to various countries around the world. Mexico is still licking some of its wounds after the big fall of the peso in the late 1994, and Indonesia, which has gone through huge social and economic dislocation in the last few years, has still to find a way out of the mess in order to avert further economic turmoil and possible disintegration. Financial crises in Brazil, Argentina (which years ago was hailed as a model of reforms following the introduction of the currency board), Turkey, etc, show how tenuous the state of affairs in many emerging countries is and how rapidly economies can fall apart - especially when aid from outside is not readily available. Rising income inequality (in rich countries, too) as well as the growing "digital divide" do not supply grounds for optimism. One can add here the bogged down reforms in many transition countries in Europe and the FSU and the rising poverty and weak institutional structures, which are becoming endemic problems. Last but not least, questionable business ethics[8] and the internationally spreading operations of organised crime, together with mounting transnational problems, would make up a gloomy balance sheet.

Both perspectives can be observed through the lenses of geopolitical dynamics. I would focus however on the less upbeat perspective. Regarding Europe, one can point out the interplay between cooperation and competition. There have been developments in the last decade, which indicate that, while the EU and the USA do cooperate extensively in many areas, they compete ever more intensely in economic matters. This competition is not devoid of frictions, which can transcend into extra-economic realms and amplify non-economic contending issues (like military and strategic goals). The EU's desire to develop its own rapid deployment force (as part of the Strategic Defense Initiative) and to assert foreign policy and security aims which may diverge from Washington's line speak for themselves. The different views of Europeans (the EU) as against the US Administration's stance in environmental issues (such as global warming for instance) and regarding the need to adopt strict rules for dealing with tax havens (in order to combat tax evasion and money laundering, etc) reinforce the competitive nature of this relationship and strain its underlying strategic alliance component.

The EU as an economic (trading) and monetary bloc, the increasing talk of creating a free trade area of the Americas and of extending the use of the dollar as a domestic currency in certain countries (Ecuador, El Salvador), and the multiplying signs that an Asian Monetary Organization is in the offing[9], are all signs that the world is heading towards the creation of major trading and currency blocs. Whereas economic and financial crises do enhance such a tendency (for blocs are seen by many as "damage-control" devices), which would clearly favor regional cooperation, it would not necessarily help the functioning of an open world system. Political and security implications can easily be imagined against the backdrop of the emergence of such blocs.

Referring to Europe again, I would emphasise the power of "attractors", of the EU and NATO in particular. Both NATO and the EU are facing major enlargement challenges, which would redefine the security and economic map of Europe. Some may be tempted to dispute such a statement[10], but I would argue that for the smaller countries - which would be either "ins" or "outs", enlargement is the overriding concern, which shapes popular perceptions and psychology, and will likely make the difference between successful reforms (modernisation) and further falling behind. Joining the EU, for most of the aspirant countries, would be an historically exceptional event (process), which is tantamount to bringing about overall modernisation and reduce considerably an economic distance of long vintage. Transition countries have already grouped in clusters which reveal different economic performances and chances to join the Clubs - the Central European countries, the Baltic countries, several groups among the Balkan countries themselves[11], and the FSU (where a wide variety of conditions can also be detected).

In this context one should not forget Russia, which, in spite of economic weaknesses, remains a major European actor with "abroad" interests and a not-negligeable reach; its growing influence in Ukraine, Belarus, Moldova is ominous.

It is striking to see that, whereas the collapse of communism terminated a historical ideological confrontation and signaled the demise of Cold War type bloc politics on the Continent, we seem, currently, to witness a sort of recreation of two major blocs - a process which has, as the major feature, the economic divide of the Continent: a rich "new West" (which would be the enlarged EU, including a few transition countries) and a "new East", a poor area made up of former communist countries. This divide existed in the past as well, but now it is becoming more visible and it acquires threatening dimensions because certain menaces cannot be contained as they might have been by the rules and mechanisms of the Cold War. As for the Partnership for Peace, it does not seem, in my view, to be capable of arresting this tendency. These blocs would shape countries' behavior according to economic performance and military and security links.

The functioning of the two blocs would increase the feeling of insecurity in countries which reside in grey areas. As a postulate, it can be submitted that the smaller a country area is, the more insecure it feels when being in a grey area. This insecurity would have consequences for these countries' economic and political evolution and would impact on neighbours.

Grey areas overlap with what I would call distress regions: the Balkans, Central Asia, the Caucasus. In these regions, economic distress combines with the struggle over scarce resources (water for example[12]), with inter-ethnic conflicts and also with military altercations. These regions show most conspicuously how ineffective regional cooperation can be and the effects of such a state of affairs.

How can cooperation be enhanced, among both major and minor actors? I would say that the juxtaposition of big and small actors is not accidental if one admits that "demonstration effects are powerful" when they shape perceptions, propensities and conduct. (If the big guys are bickering among themselves, why do they expect us to behave differently?). There are several areas in which cooperation can be tested as on a battleground. Among non-military security issues, I would range environmental concerns (pollution, global warming, etc), massive illegal migration, health hazards (diseases), organised crime, drug trafficking, and vulnerability of highly complex systems (software) at a time of very fast technological change.

Among military issues I would mention, firstly, those which pertain to the balance of power motives. How to deal with (or contain) regional conflicts is high on the agenda in a world which is not short of such conflicts - and when it is not easy to decide who should intervene, under what mandate, and who should provide the human force required to maintain peace although this may involve casualties. Arms proliferation and domestic and international terrorism are also constant policy concerns for governments all around the world.

In this context I would make a couple of references to the challenge posed by disaster areas, and I would focus in particular on the Balkans. Here the forces of fragmentation are still very much at work, the political geography is still pretty fuzzy, economic distress is ubiquitous and poverty rising, all against the background of weak state structures and high criminality. All these circumstances do not favour regional cooperation. The proliferation of "hard" and "soft" protectorates, as well as the functioning of the Stability Pact (SP), are pretty insufficient in substituting for local initiatives and institutions; they are also ineffective in dealing with what I would call the "missing party" in the equation of dialogue. This missing party is represented by groups which have specific agendas, which may be significantly at odds with the aims of local authorities and external players. These groups, some of which have more or less extremist inclinations and which thrive under current conditions, may disregard blatantly the objectives of powerful external actors (such as NATO and the EU) belonging to the loosely defined "international community". The consequences are inimical to any sort of stability and peace.

One has to admit, nonetheless, that external pressure is not without some effect and that the attraction exerted by the EU (the stabilisation and association agreements) could help the Balkan countries find a way out of the mess, but over the longer run and only following persistent and tenacious efforts; this is a process of long gestation and one should not expect miracles. In addition, the external players need to show more commitment to the area and operate as long term stakeholders; damage control can help for a while, but it does not guarantee a lasting solution. To this end it would be better to turn the SP into a "Development Pact", which should send a clearer message as to its mission and time horizon oriented endeavors.

Last but not least, cooperation needs to be enhanced in dealing with major international economic issues: trade, financial flows, business ethics,[13] etc. In this respect, there is much to do in order to bring practice in line with preaching (I am referring to big and rich actors in particular) and to acknowledge that whereas markets are the best mechanism for allocating resources and fostering entrepreneurship, at the same time they evince imperfections and asymmetries, which require public policy measures of pain alleviation and market failure correction. The havoc produced by volatile financial flows in many emerging markets should be a constant reminder of the need to formulate responsible policies and find areas of cooperation, which should bear in mind the common good.

In order for cooperation - either regional or on a broader scale - to be enhanced, actors (states) need to define common interests and areas where they can compromise in a better way. This result can be facilitated by acknowledging the existence of collective goods, whose production is indivisible. Of help would also be a more rigorous respect of norms and more adherence to the principle of non-double standards. That this aim is hard to achieve in practice - since "reality is very complex" and interests may shift in time - is an argument hard to refute. Nevertheless, statesmanship (leadership) is verified especially during duress, when one is asked to provide vision and good policy under adverse conditions. The tragic events in various parts of the world (including the Balkans) over the last decade indicate that what is ugly in the past is still with us and that we need to be better students in learning history's lessons. But to this end we need to be more candid and honest with ourselves and our fellows; to be more compassionate, less arrogant and hypocritical, and more forward-looking.

1. Remarks made during the final panel of the NATO Economics Colloquium, Bucharest, 3-4 May, 2001

2. Professor of Economics, Academy of Economic Studies, Bucharest and Visiting Professor, The Anderson School of Management (UCLA, Los Angeles); Former Finance Minister of Romania

3. Francis Fukuyama, "The End of History", New York, 1991

4. Thomas Friedman, 'The Lexus and the Olive Tree", New York, 1999

5. This is the title of one of Kenichi Ohmae's book, New York, 1995

6. Samuel Huntington, "The Clash of Civilizations", New York, 1996

7. Robert Kaplan, "The Coming Anarchy", New York, 1999

8. See in this respect the Pope's remarks quoted by the International Herald Tribune, 28 April, 2001

9. Several Asian countries have already decided to cooperate in case of speculative attacks against their currencies.

10. In a private conversation during this conference, a western expert said to me that he can hardly see any security danger for Romania in case this country is not invited to join NATO.

11. Bulgaria and Romania have started accession negotiations with the EU; Croatia is much more advanced economically and institutionally than Albania and can move relatively rapidly in upgrading its status agreement with the EU.

13. Particularly in Central Asia.

13. For instance, the conduct of big pharmaceutical companies in Africa.

THE INTERRELATIONSHIP BETWEEN REGIONAL ECONOMIC COOPERATION, SECURITY AND STABILITY
Integration or Conflict? - The Long-Term Choice for Europe

Yiannis Papanicolaou

Director General of the International Center for Black Sea Studies, Athens

There are many people who believe that the long-term real choice for Europe is either integration or conflict. As far as integration is concerned there is a demand for it (the desire to join a club) and a supply (the extent to which existing club members have an interest in admitting new ones). The determinants of such demand and supply are:

- historical, such as geography, culture and perceptions;
- economic, regarding markets, money and redistribution;
- political, meaning values, power and security.

Integration is a method of institutionalising cooperation which can powerfully reinforce expectations of compliance and offer incentives for striking successful bargains and agreeing policies. The interests of states are conditioned by a network of links between their societies and economies. The extension of globalisation since the 1970's has led to a substantial development of such links, which take the form of trade, investment and capital flows, cross border cooperation, large-scale movements of people and a sharing of information, news and ideas.

High levels of interdependence, however, do not of themselves determine either cooperation or conflict, but increase the stakes of relationships. Sometimes they foster a sense of common interest, at other times they may lead to a sense of vulnerability and threat. What matters is how and whether the interdependence is managed. When interdependence is poorly managed it can be a source of conflict. Whether conflict or cooperation will prevail depends in part on whether international institutions moderate state interests and in part on how domestic politics shape national strategies.

In order for societies to form a pluralistic security community, it is necessary for their political elites to share a basic level of political values and to be mutually responsive to one another. Post Cold War Europe has a considerable diversity of patterns of governance. The issues of governance and relationships between state and society are especially crucial for European order because the main threats to security and stability are now from internal sources. Highly charged and polarised politics, volatile swings from one direction to another and sharp challenges to government authority become more and more common. Added to this is perhaps the most important challenge to the European order - the problems of national minorities.

In order to moderate the risk of anarchy in the European state system and sustain cooperation it is desirable to strengthen the basis for the European Civil Space. The EU, together with NATO, the Council of Europe and the OSCE, are important in this respect. A "wider Europe" program should be seen as a balanced attempt to provide political order, security and economic stability at three levels; the international, the regional and the national. Such a program can be built only gradually, by opening societies to democratic scrutiny, strengthening international institutions and developing transnational links at all levels. It is therefore necessary to promote and manage interdependence between Western and Eastern European societies across a range of policy areas. A strategy of "wait and see" would risk allowing the situation in the wider Europe to deteriorate into a new confrontation.

Western Europe cannot insulate itself from the consequences of the Central and East European transition going seriously wrong. Achieving economic development in Eastern Europe is very much in the long-term common interest of all Europeans, on both economic and security grounds. Trade access, foreign direct investment, cohesion funds and regional funds are essential in order to move these countries forward. From the point of view of the interests of the countries of Eastern Europe, the most important solutions are those which open new opportunities for their inclusion into a stable European order and the wider Euro-Atlantic structures. In this context the eastward enlargement of the EU acquires a central role in reuniting Europe and making up for the divisions of the Cold War. What is equally important is an appraisal of the process of European integration on the stability and security of the countries of the European periphery.

The Enlargement of the EU

The collapse of communism was an historic opportunity to reunite Europe. The aspirations of the peoples of Central and Eastern Europe were expressed by their expectations to "return to Europe". West Europeans too felt that the EU should open its doors and eventually encompass the whole of Europe. The essence of a "Europe whole and free" was the overcoming of borders. After eleven years it is clear that borders are not about to disappear but to shift and threaten to become a new dividing line in post-communist Europe. Wherever the EU decides to draw its border, it will be seen by some as arbitrary, unfair and insulting. Yet it cannot do without borders. But at the same time, clear, firm and hard borders threaten the EU's capacity to manage its relations with the wider "Europe", some parts of which will not be able to meet the conditions of membership for many years and other parts no doubt will always remain outside.

As the prospect of "joining Europe" acts as a major motive for the candidate countries, the idea of exclusion has equally important negative consequences. Nor does ethnicity, nor religion, nor stage of economic development provide any convincing criteria of selection. There are ambiguities and the risk of inconsistency with this present enlargement and great uncertainty when it comes to questions such as where is this process of enlargement going to end. The other related question is what should the nature of the borders between the EU and its ultimate neighbours be?

The President of the Commission has already declared his objective not to create new Berlin walls. But policy makers in specific areas of cooperation have very often contradictory goals. The EU's external border cannot be treated simply as a physical line. Such an effort would increase instability by disrupting traditional, economic and cultural ties between neighbours. The external border has an enormous impact on the states on the other side and this consideration should be at the centre of the Union's own foreign policy objectives.

The EU must find ways of more active engagement in the problems of the world beyond its border. Border management implies deepening cooperation with the candidate countries and the new eastern neighbours in a wide range of fields: policing and judicial affairs, economic development, education and culture, cross-border links between local and regional authorities and communities. What is really needed is a partnership with the EU's new eastern neighbours that would support their economic development, socio-political stability and administrative capacities and respect their close historical, ethnic and cultural ties with states beyond the EU's new eastern boarders.

Central and Eastern Europe find themselves increasingly taking on the unwelcome role of a buffer zone. On the other hand these countries need to maintain good relations with their eastern neighbours. The various forms of "special relationship" between the Central and East European candidates of the first and second accession rounds and between them and their eastern neighbours are potentially a valuable asset in the development of the EU's external policy strategy and should be encouraged rather than undermined.

EU enlargement to the East has profound implications both internally and externally. Until the end of the Cold War division of Europe, the EU could enjoy the luxury of concentrating on its own internal evolution and interests. The development of the common foreign and security policy has only slowly moved up the list of the EU's priorities. All aspects of its activity need to be affected by the awareness of the new external dimension of its role in the wider Europe. Enlargement to the east should provide a new opportunity to renew the sense of the EU's original mission - that of transforming the pattern of European politics on the basis of reconciliation, cooperation and integration.

Another important issue to be addressed is the future of other international organisations (NATO, OSCE, UN, Council of Europe, EBRD) functioning in Europe which have different membership and varying effectiveness. While this international system has achieved many positive things, overall it has not managed to really facilitate the post-communist transition, at least beyond the most advanced EU accession candidates. The future role of these organisations, in the context of a pan-European order, has yet to be defined. Finally, a key related question is what should the role of Russia be in this new European architecture?

The Role of Russia

As many scholars have pointed out, Russia has belonged to European civilisation at least from the time of its Christian conversation. Since then Russian history has witnessed periods of European orientation (mainly during periods of reform) followed by periods of reaction, self-isolation and self-identification as something rather distinct from Europe. Both in the West and in Russia this ambiguous inheritance promoted the perception that Russia never truly belonged to Europe. Russia's geographical position and history as a major Euro-Asian power have resulted in controversial interpretations of Russia as the bearer of a civilisation with Byzantine and Greek orthodox roots, distinct from the Roman origins of most European nations.

Russia once again turns the page on its attempt at westernisation. Economically and politically there has been so far a failure to adopt Western norms of corporate and public governance. The vested interests in the new Russian capitalism, with its extensive oligarchic elements, make the constituency for western-style reform weak. Politically there is popular support for strong leadership. Under President Putin, more robust pragmatism in domestic policies is followed by a stronger determination to control things in the Caucasus, but the southern Caucasus is gravitating increasingly towards the EU and NATO.

In an important policy document entitled "Foreign Policy Concept of the Russian Federation"[1] it is clearly stated that; "The Russian Federation views the EU as one of its main political and economic partners and will strive to develop with it an intensive, stable and long-term cooperation devoid of expediency fluctuations". In an equally important paper called "The ways towards a mature partnership between Russia and the European Union",[2] the Russian authorities are even more explicit: "Europe is entering the new Century as a shaped bipolar whole. At the West and Centre of Europe almost all states have integrated into the European Union. In the East, the CIS is being formed on the basis of transitional economies...".

This latter document continues; "The merging of the EU and Russia is unreal and unlikely. To begin with, the great world powers - and Russia should not be hastily excluded from this category - rarely join any alliances, they rather create their own ones. Secondly, the unique Euro-Asian location of Russia rules out the exceptional orientation only towards a European direction. Thirdly, the degree of EU integration has reached a certain level at which independent economic and (very soon) foreign policies are circumscribed, while for Russia, with its own specific features, size, political system and so on, it is of the utmost importance to maintain freedom and independence in the decision-making process. Finally, in the case of accession to the EU, the obligatory convention to the acquis communaire would mean the radical breaking of the whole legal and administrative system of the country and, figuratively speaking, another "perestroika" that Russia is unlikely to deserve. Therefore, in the visible perspective, the best format of the relationship between Russia and the EU seems to be a mature contractual partnership: in politics and in economics and in forms not contradicting Russia's obligations within the CIS".

The text continues by proposing a Russia-EU cooperation in the field of Caspian Transport Corridors and the construction of Trans-Balkan oil pipelines in order to export to Europe oil from Russia, Kazakhstan and Azerbaijan. Then it mentions that the EU falls behind the USA in terms of investments in its economy, especially in the energy sector. Finally it turns to the issue of enlargement and admits that it will have for Russia major and not only economic consequences. It mentions in addition some serious security considerations plus concerns about the position of Russians living in the new accession candidates and the future of cross-border cooperation. It is thus clear that Russia is expressing a real concern about its future relations with the EU but at the same time a genuine desire to work closely with it in a wider European framework.

In our opinion, whatever direction developments in Russia take, it will remain a major European nation. Either as an uneasy great power "re-emerging" onto the European scene or as a cooperative partner, "compatible" with European civilization. It is of vital interest that there be a place for Russia in the emerging European order, whatever it looks like. The process of elaborating options for institutionalising Russo-European relations should ensure for Russia the role of an equal partner in shaping Pan-European developments. The enlarged EU must keep the relationship with Russia to a reasonably predictable, stable and cooperative status with the aid of important shared interests, for example in frontier regions and the energy sector. Another overarching challenge for the EU is to adopt coherent policies between the several regions of its borderlands and develop regional cooperative mechanisms, some of which may overlap the EU, accession candidates and neighbouring non-candidates.

Borderland Europe

Borderland Europe is defined to include, from North to South, the following regions:

• from the EU-Finnish border with North-West Russia;

• through the Baltic, Central and South-Eastern borderland of the enlargement candidate states with Russia, Belarus, Ukraine and Moldova;

• onto the former Yugoslavia;

• then Turkey and its neighbours in the Black Sea and the Caucasus;

• to the Mediterranean countries of the Barcelona process.

Borderland Europe will ultimately be defined by two parallel processes:

• The enlargement of the EU and the development of a huge economic and political entity around a core of Western European countries;

• The creation of another economic space having as its core Russia.

Borderland Europe may be viewed as a buffer zone between two big European spaces, the enlarged EU and Russia/CIS. It thus requires a different perspective from either Brussels or Moscow. Indeed, the future of Europe depends to a great extent on the future relations between the two main economic blocs and on what conditions are going to prevail in the borderlands.

The Role of Regional Cooperation

In recent years many discussions have taken place about the advantages of regional economic cooperation in promoting the development of the participating states. The issue of regional cooperation can be also addressed from another perspective. Should the countries whose aim is to be integrated into Europe join the continental and Euro-Atlantic structures individually or through some form of preliminary regional cooperation?

After the period 1989-91, many analysts perceived a process of growing integration in Western Europe and growing disintegration in Eastern Europe. According to some theorists, the more states there are in the system the greater the potential for disputes. In order words, a multi-polar system is more likely to be associated with violent conflict than a bipolar one. The existence therefore of regional formations may be instrumental in stabilising the situation and in gradually developing intra-regional cooperation with an emphasis on cross-border economic, social and cultural relations. This is the idea behind the various initiatives that have been taken in recent years in SE Europe.

It is not accidental that after every crisis in SE Europe new regional initiatives were introduced. Such a list would include: the initiative on Good Neighbourly Relations and Stability in SE Europe; the Roayammont Process; the Southeastern Cooperative Initiative (SECI); the Dayton Peace Agreements; the Southeastern European Cooperation Process (SEECP); and the Stability Pact for South Eastern Europe and the Security Council Resolution 1244 (1999). Some of these have been more successful than others.

Why is this part of Europe the area with the largest number of regional and international programs and initiatives? Because it is being recognised that the main obstacle to European integration and the enlargement process is South-East European instability. Moreover, the establishment of peace and stability in South-Eastern Europe on the basis of the European values of democracy, human rights and the rule of law is an absolute and pressing necessity both for the countries of the region and for the future of peace and security in the whole of Europe and the wider European-Atlantic space. Viewed from this wider perspective, the establishment of peace and stability in Southern Europe is an inseparable part of the goal of building a united, democratic, prosperous and secure Europe. To quote the former Secretary General of the Council of Europe, Daniel Tarschys: "it is an illusion to believe that we can maintain and develop prosperous zones of peace while neighbouring regions are devastated by conflict and misery".

Despite good intentions, it was only after Kosovo that the need was realised to move away from crisis management to a long-term

314

comprehensive policy framework for effective economic, political and diplomatic actions in all directions and that the EU should offer to all countries in the region the prospect of integration into the European structures. The implementation of regional projects of common interest, in the fields of communications, transport and energy infrastructures, trade, science and technology, protection of environment, combating of organised crime and illegal drug and weapon trafficking are the main vehicles for promoting a climate of mutual confidence and good-neighbourly relations. Such projects also promote democratic processes, respect for human rights, including the rights of minorities and the rule of law in all countries of the region. Such regional cooperation could be successful only if approved and actively supported by the EU and NATO.

At present the parallel processes of EU and NATO enlargement run the risk of reinforcing the division between those countries in Central Eastern Europe that are already most stable and secure and those that are not included. Yet there is little coordination between the two bodies to ensure that the applicants with more remote prospects for joining one or both organisations are not alienated by the processes of enlargement. However, measures directed only at the level of international institutions and interstate relations cannot deal comprehensively with problems which also crucially involve the state-society dimension. Perhaps even more important than policies at the national and international level are the transnational contacts between societies not only at the level of investments and trade, crucial as these are, but also through educational and cultural exchanges, training, links between towns, and naturally through cooperation between political parties, the media and active citizens. If through such contacts a wider sense of European solidarity develops, the prospects for cooperation among states would very much improve, because such integration is usually set in motion by the formation of core groups with sufficient cultural affinities and commonality of interests and values. The process is then further amplified by domino dynamics according to which peripheral countries may find that exclusion from the core has greater risks of unfavourable outcomes than joining a core whose policies may not be their first best choice.

From the above analysis it is very clear that regional cooperation is extremely important. Regional initiatives are very valuable because not only do they create a framework of wider cooperation within the region, but they facilitate the relations of the participating member states and the area as a whole with the outside world too.

The emerging new regionalisation is part of a process which aims at creating order when the old order (based on bipolarity, confrontation and the balance of power) has vanished. Yet we must remember that the pursuit for order still remains; the difficulty being that instead of one overarching order there seems to be a tendency towards smaller "suborders". A very interesting case of an area which was a victim of bipolarity and where confrontation has been followed by cooperation is the Black Sea region.

The Black Sea Economic Cooperation

For many decades the countries of the Black Sea belonged to two totally opposing political and military blocs. With the end of the Cold War the countries of the region have jointly decided to revive the cooperative spirit despite the fact the Black Sea Economic Cooperation (BSEC)[3] is one of the most diverse subregional groupings. Its eleven member states differ in:

• their economic and military potential, geostrategic interests and geographic size;

• their cultural, social and religious traditions;

• their affiliation with and their attitudes towards the Euroatlantic structures.

Despite these differences, the member states of BSEC have concluded that their common interests prevail and that through cooperation they can promote them in a better way. BSEC's diversity makes it also very convenient to play the role of a bridge between Europe, the Caspian Sea and Central Asia.

On the 25th of June 1992 when the Summit Declaration of the Black Sea Economic Cooperation was signed by the Heads of States or Governments of the eleven member states, its signatories set as their aim to ensure that the Black Sea becomes a sea of peace, stability and prosperity. The BSEC has so far accomplished significant progress in achieving its basic goals. The good functioning of a formation like the BSEC may be instrumental not only in stabilising the region but in facilitating its integration with the wider European structures too. The EU will not exploit its full growth potential if the BSEC area continues to stagnate and lag behind the advanced western economies. Another important function of the BSEC could be that of a bridge connecting neighbouring countries that are located in what I earlier called Borderland Europe, of which SE Europe, the Black Sea and the Caucasus were key components.

The introduction of a Black Sea Dimension to the EU along the lines of the Northern Dimension, by institutionalising the relation of the EU with the Black Sea Economic Cooperation, would be extremely beneficial for all parties. Such an initiative should combine the policy initiatives of the EU in three areas; the Balkans, the Black Sea and the Caucasus. As far as the Balkans are concerned, the EU is already very active. For the Caucasus, there are also proposals for a special Stability Pact and other similar initiatives. The EU must now develop a policy for the Black Sea region as a whole. After the accession of Romania, Bulgaria and Turkey, its borders will extend to the Black Sea. The enlargement of the EU creates a de facto new relationship between it and the Black Sea region. NATO too has a major stake in promoting political stability, economic prosperity and security in the Black Sea region. Through cooperation with the BSEC, the EU and NATO can create an umbrella of stability for the entire region from which both would benefit. The Black Sea's geostrategic importance is well known.

Europe needs an active presence in this part of the world and the BSEC is the appropriate counterpart for the following reasons:

• including Russia, it represents a vast Euro-Asian space of almost 20 million square kilometres populated by 340 million people. It possesses huge deposits of natural, particularly energy, resources;

• it is the bridge between Europe and Eurasia;

• it is important for the transportation of energy resources from the Caspian and Central Asia to the rest of the world;

• through closer cooperation with the BSEC, Europe can upgrade its relationship with a number of key countries of borderland Europe like Russia, Ukraine, Turkey and the Caspian countries. Segmentation of regional initiatives is perhaps a less efficient method of tackling regional problems. Through cooperation with the BSEC, more synergies and better quality projects can be developed.

BSEC has in this part of the world a more advanced institutional structure than all other regional initiatives. It is a fully-fledged regional organisation, since the Council of Ministers takes binding decisions. It is also supported by a Permanent International Secretariat (PERMIS) and its related bodies like the Black Sea Trade and Development Bank, the Parliamentary Assembly, the Business Council and its think-tank, the International Center for Black Sea Studies. So the BSEC possesses an infrastructure which can generate ideas, follow through on decisions, coordinate eleven administrations, and therefore ensure a more efficient cooperation process.

What is really needed is a "political" decision by the EU and NATO to recognise the BSEC as their formal partner in this region. Through an EU-BSEC and a NATO-BSEC platform of cooperation, not only would the "wider Europe" concept be substantially promoted, but the Euro-Atlantic geopolitical and economic interests would also be advanced in what is and will remain a very sensitive and important part of the world.

1. "Foreign Policy Concept of the Russian Federation", Information Bulletin (Special Issue), Ministry of Foreign Affairs of the Russian Federation, Information and Press Department, Moscow, July 10, 2000

2. Ivan Ivanov, "The ways towards a mature partnership between Russia and the European Union", "Sovremennaya Evropa", No 2, 2000

3. For an excellent paper on the Black Sea Economic Cooperation see Y. Valinakis "The Black Sea Region: Challenges and Opportunities for Europe", Chaillot Paper 36, Institute for Security Studies, Western European Union, Paris, July 1999.

FIRST EXPERIENCES AND ASSESSMENTS AFTER 20 MONTHS OF THE STABILITY PACT

Bodo Hombach

Special Coordinator, Stability Pact for South Eastern Europe

For observers of South Eastern Europe, the following conclusions can be drawn from the experiences of the Stability Pact, now with almost two years of operating experience in the field.

The Stability Pact has set new parameters for regional co-operation in South Eastern Europe and pioneered the development of a comprehensive regional approach to preventive diplomacy.

The Stability Pact is not a crisis-management organization, but a political process with a medium to long-term perspective. I do not claim that we are original in all that we do. In fact, I am proud that we have a good track record of applying recipes which have previously been successful elsewhere: the CSCE process, the EU approach to integration, and of course NATO's own very progressive approach to regional security and defence questions.

The wish of regional countries to join the European Union and NATO is arguably the strongest driving force we have for an effective and timely reform process in the countries of the region. It is obvious that we still have a long way to go in this area, and partial setbacks (for example: terrorism in Macedonia and instability in Southern Serbia) are part of the regional political equation. But generally speaking, we can agree that the trendlines have been overwhelmingly positive.

The Stability Pact framework is a two-way street. Reform and regional co-operation on the one hand are "traded" against (some cynics would say "bought with") financial support and integration within European and Euro-Atlantic structures on the other. In this sense there is conditionality on the aid given to regions. No one expects a free lunch.

The Stability Pact's main role is to provide a co-ordinating, catalytic framework, which does not attempt to duplicate or act where

319

others are clearly doing better work. As I have said, neither is the Stability Pact a classic crisis intervention instrument - we have no implementing capacities and no field structure. The Stability Pact is designed to synergise existing expertise, and we fully embrace NATO as the key player in the regional security field.

The approach pioneered by the Stability Pact has yielded tangible results:

• Politically - The main culprits of the violent disintegration of the former Yugoslavia have been removed from power through democratic means. Mr. Milosevic has been arrested. Everywhere we have democratic structures in place, which have opened the door for a new, if at times difficult, beginning.

• Security - Despite the worrisome news from Preshovo, Macedonia or Kosovo, there is no longer the danger of widespread international conflict. Internationally co-ordinated crisis management and conflict prevention measures have clearly improved the regional security outlook.

The process of joining the European Union or NATO has proven to be the vital driving force for reform, as the Stabilisation and Association Agreements signed by Macedonia, initialed by Croatia, and being negotiated with Bosnia-Herzegovina, the Federal Republic of Yugoslavia, and Albania have shown. The SAAs under negotiation or planned are important instruments to conduct reforms and to align regional legislation and institutions to those of Western Europe along the standards set by European Union, the World Trade Organization, and the Council of Europe.

Regional co-operation has improved substantially and is now a cornerstone of Stability Pact operations in the areas of refugee return, trade liberalisation, and fighting organized crime and corruption. This is reflected in SEECP's role and in the co-ordinated reaction to the Macedonian crisis. Countries in South Eastern Europe are fully aware that a proven capability for regional co-operation is also a precondition for adhesion to the European Union.

Stability Pact Activities in the Field of Security

With the fall of Mr. Milosevic, there is a unique chance to redesigning the security architecture for South Eastern Europe, including non-proliferation, arms control, and disarmament activities, confidence and security building measures and right-sizing the region's armed military forces.

The continuing contributions of NATO and the Euro-Atlantic Co-operation Council (EAPC) in this context are vital. The Southeast European Task Force, the Partnership for Peace, the Membership Action Plan process, SEEGROUP and SEECAP are some examples of the success of intensified regional co-operation.

Under the Stability Pact's Working Table III, the main activities we are dealing with are in mine action and the elimination of small arms and light weapons.

In Zagreb, the Regional Arms Control and Verification Implementation Center (RACVIAC) opened its doors last year and is now ready to assist Governments with the evolution of their armed forces in line with the current security environment.

NATO and its partners have initiated Disaster Preparedness and Prevention activities on a cross-border basis, an initiative that is designed to address an existing and serious deficit in the region.

The joint efforts of NATO and the World Bank to train demobilized military personnel for their integration into the civilian workforce serve as a shining example of what we can accomplish when we work together, building of our individual strengths for the common good. After successful beginnings in Romania and Bulgaria, these retraining programs are now also being applied in Albania and Croatia.

Stability Pact Activities in the Field of Economics

The economies of South Eastern Europe have high growth rates. The EBRD estimates are 5% on average for 2000/2001. The EBRD also noted the continuing process of major reforms in the year 2000 and sees good chances for a speedy recovery of the FRY/Serbian economy.

Foreign direct investment almost doubled in 2000 as compared to 1999 when it stood at US$2bn, an effect EBRD attributes directly to the Stability Pact's initiatives. In Bulgaria and Romania, FDI increased six-fold since 1996, in Macedonia they are now at US$120m, which admittedly is low but is 10 times more than the 1996 levels. Despite all this good news, it is vital to involve the private sector much more in the coming months.

The biggest challenges in economic policies for the near future are reforming the banking sector, strengthening governmental institutions, fighting corruption, and reducing trade barriers.

On banking: in the Federal Republic of Yugoslavia, the majority of state banks are insolvent as most credits are faulty and cannot be revoked. In other South Eastern European countries we have seen an increased interest by foreign investors. In Croatia, major financial businesses are by now foreign-owned; in Macedonia, the biggest bank has just been sold; in Bosnia-Herzegovina, we have German and Austrian investments, and Albania is experiencing a growth in foreign investment in the sector. Similar developments can be expected in Serbia and Montenegro. Whereas Romania remains difficult terrain for banking reform and restructuring, the overall regional developments in the financial sector are positive.

On institutional weaknesses and corruption: several initiatives have been designed to tackle this joint problem, such as the Anti-Corruption Initiative (SPAI) and the initiative against organized crime (SPOC). Both are difficult areas and visible results can only be expected in the mid- to long-term. Obviously, while the international community can provide moral and material support to these initiatives, the driving force has to come from the regional governments bent on cleaning their own houses.

On trade: the European Union has granted unilateral trade liberalization to all countries of the region, which has resulted in tariff-free export opportunities for 95% of the region's exports. This is very attractive for investments in the region. Additionally, the countries have now begun to reduce and eliminate intra-regional trade barriers. Up to now we had a whole range of tariff and non-tariff barriers on trade, which resulted in a fragmentation of markets. Seven trade ministers of the region (Albania, Bosnia-Herzegovina, Bulgaria, Croatia, Romania, Macedonia and the Federal Republic of Yugoslavia) agreed in January 2001 to form a network of Free Trade Agreements for the entire region by the end of 2002. This will create a market of 55 million consumers and will also facilitate political integration.

The Way Ahead

Continuing deficits in civil society and democratic institutions unfortunately parallels progress in the economic field. To address these problems the Stability Pact has developed a range of instruments, such as the Investment Compact, the Anti-Corruption Initiative, the Media Charter, the Steering Group on Refugee Return, the Szeged Process, the initiative against Organized Crime, and the Migration and Asylum initiative.

Governmental financial assistance amounted to Euro2.4bn at the Funding Conference in March 2000, which was committed to projects within the "Quick Start Package". This is a lot of money but it is not enough to solve the problems of the region. It is therefore imperative that this money is used as a strategic investment lever to foster confidence in the region in order to attract more investments, specifically greater private sector activity. So far, 9 out of 10 projects have started; and more than two thirds of the money has already been disbursed.

This year we will have two more financial conferences, one for Serbia to support the reform agenda of the new government and one for the region at large with focus on projects for democratization, institution building, refugee return, infrastructure and security.

There is a certain danger that with the region sailing into calmer waters, donor fatigue will set in. I warn against reducing efforts now. Preventive diplomacy needs a lot of stamina; the Stability Pact is a marathon. Crisis prevention is by definition a long-term process.

As recent events in Bosnia-Herzegovina, Macedonia and Kosovo clearly demonstrate, the "peace project in South Eastern Europe" still needs a vigorous security component in order to succeed. The Stability Pact can only work if Europe and the United States continue to closely co-operate. The European Union has the potential to take the political lead in this, but a strong US commitment is needed to secure this endeavor militarily. I have just returned from Washington where the Stability Pact was confirmed as a key element of the Trans-Atlantic agenda. Therefore, I am optimistic that we shall suc-ceed in bringing the Stability Pact a major step forward towards our common goals.

CONCLUDING REMARKS

Patrick Hardouin

Colloquium Chairman and Director, NATO Economics Directorate

It seems to me that the regions we have identified for study at this Colloquium - the South Caucasus, Central Asia and South-Eastern Europe - are the correct ones: Security and stability are far from being established let alone guaranteed in all three, which is why they are also high up on NATO's agenda. Of course, for South-Eastern Europe, this is absolutely clear given the Alliance's military engagement in Bosnia and in Kosovo. But NATO's concern is also to bring peace and stability to the Caucasus and Central Asia, although we do not take the lead in this process.

We also discussed the Black Sea region. It seems to me that this Colloquium amply demonstrated the key rôle of economics in these regions, and we learned a great deal about cooperation, about economic assistance by the international community, and also about the rôle of the European Union and the Stability Pact. We were also pleased to welcome the representatives of international institutions, these being the World Bank, EBRD, OECD, OSCE, United Nations, and the Stability Pact. We were further delighted to hear that the USA remains committed to international stability initiatives in the Balkans.

I would like to emphasise four short points:

• **Environment and Ecology.** I think we should look at this issue in a future Colloquium, concentrating upon the inter-relationships between economics, environment, and security. Maybe the next war will be a war for natural resources such as water, or maybe global warming is going to be a very big problem for our society and for international security.

• **Poverty.** Is poverty the cause of war or is war the cause of poverty? In NATO, we do believe that there is a link between poverty, international stability and the risk of war. Maybe on an intellectual and theoretical point of view we are wrong. But if we are right, we are also right to be concerned about high income differentials both inside societies, between regions, between ethnic groups, and between nation states. So we make an assumption in NATO, and in the strategic security concept of NATO, that there is a link between prosperity and security. Ergo, we support the creation of political, social and legal environments that foster economic development.

• **Regional Cooperation.** Maybe regional blocks are as ineffective as some participants at this Colloquium have claimed, but we are not talking about the building of regional or economic fortresses, we are talking about international cooperation in order to take advantage of and benefit from mutual cooperation to build a secure environment. We are talking about building strong links of real and concrete cooperation between economies so that war between neighbours becomes impossible. After the Second World War, France and Germany found a new trust and solidarity based on the sharing of coal and iron, at that time the very basis of both economies. This as we now know was just the start of a long and productive process of economic, political and social integration. Here in this room are represented one or two nations that have fought wars against one another and a few that are still engaged in ethnic and border conflicts, so it is very necessary to engage in conflict resolution and then to try to create better conditions for regional cooperation and economic integration. Only then will the foreign direct investment that all the countries in these three regions so desperately need be forthcoming.

• **Macroeconomic Stability, Reform and Democracy.** Naturally, all three are key to creating a prosperous economy, but of course there is a social cost to reform which can lead to political change. Thus, good leaders with good policies can run the risk of losing elections. Nevertheless, it is the historical responsibility of politicians in all the regions we have studied at this Colloquium to conduct responsible and fair administrations that promulgate sensible reforms and thereby lead their peoples towards greater prosperity. The quality of governance, institution building, liberalisation and promoting democracy are joint processes and very much linked to the building of international security. But prosperity on its own is not a factor that builds security and peace unless it is also related to the political régime. By this, I mean human rights, the rule of law, judicial independence, respect for minorities, responsibility, and democratic accountability. These are the values we share together. We will always try to help these processes of reform that relate so closely to security. But as far as the micro conduct of economic policy is concerned, NATO must take a back seat to other more specialised economic international institutions, which are very well qualified to proffer advice and suggest solutions to extant problems.

This NATO Economics Colloquium was the 29th such event to be held, the first being in 1971. Only two years have been missed, the last one in 2000 due to the knock-on effects of the Kosovo crisis. In the beginning, the NATO Economics Colloquium was devoted to analysis of the command economies of the former Soviet Union and of the countries of the Warsaw Pact. Now we are discussing how to achieve security throughout a vast area stretching from the border of China to the Atlantic Ocean, from the Mediterranean Sea to the Arctic Ocean. Indeed, we can rejoice in the fact that history has moved so rapidly over the past two decades.

I would like to thank every Colloquium participant from whatever origin, whether this be academia, the civil service, international organisations, the diplomatic corps or parliament. Parliamentarians and politicians especially have the duty and the right to know how we are working together and to give their point of view. We intend to encourage them to engage more fully with our work. Indeed, may the main message from the Colloquium be that participants from so very many states covering much of the entire Euro-Asian-Atlantic area were able, in good humour and in friendship, to discuss together economic issues related to security. Even ten years ago, such a prospect would have been considered panglossian in the extreme. Finally I would like to thank the Romanian authorities and the NATO staff involved in the organisation of this Colloquium.

2001 NATO ECONOMICS COLLOQUIUM THE INTERRELATIONSHIP BETWEEN REGIONAL ECONOMIC COOPERATION, SECURITY AND STABILITY

Bucharest, Wednesday, 2 May 2001 p.m.
Thursday, 3 May, a.m. and p.m., Friday, 4 May 2001, a.m.

Wednesday, 2 May 2001, p.m.

17.00-19.00	Registration and Administrative Details.
19.00-19.30	Briefing Session for Speakers.
20.00-21.00	Reception in Marriott Grand Hotel Hosted by NATO

Thursday, 3 May 2001

09.00-10.00 **INTRODUCTORY SESSION**

- Introductory Remarks by the Colloquium Chairman, Mr. Patrick HARDOUIN, Director, NATO Economics Directorate
- Welcoming Speech by Mr. Mircea Dan GEOANA, Minister of Foreign Affairs of Romania
- Welcoming Speech by Ambassador Klaus-Peter KLAIBER, Assistant Secretary General for Political Affairs, NATO
- Welcoming Speech by Mr. Ioan Mircea PASCU, Minister of Defence of Romania
- Welcoming Speech by Mr. Jos van GENNIP, Chairman, NATO Parliamentary Assembly Economics and Security Committee

10.00-13.00 **PLENARY SESSION**

10.00-10.30 *Lead Speeches*

- Ambassador Lazar COMANESCU, Romanian Mission to NATO
- Ambassador Nurver NURES, former First Deputy Secretary General, Black Sea Economic Cooperation(BSEC), Istanbul

10.30-11.00	**Break**

11.00-12.00   **Political-Economic Statements**

- Mr. David APTSIAURI, Vice Minister, Ministry of Foreign Affairs, Georgia
- Ms. Larissa KAPITSA, Director, Coordinating Unit for Operational Activities, UN Economic Commission for Europe, Geneva

12.00-13.00   **Discussion**

13.00-14.30   **Lunch**

PARALLEL GROUPS

14.30-18.00   **GROUP I: South Eastern Europe -** Moderator: Mr. Christopher CVIIC, EBRD, London

14.30-15.15   **Lead Presentations**

- Mr. Krassen STANCHEV, Executive Director, Institute for Market Economies, Sofia
- Prof. Vladimir GLIGOROV, Research Economist, The Vienna Institute for International Economic Studies

15.15-16.00   **Speeches and Statements by Representatives and Experts from Individual Countries and International Organisations**

- Prof. Genc RULI, Director, Institute for Contemporary Studies, Tirana
- Mr. Mihnea CONSTANTINESCU, Special Advisor on South-Eastern Europe to the Minister of Foreign Affairs, Bucharest
- Mr. Marko PAUNOVIC, Economic Adviser to the Deputy Prime Minister of the Federal Republic of Yugoslavia
- Mr. Andrey V. NIKITOV, Deputy Head of Department, Ministry of Economy, Ukraine
- Mr. Rory O'SULLIVAN, Special Representative of the World Bank Group for South-East Europe

Reconstruction, Brussels

16.00-16.30	**Break**
16.30-17.00	**Concluding Assessments**

- Prof. Katarzyna ZUKROWSKA, Warsaw School of Economics
- Prof. Ivo PAPARELA, University of Split, Croatia

17.00-18.00   **Discussion**

14.30-18.00   **GROUP II: South Caucasus and Central Asia -** Moderators: Ambassador Nurver NURES and Prof. Michael KASER, University of Birmingham

14.30-15.15   **Lead Presentations**

- Mr. Michael EMERSON, Senior Research Fellow, The Centre for European Policy Studies (CEPS), Brussels
- Mr. Friedemann MÜLLER, Senior Researcher, Stiftung Wissenschaft und Politik, Berlin
- Ms. Shirin AKINER, Lecturer, Central Asia Research Forum, London

15.15-16.00   **Speeches by Representatives and Experts from South Caucasus and Central Asian Countries**

- Mr. Altay AFANDIYEV, Head of Department of Development and Economic Cooperation, Ministry of Foreign Affairs of Azerbaijan
- Mr. Vladimir KARAPETIAN, Head of Defence Cooperation Division of the Ministry of Foreign Affairs of Armenia
- Ms. Asel ABYLOVA, Senior Researcher, Economic Analysis Department, IISS, Kyrghiz Republic
- Damir RAMILIEVICI MUZAFAROV, Institute for Strategic and Regional Studies, Republic of Uzbekistan

16.00-16.30   **Break**

16.30-17.00   **Assessments**

- Mr. Unal CEVIKÖZ, Deputy Director-General, Ministry of Foreign Affairs, Istanbul
- Mr. Cees WITTEBROOD, Head of Unit, External Relations Directorate General, European Commission, Brussels

17.00-18.00   **Discussion**

19.00-20.30   **Reception in Marriott Grand Hotel Hosted by Romania**

Friday, 4 May 2001, a.m.

09.00-12.30   **PLENARY SESSION: Reports, Assessments and Outlook**

09.00-10.15   **Reports and Assessments**

- Report on Group I (Mr. Christopher CVIIC, EBRD, London)
- Report on Group II (Prof. Martin SPECHLER, Indiana University, U.S.)
- Mr. Thomas L. PRICE, former Co-ordinator of OSCE Economic and Environmental Activities, Vienna
- Ambassador Robert E. HUNTER, Senior Advisor, RAND Corporation, Arlington, USA

10.15-10.45   **Break**

10.45-11.30   **Outlook**

- Mr. Daniel DAIANU, Professor of Economics, Academy of Economic Studies, Bucharest and Visiting Professor at the Anderson School of Management, University of California, Los Angeles
- Mr. Yannis N. PAPANIKOLAOU, Director General, International Center for Black Sea Studies, Athens

- Mr. Mugur ISARESCU, Governor of the Central Bank of Romania

11.30-12.00	**Discussion**

12.00-12.20   **Concluding Speech** by Mr. Bodo HOMBACH, Special Coordinator, Stability Pact for South Eastern Europe

12.20-12.30   **Concluding Remarks by the Chairman**

13.00   **Press Conference**

Saturday 5th May 2001

Full day excursion offered by the Romanian hosts to Bran Castle and Brasov.

60 4001706 0